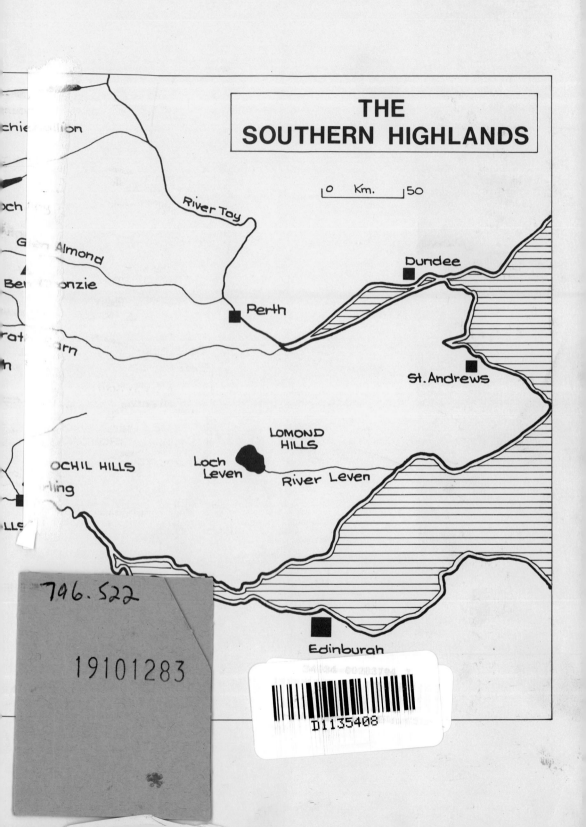

THE
SOUTHERN HIGHLANDS

|0 Km. |50

River Tay

Glen Almond

Ben ___onzie

chie___tion

och

Dundee

Perth

St. Andrews

LOMOND
HILLS

Loch
Leven

River Leven

OCHIL HILLS

___ling

Edinburgh

Scottish Mountaineering Club
District Guidebooks

THE SOUTHERN HIGHLANDS

Series Editor: D J BENNET

Published by
The Scottish Mountaineering Trust

THE
SOUTHERN HIGHLANDS

Donald Bennet

Scottish Mountaineering Club District Guidebook

PUBLISHED BY THE SCOTTISH MOUNTAINEERING TRUST: 1991
© THE SCOTTISH MOUNTAINEERING TRUST

British Library Cataloguing-in-Publication Data
Bennet, Donald John, 1928-
  The Southern Highlands
  2nd ed
  I. Title
  796.522094115

  ISBN: 0907521347

Front cover: Tyndrum hills from Beinn a'Chreachain. *D. J. Bennet*
Back cover: Ben Lui. *P. Hodgkiss*

Book design by Donald Bennet
Maps drawn by Jim Renny
Production by Peter Hodgkiss
Typeset by Westec, North Connel
Colour separations and graphic work by Par Graphics, Kirkcaldy
Printed by Pillans and Wilson, Edinburgh
Bound by Hunter and Foulis, Edinburgh
Distributed by Cordee, 3a De Montfort Street, Leicester, LE1 7HD

CONTENTS

ILLUSTRATIONS

Uncredited illustrations by the author

ACKNOWLEDGMENTS

The author records thanks to Jim Renny for his drawing a new set of maps for this edition, and to Douglas Fettes for his contribution of an article on the geology of the Southern Highlands. Acknowledgment is also given to Ken Crocket, Don Green, Peter Hodgkiss, Scott Johnstone, Jim Renny, Des Rubens and Noel Williams who made their photographs available for inclusion.

THE CLIMBER AND THE MOUNTAIN ENVIRONMENT

With increasing numbers of walkers and climbers going to the Scottish hills, it is important that all of us who do so should recognise our responsibilities to those who live and work among the hills and glens, to our fellow climbers and to the mountain environment in which we find our pleasure and recreation.

The Scottish Mountaineering Club and Trust, who jointly produce this and other guidebooks, wish to impress on all who avail themselves of the information in these books that it is essential at all times to consider the sporting and proprietory rights of landowners and farmers. The description of a climbing, walking or skiing route in any of these books does not imply that a right of way exists, and it is the responsibility of all climbers to ascertain the position before setting out. In cases of doubt it is always best to enquire locally.

During the stalking and shooting seasons in particular, much harm can be done in deer forests and on grouse moors by people walking through them. Normally the deer stalking season is from 1st July to 20th October, when stag shooting ends. Hinds may continue to be culled until 15th February. The grouse shooting season is from 12th August until 10th December. These are not merely sporting activities, but are essential for the economy of many Highland estates. During these seasons, therefore, especial care should be taken to consult the local landowner, factor or keeper before taking to the hills.

Climbers and hillwalkers are recommended to consult the book HEADING FOR THE SCOTTISH HILLS, published by the Scottish Mountaineering Trust on behalf of the Mountaineering Council of Scotland and the Scottish Landowners Federation, which gives the names and addresses of factors and keepers who may be contacted for information regarding access to the hills.

It is also important to avoid disturbance to sheep, particularly during the lambing season between March and May. Dogs should not be taken onto the hills at this time, and at all times should be kept under close control.

Always try to follow a path or track through cultivated land and forests, and avoid causing damage to fences, dykes and gates by climbing over them carelessly. Do not leave litter anywhere, but take it down from the hill in your rucksack.

The increasing number of walkers and climbers on the hills is leading to increased, and in some cases very unsightly erosion of footpaths and hillsides. Some of the revenue from the sale of this and other SMC guidebooks is used by the Trust to assist financially the work being carried out to repair and maintain hill paths in Scotland. However, it is important for all of us to recognise our responsibility to minimise the erosive effect of our passage over the hills so that the enjoyment of future climbers shall not be spoiled by landscape damage caused by ourselves.

As a general rule, where a path exists walkers should follow it and even where it is wet and muddy should avoid walking along its edges, the effect of which is to extend erosion sideways. Do not take short-cuts at the corners of zigzag paths. Remember that the worst effects of erosion are likely to be caused during or soon after prolonged wet weather when the ground is soft and waterlogged. A route on a stony or rocky hillside is likely to cause less erosion than on a grassy one at such times.

Although the use of bicycles can often be very helpful for reaching remote hills and crags, the erosion damage that can be caused by them when used 'off road' on soft footpaths and open hillsides is such that their use on such terrain must cause concern. It is the editorial policy of the Scottish Mountaineering Club that the use of bicycles in hill country may be recommended on hard roads such as forest roads or private roads following rights of way, but is not recommended on footpaths and open hillsides where the environmental damage that they cause may be considerable. Readers are asked to bear these points in mind, particularly in conditions when the ground is wet and soft after rain.

The proliferation of cairns on the hills detracts from the feeling of wildness, and may be confusing rather than helpful as regards route-finding. The indiscriminate building of cairns on the hills is therefore to be discouraged.

Climbers are reminded that they should not drive along private estate roads without permission, and when parking their cars should avoid blocking access to private roads and land, and should avoid causing any hazard to other road users.

Finally, the Scottish Mountaineering Club and the Scottish Mountaineering Trust can accept no liability for damage to property nor for personal injury resulting from the use of any route described in their publications.

Ben Lomond from Beinn Narnain

Introduction

The area covered by this volume of the Scottish Mountaineering Club's series of District Guidebooks extends from the Central Belt of Scotland northwards to the line of the River Awe, Glen Orchy, the southern edge of the Moor of Rannoch, Loch Rannoch and Loch Tummel. From there the eastern boundary follows the rivers Tummel and Tay to the sea, and includes the Kingdom of Fife. On the west the area is bounded by the much indented coastline from the Firth of Clyde round the Cowal peninsula to Kintyre and up the west coast to Oban and the lower reaches of Loch Etive.

This area is not entirely mountainous. It shows within its boundary most of the aspects of Scottish landscape from the urban fringe around the northern perimeter of Glasgow and the rich farmland of Fife through the moorland, low hills and forests of the transition zones between lowland and highland to the great mountains of Argyll and Breadalbane where the Highlands really begin. In the west part of the area there is a rich variety of scenery in Cowal, Knapdale and Argyll, characteristic of the west coast where the seaboard is much indented by long narrow lochs and adorned by a host of offshore islands. However, this western seaboard is low-lying with no hills or mountains of note, and in this book, which is devoted to the mountainous parts of the land, it is consequently neglected. The larger mountainous islands such as Arran and Jura are described in a companion guidebook in this series, *The Islands of Scotland including Skye*.

Many of the lower hill ranges are of particular interest. The Luss Hills, the Trossachs, Ochils, Lomonds of Fife and Campsies are all hills on the doorsteps of the urban areas of Central Scotland, so they have a special place in the affections of those who live close by. They are the hills that can be walked on a Sunday afternoon, and the hills on which many took their first upward steps. Their place in the landscape of Scotland and the affection of those who live near them transcends their modest height.

To the north of these lower hills the Scottish Highlands achieve their full stature and the mountain heights rise to over a thousand metres. Forty-five mountains in the Southern Highlands are classified as 'separate mountains', and a further twenty-two are classified as 'tops' in *Munro's Tables*. With only eleven exceptions, all the Munros in the Southern Highlands lie wholly or partly in the catchment area of the River Tay and its tributaries, so the area is dominated geographically by the upper glens and straths of this river, which lie in a roughly west to east direction.

The character of the Southern Highlands may perhaps be best seen on a clear day from one of the high peaks, such as Stuc a'Chroin, that stands on the dividing line between Highlands and Lowlands. Looking in the northern arc many of the Munros of the area can be seen, but only a few are outstanding. Ben Lawers and the Tarmachan Hills are prominent to the north, the great twins Ben More and Stob Binnein dominate the north-western view and to the west Ben Lomond and the Arrochar Alps are visible along the horizon. Between and beyond these outstanding peaks there is a host of other hills and mountains, most of them rounded and, when seen from a distance, lacking distinctive features although closer acquaintance may well contradict this impression. In the southern arc from Stuc a'Chroin one sees a very different picture across the whole of central Scotland. Near at hand there are extensive tracts of high moorland running down to Strath Earn, and to the south-west is the wide flat plain of Flanders Moss through which meanders the River Forth on its way from the corries of Ben Lomond to the North Sea. Beyond these valleys are the ranges of low hills, the Ochils and the Campsies, with a few prominent little summits such as West Lomond, Meikle Bin and Dumgoyne peeping above the flat horizon.

Although views such as this may give one a general impression of the Southern Highlands, they miss many of the details that give individual hills and glens their character. One must penetrate more deeply to discover the richly wooded glens of The Trossachs, the spectacular rock architecture of The Cobbler, the tranquility of Loch Voil and the remnants of the fine Old Caledonian forest in Glen Lyon and elsewhere.

HILLWALKING

The mountains of the Southern Highlands are notable for the absence of massive rock features such as the buttresses, gullies, ridges and corries that characterise the mountains further north. Although many of the hills are quite rugged and have rock outcrops, these outcrops tend to be modest in size and vegetatious in nature. Nowhere are there great sheets of slabs, towering cliffs or deep chasms forming gullies on the mountainsides such as one sees , for example, in Glen Etive and Glen Coe further north. There are , of course, some exceptions such as The Cobbler, which can hold its own in the company of any Scottish mountain and is justly famous for its rock-climbing, and the Bridge of Orchy mountains can in a hard winter give ice-climbing which in the opinion of their devotees is the equal of Glen Coe. Elsewhere throughout the area there is plenty of rock-climbing on low-level and small crags. However, it is probably true to say that the mountains of the Southern Highlands are first and foremost hillwalkers' mountains, and this is therefore mainly a hillwalker's guidebook.

In dealing with hillwalking routes on the mountains it is the policy to describe no more than two or three routes on any mountain. The routes chosen are those with climbing or scenic interest, routes following well-defined mountain features such as

Ben Lomond from the north end of Loch Lomond

ridges, and routes following rights of way, paths or tracks. It is possible to climb any mountain in the Southern Highlands by any one of several different routes, but it is not always expedient to do so. The experienced hillwalker, equipped with a map and excercising good judgement, can chose a way that is interesting, safe and has minimum impact on the environment.

There are also many good low-level walks through the mountains following paths, tracks and rights of way. Many of these are referred to in the text, but unless it is specifically stated that these walks follow rights of way, it should be assumed that they do not. The Forestry Commission usually permit access through forests along forest roads and waymarked paths. Most landowners tolerate walkers and climbers walking along private roads and stalker's paths outwith the stalking and shooting seasons, but one should respect such tolerance by not causing any damage nor infringing privacy. During the stalkng and shooting season it is diplomatic to make contact with landowners or their factors or keepers before going onto the hills. The booklet *Heading for the Scottish Hills* published by the Mountaineering Council of Scotland and the Scottish Landowners Federation is intended to enable climbers and walkers to do this by providing names, addresses and telephone numbers for many estates in the Highlands.

The North Peak of The Cobbler

ROCK-CLIMBING

As already mentioned, the Southern Highlands are not noted for their rock-climbing potential. The one exception to this generalisation is The Cobbler, where there is some very fine climbing. In the nineteen thirties, and again in the forties and early fifties The Cobbler was a crucible of Scottish climbing, where some of the finest climbers of their day perfected their skills and raised the standards of Scottish rock-climbing to unprecedented levels. Nowadays there may be fewer new routes being done, but those that have been achieved in the last few years have maintained the position of The Cobbler as a superb climbers' mountain on which the spectacular quality of some of the routes puts them in a class by themselves.

The rock-climbing on some of the other peaks of the Arrochar Alps, for example Beinn Narnain, Creag Tharsuinn, Beinn Ime and The Brack, may suffer by comparison with The Cobbler, but those peaks have their routes, albeit rather vegetatious. One feature that all these mountains have in common is the very slippery and treacherous nature of the mica-schist rock when it is wet.

On the Bridge of Orchy mountains there has been some rock-climbing done on the high crags, but they too are very vegetatious and the few climbs that have been done have never become popular. This is hardly surprising as one only has to go twenty miles further to reach the much better climbing of Glen Coe and Glen Etive.

There remain the lower hills and low-lying crags, of which there are many, which give climbing practice and sport within fairly easy reach of the towns and cities of central Scotland. The little rocky peak of Ben An in The Trossachs might take pride of place among these, not for the difficulty of its routes but for its situation, outlook and delightful character. The Whangie, Craigmore and Auchinstarry Quarry at Kilsyth give western climbers their local training grounds. Elsewhere, to mention just a few of the better-known crags, Dumbarton Rock is noted for its very serious and difficult climbs, Aberdour for its delightful sea-cliffs at Hawcraig and there is a host of other crags between Dun Leacainn beside Loch Fyne in the west and Balnacoul Castle far to the east above Glen Lednock.

It is not the intention in this guidebook to give comprehensive information and route descriptions for all these rock-climbs. In each chapter (where relevant) brief information is given about climbing possibilities and a few of the most noteworthy routes are mentioned. For full information the climber is referred to the following Scottish Mountaineering Club guidebooks:-

Climbers Guide to Arran, Arrochar and the Southern Highlands. K.V.Crocket and A.Walker. (1989).

Climbers Guide to Central and Southern Scotland. Editor J.Handren. (1986). New edition to be published in 1992.

Climbers Guide to Highland Outcrops. Editor K.Howett. To be published in 1992.

WINTER CLIMBING

The Southern Highlands have much more to offer by way of winter mountain-eering than rock-climbing. Crags which in summer are loose and vegetatious, and corries which are unpleasant slopes of steep grass and scree can in winter give excellent climbing when they are bound by frost and covered with snow and ice.

The Arrochar Alps cannot be relied on to give good conditions for winter climbing because of their modest height and closeness to the western seaboard. However, when good conditions do exist there is very good and hard climbing on crags such as Creag Tharsuinn, *Fan Gully Buttress* of Beinn Ime and the north-east face of the South Peak of The Cobbler.

Going further north, Ben Lui has for a hundred years been the most popular mountain in the Southern Highlands for the winter mountaineer, although this position may be challenged nowadays by one or two of the Bridge of Orchy peaks. Despite the fact that the climbs in the north-east corrie of Ben Lui, such as the classic *Central Gully*, may be easy by modern standards, they have a quality and ambience on a peak of Alpine character that gives them lasting appeal.

The Bridge of Orchy mountains have been well developed in the last twenty years and there is excellent climbing on several of them. Beinn Udlaidh above Glen Orchy and Beinn an Dothaidh above Loch Tulla are probably the two best mountains for the number and quality of their ice-climbs. There are some who claim that the quality of winter climbing on these hills equals that on the Glen Coe peaks. This may be a flattering comparison, but there is no doubt that the accessibility of the climbing, twenty miles closer to Glasgow than Glen Coe, makes it very attractive on short winter days.

Elsewhere in the Southern Highlands there are high crags and corries which once were climbed in winter, but now seem to be out of favour. The east face of Stuc a'Chroin and the summit cliffs of Ben Lomond are just two examples. Certainly by present standards the climbing on these crags is not sufficiently challenging for modern young climbers, but as the New Routes section of the *Scottish Mountaineering Club Journal* proves, there are still opportunities for exploratory climbing on the ice-bound crags of the remote and unfrequented corries of the Southern Highlands.

As is the case with rock-climbs, it is not the intention of this guidebook to give detailed information about all winter climbs in its area. This information will be found in the Scottish Mountaineering Club's *Climbers Guide to Arran, Arrochar and the Southern Highlands* by K.V.Crocket and A.Walker (1989). More recent information about routes done since the publication of this guidebook can be found in the *Scottish Mountaineering Club Journal*, published annually.

The ascent of Beinn Ghlas from Coire Odhar

SKI MOUNTAINEERING

The relatively smooth grassy nature of many of the Southern Highland mountains, and the absence of steep corries, extensive crags and rocky outcrops on them provides good terrain for ski mountaineering. There is a wealth of good climbs, tours and traverses that can be done on skis, particularly on the Breadalbane mountains which are high and remote from the mild influence of the western seaboard.

Ben Lawers is the mountain par excellence for ski touring. Its even slopes, broad ridges and open corries give a wide choice of expeditions on skis, from the simple ascent of Beinn Ghlas from the National Trust for Scotland's visitor centre to the complete traverse of the six peaks of the range. The latter is one of the finest day's ski mountaineering in Scotland. It is worth recalling that Ben Lawers was in the nineteen-thirties the focal point of Scottish skiing, the earliest ski races were run there in Coire Odhar and the Scottish Ski Club built its first hut on the slopes of the mountain at that time. Now, with the development of ski resorts elsewhere in Scotland, the downhill skiers have left Ben Lawers, but the ski mountaineers remain.

Elsewhere in the Southern Highlands there are many mountains that in reasonably snowy winter conditions give good tours. The Carn Mairg range on the north side of Glen Lyon is a long but easy traverse. Further west Beinn Heasgarnich is probably the best of several mountains round the head of Glen Lochay. The traverse of Stob Binnein and Ben More is second only to the Ben Lawers traverse in the Southern Highlands, but it is not a tour to be undertaken lightly for the skiing is on long steep slopes and corniced ridges. Much easier is Beinn Dubhchraig to the west of Crianlarich which, with its neighbour Ben Oss, gives a fine easy traverse with one short steep section.

If Scotland's winter climate were a bit more favourable, Crianlarich would be an excellent centre for ski mountaineeering for there are within easy reach a dozen eminently skiable mountains.

Further north the Bridge of Orchy mountains give good skiing individually, and the traverse of the four big ones is an excellent expedition, quite long for a short winter day.

Detailed information about these and many other ski mountaineering tours in the Southern Highlands is contained in the Scottish Mountaineering Club's guidebook *Ski Mountaineering in Scotland* edited by D.J.Bennet and W.Wallace.

MAPS

The best maps for the climber and hillwalker are without doubt the Ordnance Survey 1:50,000 maps. The current 'Landranger' series has the detail that is required for accurate navigation through the hills in bad visibility and also contains a lot of useful information. The maps presently available for the Southern Highlands have all been recently revised, most within the past five years, and they are up to date in showing features of importance such as forests. There are, however, a very few instances where forests, tracks and paths are not correctly shown and where important these discrepancies are mentioned in the text. Hill and mountain heights quoted in the text are taken from the 1:50,000 maps except in some cases where presumably more accurate heights are available from more recently published 1:25,000 maps. To avoid confusion, the spelling of place names used in this book corresponds with spellings on the 1:50,000 map.

Bartholomew's series of 1:100,000 maps is very suitable for tourists and walkers who do not require the detail shown by the 1:50,000 maps, and their colour contouring gives a very clear impression of the country at a glance.

HYDRO-ELECTRIC POWER

There are several hydro-electric power schemes in the Southern Highlands, and although the developments are not as extensive as those in the north-west, two of Scotland's earliest hydro-electric schemes, Tummel and Sloy, are in this area.

Looking across Loch Lomond to Sloy Power Station

The Sloy scheme has its reservoir high in the mountains between Ben Vane and Ben Vorlich, although it collects water from a much wider catchment area extending south to The Cobbler. The generating capacity of the Sloy Power Station at Inveruglas on the side of Loch Lomond is 130MW, making it the most powerful conventional hydro-electric power station in Scotland.

A few kilometres north-west of Loch Sloy the reservoir at the head of Allt na Lairige supplies a small power station (6MW) in Glen Fyne. To its west, on the other side of Beinn Bhuidhe, Lochan Shira supplies water to the small Sron Mor generator (5MW) and the larger Clachan Power Station (40MW) at the head of Loch Fyne.

The Tummel scheme draws water from as far away as Loch Cuaich near Dalwhinnie and Loch Ericht, and this water supplies the Rannoch Power Station (48MW). A few kilometres west of the head of Loch Rannoch the Gaur Power Station (6.4MW) takes its water from Loch Eigheach. Downstream from Loch Rannoch the Tummel (34MW), Clunie (61.2MW) and Pitlochry (15MW) power stations are all part of the extensive Tummel scheme whose catchment area is a huge tract of the Grampians between the Moor of Rannoch and Gaick Pass. The Errochty Power Station (75MW) at Trinafour is also part of this system.

In Breadalbane Loch an Daimh (to the north of upper Glen Lyon) is the reservoir for Cashlie Power Station (11MW) in Glen Lyon, and the Lubreoch Power Station at the Loch Lyon dam generates 4MW. The combined flow from these two sources flows from Stronuich Reservoir to the Lochay Power Station (47MW) in Glen Lochay a few kilometres north-west of Killin. Lochan na Lairige between Ben Lawers and the Tarmachan hills supplies the Finlarig Power Station (30MW) at the west end of Loch Tay.

To the south of Loch Tay, Loch Lednock supplies the Lednock (3MW) and St Fillans (21MW) power stations, and a few kilometres down the River Earn from St Fillans is the Dalchonzie (4MW) Power Station.

In Cowal the Striven Power Station (8MW) situated at the head of Loch Striven takes its water from Loch Tarsan.

FORESTRY

As in many other parts of the Highlands, the activities of the Forestry Commission and private forestry companies are obvious to see in the Southern Highlands. Blanket afforestation has a very considerable impact on the landscape and on access to the mountains. Poor forest design and practice in the past have resulted in much unsympathetic planting, both from the visual point of view and as regards impeding, and often making quite impossible, access from glens onto hills. Many traditional hillwalkers routes have been completely blocked by densely planted conifers. Hopefully the situation is improving, and present guidelines for forest planting stress the need to preserve access routes by, for example, leaving clearings between forests and streams.

As a general rule it is more or less essential when going through forested areas to follow a path or track. Otherwise progress is likely to be slow and painful as one struggles through closely planted trees and across drainage ditches, and in newly planted forests there is the probability that young trees will be damaged. In many forests that are now mature, felling results in even more difficult terrain as the aftermath of felling usually leaves small branches, logs and tree stumps in a tangle that makes progess extremely slow if not actually dangerous. A sprained or broken ankle can easily result from a stumble in such treacherous ground.

There are two Forest Parks in the Southern Highlands. The Queen Elizabeth Forest Park covers a large area from Ben Lomond to The Trossachs, and the Argyll Forest Park extends from Cowal to the Arrochar Alps. In both parks the existence of trails, many of them waymarked, provides access through the forests onto the higher hills and also a network of low-level paths and forest roads that give good walking and cycling. Guides and maps published by the Forestry Commission give full information about these parks.

Elsewhere there are several remnants of the old Caledonian Forest whose gnarled Scots pines seem to symbolise the character of the mountain land. The Black Wood of Rannoch, Crannach Wood below Beinn Achaladair and the Coille Coire Chuilc at the foot of Beinn Dubhchraig are some of the remnants of the old forest in the Southern Highlands, but the trees are not regenerating and the forest is slowly dying.

ACCESS AND TRANSPORT

Access to all parts of the Southern Highlands is very easy by public roads, and there are very few hills more than six or seven kilometres from a public road. The mention of private roads or forest roads in this book does not mean that it is permissible to drive along them, and permission should be sought before driving along such roads.

Public transport services are noted in each chapter, but it should be borne in mind that these services can change and the information given may thus be rendered out of date. Apart from the railway from Glasgow to Arrochar, Crianlarich and Tyndrum, and from there to Oban on one line and Fort William on the other, the public transport services available in the Southern Highlands are provided by buses and postbuses.

There are services operated by the bus companies in central Scotland, and Scottish Citylink Coaches Limited operates from Edinburgh and Glasgow to many destinations in the Highlands. In addition postbus services operated by Royal Mail provide public transport in more remote rural parts of the country.

A very useful publication for those depending on public transport in the Highlands is *Getting Around the Highlands and Islands,* published by FHG Publications Ltd in association with the Highlands and Islands Development Board. Royal Mail publishes a *Postbus Timetable for Scotland* which can be obtained from many post offices. Many of the towns and bigger villages in the Southern Highlands, particularly those with much tourist business, have information offices which can provide complete information about all local public transport services.

ACCOMMODATION

An indication of the accommodation available is given in each chapter. The publications of the Scottish Tourist Board give a comprehensive listing of different types of holiday accommodation under the title *Where to Stay in Scotland.* There are four such booklets describing hotels amd guest houses, self-catering accommodation, camp and caravan sites and bed and breakfast accommodation. These books are available in bookshops and tourist information offices, or from the Scottish Tourist Board, 23 Ravelston Terrace, Edinburgh EH4 3EU. Information about accommodation may also be obtained from information offices in towns and villages.

The Scottish Youth Hostels Association also has several hostels in the Southern Highlands. The relevant ones are noted in each chapter.

There are two huts owned by mountaineering clubs in the Southern Highlands. The Ochils Club has a small cottage at the east end of Crianlarich beside the Ben More Restaurant, and the East Kilbride Mountaineering Club has a hut in Glen Croe below The Cobbler. These huts are available to members of clubs which are members of the Mountaineering Council of Scotland and the British Mountaineering Council and to Associate Members of these organisations, and bookings should be made by club secretaries to the hut custodians. The Mountaineering Council of Scotland publishes annually a list of climbers' huts in Scotland and the addresses of their custodians.

The Glencoe Ski Club has a lodge near Bridge of Orchy which is available for groups of twenty or more (maximum forty) at all times of the year except weekends in the skiing season (December to April inclusive). Application to use this lodge should be made to the custodian, Mrs C.Thomson, 85 Durward Avenue, Glasgow.

In addition to the many organised camp sites in the Southern Highlands, wild camping is possible in many glens and on the mountains. However, campers should bear in mind that it is an offence to camp or light a fire on private land without the owner's permission. It is therefore prudent to seek permission, particularly if camping near any habitation.

ACCESS TO THE HILLS

The law regarding access to private land in Scotland is different from that in England and Wales. In Scotland, although it is an offence to go on private land without permission, the owner cannot raise an action against the person concerned unless damage has been caused. He can, however, ask the person concerned to leave his land and if the latter does not do so, he may use reasonable force to eject him. As far as the writer knows, 'reasonable force' has never been defined, but thanks to the tolerance and good sense of both walkers and landowners, it seldom has to be used. There has for many years existed in Scotland, and hopefully will continue to exist, a *modus vivendi* between landowners on the one hand and walkers and climbers on the other which has allowed considerable (if not complete) freedom of access to the hills outwith the stalking and shooting seasons. Climbers and walkers should recognise the important economic role that stalking, shooting and fishing play in the viability of Highland estates, and should not jeopardise it by their actions. Unfortunately, in recent years some landowners and their stalkers have interpreted the stalking season as continuing to mid-February, the end of the hind culling season. This is a development which could strain good relations between climbers and landowners.

As mentioned earlier in this Introduction, the booklet *Heading for the Scottish Hills* published by the Mountaineering Council of Scotland and the Scottish Landowners Federation provides information to enable climbers and walkers to make contact with estate factors and stalkers to get advice about stalking and similar activities before going onto the hills.

DROVE ROADS AND RIGHTS OF WAY

Cattle droving was for three centuries an important part of Highland life and commerce. Every year, as summer drew towards its end, herds of cattle fattened by long days of grazing in the lush pastures of the Highland glens started their long journey to the markets of the south. There was a great demand for cattle in southern

Scotland and England, and the animals provided their own transport to the markets. Thus droving was a natural way to export this valuable product of the Highlands. For the Highland drovers, also, it was a natural activity, relying on their ability to endure hardship in the open for day after day.

Although droving has long since passed into history, the drove roads followed by the cattle have remained as rights of way and are a valuable part of the social heritage of the Highlands. Other rights of way have come into existence for other reasons. They may have been traditional routes for Highlanders to and from their churches and burial grounds, and many rights of way are known as coffin routes. The cairns along them mark the places where the carriers rested from their heavy labours. Other rights of way came into existence simply as the usual route on foot from one village to the next.

The network of rights of way in the Highlands remain as a most valuable heritage. These are ways along which everyone has the right to walk, without obstruction, at any time of the year. In many cases the original path or drove road may have disappeared through lack of use, but the right remains so long as once every twenty years (the prescriptive period) someone walks along it.

A public right of way is defined as a right of passage, open to the public, over private property by a route which is more or less well-defined. Rights of way can be of three types: vehicular routes, drove roads and footpaths. Only the two latter categories are of relevance in the rough terrain of the Highlands, and both confer right of passage for walkers. A drove road also confers a right of way on horseback, or leading a horse. It is considered that a pedal cyclist has the same rights as a pedestrian, but this has not been definitely established in law.

The essential elements of a right of way are that it should at some time in the past have been in continuous use for a period of not less than twenty years, that its use is a matter of right and not due to tolerance on the part of the landowner, that it must connect two public places or places to which the public habitually and legitimately resorts, and that it follows a more or less well-defined route. It is not at present considered that mountain tops, even the most popular ones, can be regarded as public places, and this is an important point because if they were, then many of our mountains could be considered to have rights of way to their summits. As regards the definition of a well-defined route, it is not necessary that there should be a visible path, rather that it should be established that the public has followed a more or less consistent line during the period in question. Minor deviations such as might be required to cross a stream or circumvent a loch whose level has been raised by damming do not invalidate a right of way.

It is to be hoped, however, that walkers along rights of way will have regard for the legitimate interests of those who live in the country and earn their livelihood there.

For further information the reader is referred to the booklet *Rights of Way, A Guide to the Law in Scotland* published by the Scottish Rights of Way Society Limited, John Cotton Business Centre, 10/2 Sunnyside, Edinburgh EH7 5RA.

MOUNTAIN SAFETY

The routes described in this guidebook range from simple walks on well-defined tracks and paths to serious climbs demanding skill, knowledge and the right equipment. However, it must be stressed that any expedition which in good weather is perfectly simple and safe may become very different if the weather deteriorates or mist comes down. Such changes can occur very rapidly. Similarly, routes which in summer conditions present no difficulty may become difficult or dangerous in winter conditions, especially to a party not experienced or equipped for winter climbing. To generalise, practically any expedition on the mountains is potentially dangerous should severe weather or snow conditions occur, and the party be unable to deal with such conditions.

It is a good rule for a party, before setting out, to leave information at its hotel, hut or car or with friends as to its objective, route and estimated time of return. This may save many hours of searching by a mountain rescue team in the event of an accident or benightment.

A party should always stay together, particularly in bad weather. The pace of a party should be dictated by the slowest member, and the party should be prepared to turn back if weather conditions become very bad or if any member is going very slowly or is exhausted.

Whilst care should be excercised at all times, this is most important on the descent, particularly if the route is unknown. During and after rain, rocks, boulders and grass may become very slippery if one is wearing rubber-soled boots. Do not run downhill, as a minor slip or fall may result in a sprained ankle and a mountain rescue team may have to be called out.

Three is the minimum number to ensure safety in the event of an accident. In such an event which requires a mountain rescue team at least one member of the party should stay with the injured climber while one or two go down for help. If there are only two in the party, the injured climber should be left with all the spare food and clothing, and a whistle and torch, while his companion goes down for help. The position of the injured climber should be marked by reference to some conspicuous landmark nearby. The person descending to the valley should get to a telephone as quickly as possible and inform the police.

MOUNTAIN RESCUE

There are several mountain rescue posts and teams in the Southern Highlands. However, the standard advice to anyone seeking assistance in the rescue of an injured climber or the search for a missing one is to contact the Police (telephone 999) who will set in motion a rescue or search operation and liase with mountain rescue teams.

The Geology of the Southern Highlands
by D J Fettes

Anyone looking northward across the Midland Valley of Scotland will be impressed by the abruptness of the 'Highland Boundary' with rolling grassy land giving way to heather-covered, craggy hills. This sudden change in topography marks one of the fundamental features of Scottish geology, the Highland Boundary Fault, a huge shatter zone which brings together the ancient crystalline schist of the Highlands with the softer, younger sediments of the south. The fault runs from Bute in the south-west to Stonehaven in the north-east through such well-defined features as Glen Artney. The major movements of this great fault took place hundreds of millions of years ago, but tremors are still occasionally felt at the present time.

To the south of the Highland Boundary Fault lies a wide expanse of sandstone and lava belonging to the Old Red Sandstone, overlain to the south by the mixed sediments and lava of the Carboniferous. Sedimentary rocks such as limestone and sandstone are relatively soft, thus the sediments of the Midland Valley have been planed by the forces of erosion to a smooth profile. This feature has been enhanced by the glaciers of the Ice Age which, some twenty thousand years ago, scoured the rocks and then in their dying stages plastered them with debris scraped from the Highland hills. Lava, however, is tougher and more resistant to erosion, and in consequence the lavas of the Old Red Sandstone are preserved in the Ochil Hills which stand out prominently from the surrounding land. Similarly the lavas of the Carboniferous period are preserved in the Kilpatrick and Campsie Hills. When lava is erupted, the base of the flow becomes cold and broken and mixed with the debris on the ground. The surface of the flow cools more slowly and cracks, and before being covered by subsequent flows it may be badly weathered and covered by ash, dust and possibly sediment. Consequently, hills formed by an accumulation of lava flows are marked by a succession of layers which may consist of rotten and broken rocks. Thus, although lava hills present steep features and impressive scarps, they seldom offer rock-climbing of any great length or quality.

At the same time as the Carboniferous lavas were pouring out onto the surface, molten igneous rock was intruding the underlying sediment at depth. Dark basic rocks (dolerites) thus formed now lie exposed at the top of the Lomond Hills in Fife. This capping of tough igneous rock has protected the sediments below from erosion, so that the Lomonds stand out from the denuded plains around them. Similar rocks outcrop on the coast of Fife and on the Isle of May.

To the north of the Highland Boundary Fault lie two great rock assemblages, the Dalradian and the Grampian Group (formerly correlated with the Moine rocks of the western and northern Highlands). The former is a mixed group of schists, quartzites and marbles, and the latter is a monotonous series of flaggy quartzite rock which stretches from the northern part of Perthshire to the Great Glen. These two assemblages were once sediments very similar to those now found in the Midland

Valley; however, during the Caledonian Orogeny (some four or five hundred million years ago) these rocks were subjected to great stresses and were thrown into a series of gigantic folds to become strongly deformed and cleaved.

The accompanying high pressures and temperatures recrystallised and metamorphosed the rocks. In general the degree of metamorphism increases northwards so that shale bands near the Highland edge have been changed to slate, whilst further north they have recrystallised to give the well-known mica-schist which is often characterised by large pink garnets. Sandstones have been fused to form quartzites, and intercalated lavas and intrusive igneous rocks are now found as the dark green hornblende-schists so typical of the south-west Highlands.

The structure of the area is complex, with folds of all sizes deforming and twisting the rocks. However, one huge fold dominates the area, rising from the ground to the north of Ben Lawers, stretching horizontally southwards and dipping steeply downwards near the Highland Boundary. This great structure has given the majority of the rocks in the area a predominantly flat- lying attitude, although large rolling folds locally steepen the dip and repeat different rock groups on the ground. These rock groups lie as bands roughly parallel to the Highland Boundary Fault, commonly stretching the entire breadth of Scotland. The youngest rocks are found adjacent to the Highland Boundary Fault, and they become progressively older northwards.

During the passing of geoloical time, the forces of erosion have worn away the Highlands. The most important agents of erosion were the glaciers of the Ice Age. These sculpted the rugged features of the hills, gouging out the valleys and plucking rocks from the backs and sides of corries to deepen and enlarge them. Soil and broken rock which had accumulated over the aeons were scraped off and carried away down the valleys. Two important features control the reaction of the rocks to this great abrasive force - the inherent toughness of the rock type and the degree and attitude of planes of parting, such as schistosity planes. Gullies and cracks are often formed by the preferential weathering out of igneous dykes and shatter zones.

The rocks forming the southern half of the Dalradian Assemblage, i.e. the southern half of the Highlands, are a series of schistose grits with intercalated quartz-mica-schists, the mica-schists dominating in the north. Near the southern edge of the Highlands an important slate band is marked by a series of quarries on the line between Birnam and Aberfoyle. The schistose grits are one of the toughest of the rock groups and form several impressive mountains such as Ben Venue, Ben Lomond, Ben More, Ben Ledi, Ben Vorlich and Ben Chonzie, as well as many lesser craggy tops. On the lower northern slopes of Ben Venue bands of green epidotic grit can be seen which may represent the ash thrown out by ancient volcanoes. The schistosity of the rock in these areas is usually relatively flat, the dip seldom exceeding 30 or 40 degrees. As a result, weathering along the schistosity planes tends to produce 'step-like' features in the rock. It is this favourable combination of sound rock type and flat-lying structure which has given rise to some of the best climbs in the hills around Arrochar. Also, because the grits do not readily break down into sand and soil, vegetation finds little foothold on the cliffs, and the rocks are generally clean.

Proceeding northwards from this group, there is an intermittent band of limestone which, although recrystallised to marble, is still softer than the surrounding rock and usually lies in unexposed depressions. North again, calcareous mica-schists predominate. These are relatively soft rocks, easily weathered so that they do not produce the dramatic rock scenery of the mountains further south. Thus Ben Lawers, which is formed of this type of rock, although the highest mountain of the area is notably less craggy than many of its neighbours. The Killin Hills such as Meall nan Tarmachan and Beinn nan Eachan show some impressive cliffs, although they are also formed of calcareous mica-schist. The rock, however, is crumbly and soft and does not form the 'steps' of the tougher grits. The crumbled and rotten rock provides a good foothold for vegetation and consequently climbs where they exist are of poor quality. The junction between this calcareous mica-schist and the quartz-mica-schist of the more southerly hills passes near the foot of the north-east corrie of Ben Lui.

The northernmost and oldest significant rock group of the Dalradian is a thick band of quartzite. One of the hardest rocks, quartzite has little or no schistosity and is fairly homogeneous. In consequence it weathers uniformly and although forming prominent hills such as Schiehallion and Carn Mairg, it does not form spectacular cliffs. Rock-climbs on quartzite are usually short but of good quality.

The Dalradian is succeeded northwards by the flaggy quartz-mica-schists of the Grampian Group. Many of the hills around Bridge of Orchy, such as Beinn a'Chaisteal, lie wholly within the Grampian Group; others such as Beinn Udlaidh and Beinn Dorain straddle the boundary between it and the Dalradian. The lower slopes of Beinn Dorain and Beinn an Dothaidh are composed of Grampian Group quartz-mica-schists, with limestone and mica- schists of the Dalradian forming the highest parts. A prominent north-east trending fault passing through the summit of Beinn Udlaidh brings a small patch of Dalradian mica-schist to the south-east into contact with the quartz-mica-schists of the Grampian Group.

One reason why the hills of the Southern Highlands do not have more good rock-climbing areas is the absence of large igneous complexes such as those of the Cairngorms, Glen Coe, Ben Nevis and Skye. Although small patches of diorite and granite occur around Comrie and on the north side of The Cobbler, they do not provide notable rock features. The Lorne plateau lavas belong to the Old Red Sandstone, but as the name suggests, there are no prominent summits.

Over much of the Southern Highlands the schistose grits are cut by a system of steep regular fractures or joints. During the closing stages of the Ice Age melt water flooded these joints such that the resulting internal pressures caused widespread rock slippage on the valley sides. In some places the movement was of local extent and shows up as deep parallel crevasse-like fissures. These can be seen on Ben

Vorlich (Loch Lomond), Beinn an Lochain, Ben Donich and Cruach Ardrain. Elsewhere total collapse of hillsides have occurred, with steep headwalls rising above extensive slopes of large boulders and blocks. Collapses of this type are well displayed on The Brack, Ben Donich, Beinn an Lochain and above Hell's Glen. The spectacular shape of The Cobbler probably results in part from block collapse with the cave at the foot of the North Peak formed by the ill-fitting junction between the fallen blocks.

Some notable faults occur in the area with a north-east to south-west trend. One such passes through Loch Tay and another from the head of Loch Fyne via Tyndrum to Strathspey. At Tyndrum this latter fault brings rocks of the Grampian Group against Dalradian schists. Lead and silver mineralised rocks on this fault have been

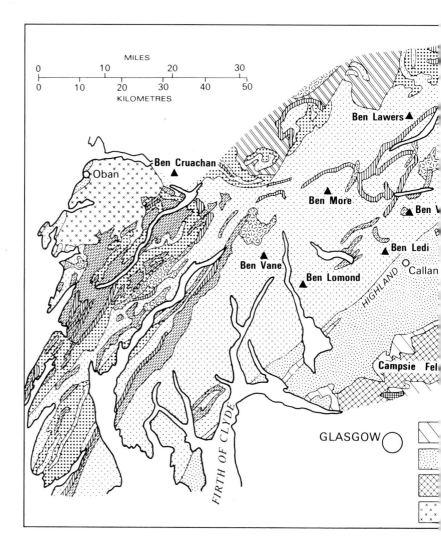

mined and the scars of the old workings can still be seen on the hillside south of the road from Tyndrum to Oban. Sporadic mining has also been carried out at various other places in the area during the 18th and 19th centuries, but the only other notable examples were the copper mines at Tomnadashan on the south side of Loch Tay and at Kilfinan on Loch Fyne. In more recent years a number of areas have been investigated for gold mineralisation, the most significant example being the slopes of Beinn Chuirn above Cononish (near Ben Lui) where adits have been driven into the hillside close to the site of old lead mines. Another modern mine lies in the hills north of Aberfeldy near Foss, where bedded barytes occurs in the Dalradian schists. These mines are being actively developed at the present time due to the importance of barytes as a constituent of 'drilling-mud' for North Sea oil exploration.

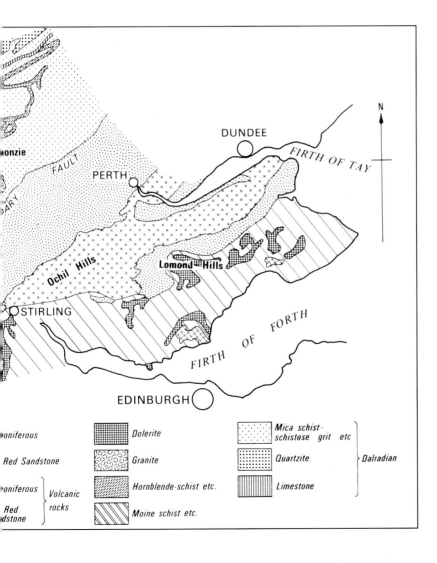

CHAPTER 1

The Kilpatrick, Campsie and Fintry Hills

Duncolm	401m	471 775
Earl's Seat	578m	570 838
Dumgoyne	427m	541 828
Meikle Bin	570m	667 822
Stronend	511m	629 895

ACCESS
The following roads pass round or through the hills described in this chapter:- Glasgow to Balloch (A82), Glasgow to Drymen (A809), Glasgow to Killearn (A81), Glasgow to Kilsyth (A803). Strathblane to Kilsyth (A891), Drymen to Stirling (A811), Lennoxtown to Kippen (B822) and Killearn to Denny (B818).

TRANSPORT
Bus: Services from Glasgow and Stirling to Blanefield, Lennoxtown, Killearn, Drymen, Kilsyth, Gargunnock and Kippen. Daily.

ACCOMMODATION
There are hotels in the villages mentioned above.

MAPS
Ordnance Survey 1:50,000, Sheets 57 and 64.
Bartholomew 1:100,000, Sheet 45.

These groups of low hills form a more or less continuous range across the centre of Scotland between Dumbarton and Stirling. The Kilpatricks overlook Dumbarton and the north shore of the River Clyde as far upstream as Clydebank. North-east of them, across the wooded Strath Blane, are the Campsie Fells which, extending eastwards to join the Kilsyth Hills, form the most extensive and highest area of hills described in this chapter. North-east of the Campsies, across the forested Carron Valley with its large reservoir, are the Fintry and Gargunnock Hills which present an almost continuous escarpment to the north overlooking the villages of Kippen and Gargunnock.

Duncolm, the highest of the Kilpatrick Hills

These hills are of volcanic origin and are composed of lava sheets worn down by ice in past ages. Some of the prominent rounded tops such as Dumgoyne are the vent plugs of ancient volcanoes whose hard cores have weathered more slowly than their surrounding rocks.

The principal characteristics of all these hills are similar. Their tops, with one or two exceptions such as Dumgoyne and Meikle Bin, are flat and grassy with considerable areas of eroded peat bog. These plateaux are intersected by many small streams. The flanks of the hills on the other hand are in many places steep, and there are quite considerable escarpments and cliffs overlooking Blanefield, Lennoxtown, Fintry and Gargunnock. In general the hills give rather rough and tiring walking as the grass of their summits is very tussocky and the peat bogs are in places extensive. There is also increasing afforestation, and not all the most recent plantings are shown on the present Ordnance Survey maps.

It is probably true to say that the most interesting features of these hills are to be found not on their summits, but on their flanks. For example, the strange rock formation at The Whangie on the northern edge of the Kilpatricks, the Corrie of Balglass on the north side of the Campsies and the beautiful glens holding the Ballagan and Finglen burns have more interest for the climber and walker than the rather featureless tops. At the Spout of Ballagan, where there is a small nature reserve, the hillside is cut away steeply, and the geological strata are exposed in a series of clearly defined layers.

It should be borne in mind that the principal land use in these hills and the low ground surrounding them is sheep and cattle farming. Great care should be taken when crossing this low ground to reach the hills to avoid causing any damage or disturbance to livestock.

THE KILPATRICK HILLS

The southern slopes of these hills rise quite steeply above the River Clyde between Clydebank and Dumbarton. The interior is high undulating moorland dotted with about a dozen reservoirs and some quite extensive areas of afforestation. Northwards this moorland drops gradually towards the rather featureless expanse of Dumbarton Muir and Stockie Muir, beyond which lie the wide valleys of Strath Endrick and Strath Blane.

The Kilpatricks are mainly of interest as providing some good moorland walks within easy reach of Glasgow, and literally at the back door of Duntocher and Clydebank. There is access to the hills by paths and private roads which strike northwards from Milton, Duntocher and Faifley on the north side of the River Clyde, and westwards from Craigton, Carbeth and Auchengillan on the A809 road from Glasgow to Drymen.

Most of the hills are mere swellings in the undulating moorland which characterises the Kilpatricks, and only the highest of them, Duncolm (401m), is in any way outstanding. Its circular summit rises about 70m above the surrounding moor and on its north-east side there are some steep basalt rocks. Fynloch Hill (400m) is half a kilometre south-west of Duncolm, but it is quite featureless.

Duncolm is probably most easily reached from the south-east, leaving the public road at the north edge of Hardgate at grid reference 497 737. Walk up the private road past Wester Cochno farm to Greenside Reservoir, go round the east end of the reservoir and continue north then north-west along a dry stone wall to the final steep slopes of the hill.

Cochno Hill (347m) is a good viewpoint and easily accessible from the road between Wester Cochno and Greenside Reservoir.

Doughnot Hill (374m), two and a half kilometres west of Duncolm, is also a good viewpoint. The ascent is from Milton on the A82 road a few kilometres east of Dumbarton. Follow the private road past Greenland farm and north through forest to Black Linn Reservoir. Cross the dam and climb half a kilometre north to the summit. The return may be varied by going further west along the top of the Lang Craigs to descend towards Middleton farm and the road down to Milton

On the north side of the Kilpatricks, Auchineden Hill (357m) is the most popular hill, being easily accessible from the Queen's View car park on the A809 road and commanding a very fine view in the northern arc to the Luss Hills, Ben Lomond and round north-eastwards to Ben Vorlich beyond the flat expanse of Flanders Moss.

Looking across Strath Blane to Dumgoyne

The most notable feature of Auchineden Hill is The Whangie, a short distance north-west of the summit. A long, narrow flake of rock has split from the hillside (possibly as a result of glacier plucking) to leave a deep and narrow cleft. The flake is about a hundred metres long and is vertical on both sides. The crest is very narrow, generally less than a metre wide, and can be reached by easy scrambles at both ends and at an intermediate point. The traverse along the crest of the flake is an airy scramble. At the northern end of The Whangie there is a smaller flake known as The Gendarme, whose top can be reached by a moderate scramble. Its bizarre rock scenery gives The Whangie a rather unique character.

Access to The Whangie is along a well-marked path from the Queen's View car park. After climbing beside a wood for half a kilometre, the path follows a horizontal traverse just below the northern escarpment of Auchineden Hill. A higher path above the escarpment leads across the level top of the hill to the trig point at its summit.

A good cross-country walk over the Kilpatricks (making use of the local bus services) can be made by climbing Duncolm from Hardgate by the route described above. From its summit descend north and cross the moorland to the dam at the north-west corner of Burncrooks Reservoir. From there reach the A809 road either by the track past the water treatment works to Lower Auchengillan, or over Auchineden Hill and down to the Queen's View. (11 kilometres).

Dumgoyne from Craigallian Loch

THE CAMPSIE FELLS

These hills are the highest and most extensive of the groups described in this chapter. They are prominent in views north from Glasgow, and the southern slopes drop steeply to Strath Blane and the wide valley of the River Kelvin. To the north the hills are bounded by the Endrick Water and the Carron Valley Reservoir.

At the western end Dumgoyne (427m) is a prominent conical hill, certainly the most distinctive of the Campsies. The highest hill, Earl's Seat (578m), is about three kilometres north-east of Dumgoyne, but being the highest point of a gently undulating plateau it is not very distinctive. Slackdhu is the highest point of the very prominent line of crags overlooking Blanefield.

Further east the Campsies are bisected by the B822 road from Lennoxtown to Fintry, known locally as the Crow Road, which reaches 333m at its summit. To the east of this road Meikle Bin is the highest hill, and it is a distinctive point when seen from a distance to the north or south. There are forestry plantations all round the hill, those on the north side of many years standing and those on the south and west of more recent planting. Eastwards from Meikle Bin the fells drop gradually to the road between Kilsyth and Carronbridge.

The south side of the Campsies have some steep, rocky escarpments overlooking Blanefield and Lennoxtown, and on the north side the Corrie of Balglass and the

Winter morning in Strath Blane

smaller corrie to its west are fine features. The Spout of Ballagan (now a nature reserve) and the Fin Glen are beautiful spots, with the streams in these two glens tumbling down in many falls over the successive layers of lava. Above these crags and glens the undulating plateau of the Campsies extends for more than sixteen kilometres from west to east without dropping below 300m. It is for the most part featureless and devoid of paths save for those made by sheep, and walking across this plateau of tussocky grass and eroded peat bog is very rough in places.

Dumgoyne is probably the most popular hill in the Campsies by reason of its isolated position and striking appearance. It commands a very fine view of Loch Lomond and the hills beyond. The shortest approach is from the A81 road two kilometres north-west of Blanefield up the private road past Craigbrock farm to Cantywheery cottage. Alternatively, reach the same point from the church in Blane-field along the 'Pipe Road' which follows the line of the aqueduct from Loch Katrine to Glasgow. About one hundred metres north-west of the cottage a gate gives access to a grassy track which goes north-east up the hillside towards a prominent little crag. Beyond the crag bear north-west over a burn and horizontally across the slopes of Dumfoyn (as Dumgoyne's twin neighbour is called) to make the final ascent of Dumgoyne by a rising traverse to reach the south-west ridge, thereby avoiding the rather steep and rocky slopes just below the summit on its south and east sides.

The ascent of Earl's Seat can be combined with Dumgoyne. From the prominent little crag above Cantywheery climb north-east up the Cauldhame Glen to Graham's

Cairn at a fence and continue in the same direction across flat featureless ground at the head of the Ballagan Burn to the steeper rise to Earl's Seat, where three fences meet at the trig point.

Slackdhu (496m) can also be climbed by the same approach. From a point just above the prominent little crag bear east up a grassy ridge past the edge of the escarpment and across the rising plateau to the top which is not well defined.

The Spout of Ballagan is a nature reserve owned by the Scottish Wildlife Trust. Visitors should obtain a permit to visit the reserve from the warden, (at the time of writing, Mr G.Durant at Ballagan House). The Ballagan Burn tumbles down a narrow, steep-sided glen in a series of falls, the lowest of which forms a beautiful curtain behind which one can walk along a narrow rock ledge. On the west side of the glen close to the fall the horizontal strata of lava are clearly exposed.

The Corrie of Balglass on the north side of the Campsies is another fine feature with a lovely little waterfall at its head. Access to the corrie from the B818 road between Killearn and Fintry is across farm land; a discreet approach is needed. A private road leads to Mount farm, and beyond it a track continues up the Balglass Burn towards a recently afforested area on Ballikinrain Muir. To reach the corrie leave the track a few hundred metres beyond the farm, after crossing the Balglass Burn, and bear south-east across grassy slopes.

The Campsie plateau at Allanrowie can be reached from the same track south of Mount by climbing the broad grassy slope west of Corrie of Balglass. Towards the top of the slope there is a grassy path just east of the stream which comes down from the plateau. Just to the west of this stream is Jock's Cairn (478m), a prominent pointed top on the edge of the northern escarpment of the Campsies.

The Crow Road gives access to the central part of the Campsies. Probably the best walk from it starts at the car park at the bend in the road near Jamie Wright's Well and goes east along an easy-angled grassy ridge, with the escarpment above Lennoxtown on one's right, to Lairs (504m). The walk can be continued to Cort-ma Law (531m) and north-west across rough boggy ground to Lecket Hill (546m), from where the descent goes west-south-west to avoid recent forestry further north.

Meikle Bin (570m) is most easily climbed from the Crow Road two kilometres north of its summit. Take the track to Waterhead farm and follow a new forest road round the north side of the farm and southwards towards Lecket Hill. The slopes of this hill have been extensively forested right down to Waterhead. At a junction turn left to the road end and descend a grassy bank to the Bin Burn. Cross the burn and climb up a clearing beside a fence between old and newer forest to reach a higher road. Go left along this for a short distance to a path which leads to the top of Meikle Bin.

Another longer route starts at the west end of the Carron Valley Reservoir and goes along the forest road south to the bridge over the River Carron. Continue up another road south-west past Little Bin to the upper slopes of Meikle Bin where the route described above is joined. It is possible for those who are fit to cycle almost all the way.

Another route to Meikle Bin starts at Queenzieburn on the A803 road between Kirkintilloch and Kilsyth. Go north up a narrow road to Corrie and continue by a path to the dam at Birkenburn Reservoir. From the north end of the dam go north-west across the slight rise of Black Hill and follow a path through the recently planted forest to reach Meikle Bin.

THE FINTRY HILLS

This small group, together with the Gargunnock and Touch Hills further east, form the eastern third of the range of hills across Scotland from Dumbarton to Stirling. The most striking feature of these hills is the long and almost continuous escarpment on thier north side .

The highest and most prominent hill is Stronend (511m) at the western end of the escarpment. The shortest approach to it is from Fintry along the private road to Culcreuth Castle. On reaching a little loch before the castle turn right up a path to reach a higher track which is followed past a cottage and up the hillside. At a gate where the track reaches the open hillside turn north-east uphill and climb easy grassy slopes to reach the gently rising plateau one kilometre south of the summit.

There is a good cross-country walk across the Fintry Hills from the west end of the Carron Valley Reservoir to Ballochleam near Kippen. Follow a road through the forest and then a track onto the open moor towards the derelict cottage at Cringate. Continue up the Endrick Water past the ruins of Burnfoot to reach another track which goes past the Spout of Ballochleam and down to the farm of the same name. (9 kilometres). Stronend may be included in this walk as it is only two kilometres west of the Spout of Ballochleam.

CLIMBING

Nearly all the rock climbing in the area of this chapter is on low-lying crags and outcrops, although Dumbarton Rock deserves to be regarded as something rather bigger and more serious than a mere outcrop. Full details of nearly all the recorded climbs on these crags are given in the *Climbers' Guide to Central and Southern Scotland*, edited by J.Handren and published by the Scottish Mountaineering Trust (1986). An updated edition of this guide will be published in 1992. The following notes summarise the principal climbing grounds.

Dumbarton Rock is a prominent volcanic plug rising to a height of over 70m above the muddy flats of the River Clyde near the mouth of the River Leven. Dumbarton Castle, the site of an ancient stronghold of the Britons, stands on top of the rock and is a Historic Monument. The most impressive feature of Dumbarton Rock is its north-west face, which overhangs to a considerable degree. The routes on it, the longest of which are 45m, are very hard (up to E7) and serious. At the base of the north-west face there are a number of boulders which give short climbs of all grades, but very much shorter and less serious than the Rock itself.

The Whangie on the north side of Auchineden Hill has already been mentioned. It was the first of the Glasgow outcrops to be explored, but now it seems to be less popular than other crags such as Craigmore and Auchinstarry Quarry. This is a pity, because The Whangie has an ambience and outlook across Stockie Muir towards Ben Lomond which few other crags can match.

There is a thirty minute walk from the Queen's View car park to reach The Whangie, and the first feature to be encountered is The Gendarme, a small 6m high flake. Beyond it is the main crag forming a long flake with a narrow passage between it and the steep vegetatious wall which is part of the escarpment of Auchineden Hill. Climbs on this wall are unpleasantly grassy and loose, but on The Gendarme and The Flake itself there are many good short routes up to 15m on both the outside and

Backstep Chimney, a classic problem at The Whangie

inside faces. *Backstep Chimney* (Severe) on the outside wall of The Flake is one of the best-known of these climbs.

Craigmore (at grid reference 527 797) is a popular outcrop less than five minutes from the B821 road between Carbeth Inn and Blanefield, just opposite Carbeth House. The crag faces north and gets little sun. The rock is basalt with many of the characteristics of gritstone, being sound and rough, and there are over a hundred recorded routes up to 15m long.

Other crags of less interest in the same area include Pillar Crag on the south side of the B821 road one and a half kilometres east of Craigmore, Craigton crag on the hillside behind High Craigton on the A809 road four kilometres north of Bearsden, and Dunglass, a small volcanic plug opposite the foot of the Ballagan Glen near Strathblane.

The climbs on the high escarpment below Slackdhu seem to have been neglected since the discovery of lower outcrops such as Craigmore. The line of cliffs, which is rather discontinuous and broken into tiers by horizontal grass ledges, is about two kilometres long. At the left end is *North-west Gully* and near the centre is *Coffin Gully*; neither is of interest in summer, but they might give pleasant winter routes. The best rock climbing is on a small crag about half a kilometre south-east of Coffin Gully which is recognisable in wet weather by a small waterfall down a chimney, *Jenny's Lum*. The cliff immediately to the left of the Lum, although only 10m high, is steep and its north-west edge is *Jenny's Lum Arête*, a very fine little climb (Hard Severe). There are several other easier routes to the right of Jenny's Lum, and far to its right, directly above Strathblane, is Black Craig, a loose and vegetatious crag (apparently held together by ivy) which was the scene of a tragedy in 1935, and has probably been seldom climbed since then.

Finally, far to the east near Kilsyth (at grid reference 791 771) is Auchinstarry Quarry. This is reputed to be Glasgow's most popular quarry, and it offers excellent climbing at all grades. The rock is quartz-dolerite, and the quarry's southerly aspect means that the rock dries quickly after rain. The 1986 guidebook lists over a hundred and twenty routes in the quarry.

SKI TOURING

The Campsies were the scene of one of the earliest attempts to ski on the hills in Scotland, by W.W.Naismith in 1892. He described his sortie on a pair of wooden planks with enthusiasm, but the Campsies have not become a popular ski resort. The best that can be said of them is that in conditions of heavy snow (when the roads to the north may be blocked) they can give good excercise of the langlauf variety. The road from Lennoxtown to Fintry provides a good high starting point for excursions to the east or west. Unfortunately, the very tussocky nature of the Campsies, the afforestation and the ditches that cross the hills all combine to make the terrain less than ideal for skiing. Enthusiasts will overlook these shortcomings and get some good days when the sun shines and the snow is deep.

CHAPTER 2

The Lomond and Ochil Hills

West Lomond	522m	197 066
Benarty Hill	356m	154 979
Dumglow	379m	076 965
Ben Cleuch	721m	903 006
Andrew Gannel Hill	670m	919 006
King's Seat Hill	648m	933 999
Tarmangie Hill	645m	942 013
Blairdenon Hill	631m	866 018
Dumyat	418m	836 976

ACCESS
Many major and minor roads encircle these hills and make access easy. In particular the
A91 road from Stirling through Menstrie, Alva, Tillicoultry and Dollar gives close access to
the south side of the Ochils, and the A91, A911 and A912 roads encircle the Lomond Hills

TRANSPORT
Bus: Service from Stirling to St Andrews passes through Menstrie, Alva, Tillicoultry, Dollar
and along the north side of the Lomond Hills through Strathmiglo; daily.
Service from Milnathort to Leslie passes through Wester Balgeddie, Easter Balgeddie and
Kinnesswood on the west side of the Lomond Hills; daily.
Service from Glenrothes to Falkland passes along the east side of the Lomond Hills; daily.

ACCOMMODATION
Hotels in all neighbouring towns including Bridge of Allan, Menstrie, Alva, Tillicoultry, Dollar,
Rumbling Bridge, Milnathort, Kinnesswood and Falkland. Youth hostels in Stirling, Glen-
devon and Falkland.

MAPS
Ordnance Survey 1:50,000, Sheets 57,58 and 59
Bartholomew 1:100,000, Sheets 45,48 and 49.

The Ochils and the Lomonds together with a few smaller hills between them lie
between the Forth and Tay valleys in the counties of Fife, Kinross and Clackmannan
and a small part of Perthshire. This is not by any stretch of the imagination a
mountainous part of the country, and these hills are much lower than their Highland
neighbours. However, their position in Central Scotland rising abruptly from low-

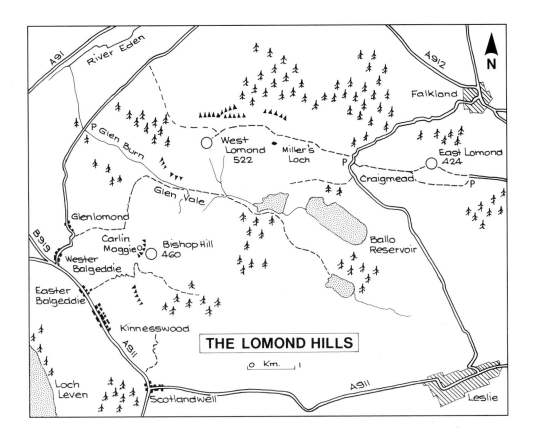

lying country and facing across the Firth of Forth makes them conspicuous features of the landscape seen from all the towns and villages between Edinburgh and Stirling. The Ochils form a fairly continuous range of rounded hills which rise steeply above the hillfoot towns from Bridge of Allan to Dollar, and West Lomond, the highest of the hills of that name, is one of the most conspicuous of the little hills of Scotland, visible from many distant viewpoints.

THE LOMOND HILLS

The Lomond Hills in Fife form a small group of three distinct tops - West Lomond, East Lomond and Bishop Hill. They are partly situated within the Fife Regional Park. Around their northern and western perimeter the hills rise very steeply from the farm lands of Fife; in places the escarpment is quite rocky and near its middle it is split by the narrow valley of Glen Vale which separates West Lomond from Bishop Hill. To the south and east the hills drop much more gradually towards the River Leven across an area of high moorland dotted with reservoirs, plantations and hill farms and crossed by a number of narrow private roads. A narrow public road crosses the hills from Leslie to Falkland, reaching a height of almost 300m between West and East Lomond.

West Lomond and Bishop Hill from the north

The surrounding area is also full of interest. The town of Falkland nestles at the foot of East Lomond; it is one of the historic towns of Scotland and Falkland Palace was once a royal Scottish palace, the home of the Stuart kings who used to hunt on the forested slopes of the Lomond Hills before those forests were felled. Now the palace is in the care of the National Trust for Scotland, and a visit to it is an excellent complement to half a day's hillwalking on the Lomonds. To the west of the Lomonds, Loch Leven is a Nature Reserve, noted for its birds and the Royal Society for the Protection of Birds has a Nature Centre at Vane Farm on the south side of the loch.

West Lomond (522m)

This is the highest of these hills and the summit dome rises 100m above the high moorland round its base. To the north and west the escarpment round the hill is quite steep, and to the south slopes of heather and grass drop to Glen Vale where one of the caves in the rocky walls of the glen is known as John Knox's Pulpit. The glen itself is also known as the Covenanters' Glen, so there would seem to be a religious connection dating back a few hundred years. It is a beautiful little glen with white cliffs and miniature waterfalls.

To the east from the summit of West Lomond grassy moorland drops gradually for three kilometres to the road between Falkland and Leslie. From the summit of this road at Craigmead, where there is a car park and visitor centre, a good track

Seamab Hill in the Ochils from the River Devon

leads across the moor to West Lomond and gives the easiest ascent of this hill. Other routes to the hill from the north-west start from the minor road south of the village of Gateside; one goes up a path starting one kilometre south of the village, and another goes up the Glen Burn to reach Glen Vale from where there is a steep climb up tussocky grass to the top.

Not surprisingly, the view from West Lomond on a fine day is superb, not least the mosaic of fields and woodland surrounding the foot of the hill in this fertile corner of Fife. Further north the Highland hills stand in a great range on the horizon, but it difficult to identify many of the individual hills.

East Lomond (424m)
This is another prominent little hill, but being almost a hundred metres lower than West Lomond, it is not nearly as easily recognised in distant views. It is a particularly good viewpoint looking across the eastern half of Fife. The ascent may be made from four starting points. The shortest climb is from the east, starting at the car park at the top of the Purin Hill road half a kilometre from the summit; there is also a path from the car park at Craigmead, and another climb starts in Falkland and goes steeply up through woods on the north-east side of the hill. A waymarked path from Pitcairn on the north edge of Glenrothes leads to the summit via the Purin Hill car park.

Bishop Hill (460m)

This is the highest point of the long west-facing escarpment of the Lomonds, although the actual summit is little more than a knoll on the edge of the plateau overlooking Loch Leven. A farm track starts in Easter Balgeddie and after passing beside some fields a higher path is reached which climbs steeply up the grassy scarp to reach the plateau a little south of the highest point of Bishop Hill.

There is a pleasant high-level walk northwards from the summit to Glen Vale from where the return to Easter Balgeddie can be made by a low path which goes down the glen for a short distance before turning south along the foot of the escarpment to reach Glenlomond Village (named Glenlomond Hospital on the 1:50,000 map) one and a half kilometres north of Easter Balgeddie.

Just to the west of the summit of Bishop Hill the top of the escarpment has some low cliffs in front of which stands a spectacular little pinnacle called Carlin Maggie. It can be reached by a steep climb from the path above Glenlomond Village, or more easily by descending a short distance west from the top of Bishop Hill, but this should be done with care for there are some steep rocks just above the pinnacle.

Benarty Hill (356m) rises steeply above the south side of Loch Leven. The rocky escarpment of the north face of this hill gives it an impressive appearance as seen from the B9097 road along its foot. To avoid walking through farmland on the north side of the hill, the ascent is probably best made from the south. There is a path starting from the road west of Ballingry at grid reference 159 970 which leads uphill through the west end of Benarty Wood to reach the open hillside half a kilometre south-east of the summit.

The highest point between the Lomonds and the Ochils is Dumglow (379m) in the Cleish Hills. It is a prominent little hill, its summit rising above the forestry plantations which surround it on three sides. There is access along the roads through the forest on the east side of the hill. Access from the north is possible at present, but may be impeded as newly planted forests grow.

THE OCHIL HILLS

The Ochil Hills extend for about 30 kilometres from west to east and 13 kilometres from north to south at their broadest point. The range is divided in two by Glen Devon and Glen Eagles, with all the highest hills to the west of this line. To the east of Glen Devon the hills are relatively low, none exceeding 500m, but there is plenty of good hillwalking in a quiet area of grassy hills and sheep farms.

The main hills of the Ochils lie to the west of Glen Devon, and on their south side they form a steep and imposing front overlooking the valley of the River Forth. The name Ochil is derived from the old Brittonic word *uchel* meaning high, an appropriate name when one considers that to the early people of central Scotland these hills would probably seem quite mountainous, being much higher and steeper than the Pentlands or the Campsies. On their north side the hills fall away in long gentle slopes towards Strath Allan and Strath Earn and their appearance from those straths is much less impressive. From most viewpoints the Ochils appear as a rather continuous range of undulating hills rather than as well-defined and separate summits. This impression is quite correct as in the 10-kilometre long range from Glen Devon to Sheriff Muir the highest point, Ben Cleuch, is 721m and the broad ridge never falls below 540m.

Nearly all the hillwalkers' access routes to the Ochils are from the south, starting from the hillfoot towns from where there are several paths leading up into the hills. It is advisable to use these as the southern hillsides are quite steep and in places craggy, and anyone wandering off the paths and attempting an ascent or descent on the south side of the hills could well get into difficulty. On the other hand the paths up some of the glens such as Alva Glen or the Mill Glen above Tillicoultry are delightful and give good walks even if one does not continue onto the hills.

Higher up, above the steep lower slopes, the Ochils are fairly smooth and grassy hills with little heather and a few areas of eroded peat bog. One can wander almost anywhere. There are few well-defined paths, and many sheep tracks which do not always take the walker in the right direction. In very thick weather the rather featureless nature of the high ground may make route-finding difficult, but the existence of fences along most of the ridges and over the summits makes the task of navigation in bad weather much easier.

Ben Cleuch (721m)
This is the highest and in many ways the most attractive of the Ochils. Its summit is well-defined and stands clearly as the topmost point of the range, and it commands a correspondingly good view, with an indicator on its summit.

The most direct ascent is from Tillicoultry, starting at the car park in the north-west corner of the village. Either the Glen Path or the Hill Path can be taken, the former is scenically more attractive. Both paths lead to the junction of the Daiglen and Gannel burns where a footbridge gives access to the foot of the south ridge of The Law (638m). The path continues up this ridge, over The Law and north-west across flatter ground to Ben Cleuch.

An alternative ascent from Alva starts at the north edge of the village just east of the Alva Burn. A footpath leads east across the hillside to join a track which in turn leads up the Silver Glen. From the col between The Nebit and Ben Ever climb north up the ridge to Ben Ever (622m) and continue across a col north then east to reach Ben Cleuch.

Andrew Gannel Hill (670m)
This is the eastern outlier of Ben Cleuch, separated from it by a high col at 630m. Like Ben Cleuch, it is most easily climbed from Tillicoultry, either following the path over The Law (as for Ben Cleuch) and then bearing north-east, or by following the Hill Path up the south side of the Gannel Burn to the col one kilometre east of the summit. From this col the path (which is a right of way from Tillicoultry to Blackford)

goes north-west towards Maddy Moss and Skythorn Hill, and the way to Andrew Gannel Hill goes west up easy grassy slopes.

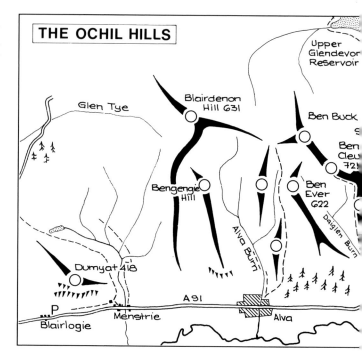

King's Seat Hill (648m)
This hill is fairly conspicuous in views of the Ochils from the south as it stands in front of the range, rising directly above the River Devon between Tillicoultry and Dollar. It can be climbed from Tillicoultry by the path up the Gannel Burn, or from Dollar by a path from the north side of the town up Dollar Glen to Castle Campbell and from there up easy grassy slopes on the south side of the Burn of Sorrow.

Castle Campbell stands in a splendid position above the confluence of the Burn of Sorrow and the Burn of Care. There are some paths in the glen below the castle which give a good short walk from Dollar.

Tarmangie Hill (645m)
This is the highest point of a ridge of three hills between Glen Sherup and Glen Quey to the north of Dollar. The other two are Whitewisp Hill (643m) and Innerdownie (611m). The three hills can be traversed in a good walk from Glen Devon, starting near Glenquey Reservoir, and following the crest of the ridge with forest on the north side. From Tarmangie descend south-west towards the headwaters of the Burn of Sorrow and either descend by a grassy path on the south-west side of this burn to Dollar or climb again to the col between King's Seat Hill and Andrew Gannel Hill to descend the path to Tillicoultry.

Blairdenon Hill (631m)
This is the westernmost of the high hills of the Ochils, but it is flat-topped and not very distinctive. Three fences meet at the top of the hill, making it relatively easy to find in mist.

The shortest ascent is from the Sheriff Muir road to the west, starting from the Inn at the foot of Glen Tye. This is, however, not a particularly interesting way.

The path up the Alva Glen is probably the finest of the Ochil glen walks, up a beautiful wooded gorge, and it is possible from the end of the path to climb steep

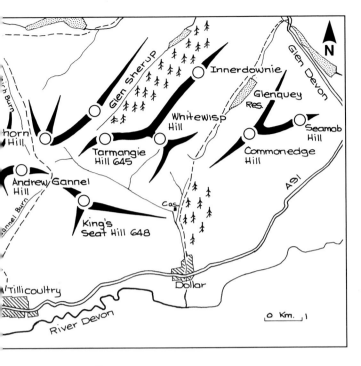

slopes westwards to gain the ridge of Bengengie Hill and continue north over it and across one and a half kilometres of featureless ground to Blairdenon Hill.

Dumyat (418m)

Although it is much lower than the main group of Ochil hills, Dumyat is as well known as any of them by virtue of its position at the west end of the range overlooking Stirling, and its fine rocky appearance. It rises very steeply in craggy slopes above the road between Blairlogie and Menstrie, and a prominent feature of this steep hillside is the big gully which divides the south face just west of the summit.

Possibly the easiest route of ascent starts from the minor road between Bridge of Allan and Sheriff Muir at grid reference 813 980 and goes up a good path for just over two kilometres to the top where there is a beacon.

Another route starts at a car park about two hundred metres east of Blairlogie on the A91 road. Walk east along a track at the foot of the hill for a few hundred metres until below the big gully on the south face and then climb steeply uphill, following a faint overgrown path through bracken and whins, at first on the west side of the gully. Higher up follow the path up the gully itself between crags to reach flatter ground to the west of the summit where the path of the previous route is joined.

From Menstrie one can climb from the north edge of the village (on the west side of the Menstrie Burn) uphill by a path leading north-west to the waterworks on the hillside above, where a track is reached. Leave this track a short distance further north and climb a good grassy path north-west to reach the summit of Dumyat from the east.

The best hillwalking expedition on the Ochils is the complete traverse from Glen Devon to Sheriff Muir taking in all the 600m tops. There are twelve of them if minor bumps such as Cairnmorris Hill, Skythorn Hill and Ben Buck are included, and the distance from Castlehill Reservoir in Glen Devon to the Sheriff Muir road is about 25 kilometres.

PATHS AND WALKS

Blackford to Tillicoultry. The north end of this right of way starts at Blackford village beside the busy A9 road. Take the track past Kinpauch up the Glen of Kinpauch and down Glen Bee to the Upper Glendevon Reservoir. Go round the west end of the reservoir and reach the path which goes up the Broich Burn high on its east bank. This leads to the col between Skythorn Hill and Andrew Gannel Hill at Maddy Moss, and from there the path goes south-east for a short distance before turning south-west down the Gannel Burn to Tillicoultry. (15 kilometres).

Dollar to Glendevon. Take the path or road from Dollar up the east side of the Dollar Glen to the cottage just east of Castle Campbell. From there continue north along a path up the Burn of Care to Maiden's Well and down to Glenquey Reservoir to reach Glendevon. This is a right of way. (8 kilometres).

It is possible to extend this walk north from Glendevon by the path through Borland Glen and down the Coul Burn to Coulshill where a minor road is reached which leads to Auchterarder.

CLIMBING

Many years ago J.H.B.Bell pioneered climbing on the Lomonds. *The Split Nose* on Craigengaw was a notoriously loose and unpleasant route. On Bishop Hill, Carlin Maggie and the small cliffs near to it were also climbed, and on Dumyat the crags on the south side of the hill seem to have had a brief period of popularity. The earliest climb on Dumyat was almost certainly *Raeburn's Gully* (50m, Difficult), a narrow cleft high up on the east side of the big gully on the hill's south face.

However, these hills and climbs are now out of fashion. Carlin Maggie has an old decaying sling round her neck to show that the last climber to abseil from her did so many years ago, and Raeburn's Gully is overgrown with weeds and nettles.

Modern rock climbers prefer the sea-cliffs at Hawcraig near Aberdour, which is the most popular crag in Fife. There are also a few modern routes on Benarty Hill on the south side of Loch Leven. Limekilns to the west of Dunfermline enjoyed several years of popularity, but is now out of bounds. Details of these climbs are contained in the *Climbers Guide to Central and Southern Scotland*, edited by J.Handren (1986), to be revised in 1992.

SKI MOUNTAINEERING

The Ochils give excellent ski touring of the langlauf variety when the snow cover is good. Many different tours are possible, of which the complete traverse from east to west is the best.

Carlin Maggie, a portrait taken before her head fell off

CHAPTER 3

The Trossachs Hills

Ben Venue	729m	474 064
Ben An	454m	502 082
Ben Ledi	879m	563 098
Benvane	821m	535 137
Stob Fear-tomhais	771m	474 163
Stob a'Choin	869m	417 160

This chapter includes not only The Trossachs, but also the surrounding hills and lochs. The area occupies a strategic position in the centre of Scotland between the low-lying valley of the River Forth and the mountains of the Highlands. There is a wonderful gradation of scenery as one goes from the parkland and cultivation around the Lake of Menteith to the Braes of Balquhidder and the high mountains to the north-west of Loch Voil.

The area described in this chapter is bounded on the south by Glen Gyle, the west end of Loch Katrine and the roads from Stronachlachar to Aberfoyle (B829) and from there to Callander (A81). The northern and eastern boundaries are formed by the River Larig which flows eastwards from its source near the head of Glen Gyle, through lochs Doine and Voil and then, having become the River Balvag, it turns south past Strathyre, through Loch Lubnaig and cascades down the Falls of Leny to become the River Teith at Callander.

The name Trossachs applies, strictly speaking, only to the short wooded glen between Loch Katrine and Loch Achray, an area of no more than a few square kilometres. However, by common use the name has come to be applied to a much larger area embracing the country from Loch Ard and Aberfoyle northwards to lochs Katrine, Achray and Venachar.

The Trossachs have for many years been one of the most popular areas in Scotland for the traveller and the tourist. At the beginning of the nineteenth century William and Dorothy Wordsworth travelled on foot through Glen Gyle, along Loch Katrine and over the hills from there to Loch Voil and Strathyre. Their journey was recorded

ACCESS
From Stirling by the A84 road to Callander, Strathyre and Kingshouse Hotel and the A873 road to Aberfoyle. From Glasgow by the A81 road to Aberfoyle. From Aberfoyle by the B829 road to Inversnaid, and by the road over the Duke's Pass to The Trossachs. From Callander by the A821 road to The Trossachs. From Kingshouse Hotel by road to Balquhidder and Inverlochlarg farm (public road ends before the farm).

TRANSPORT
Bus: Glasgow to Aberfoyle; daily.
Stirling to Callander; daily.
Callander to Strathyre; Mondays to Fridays.
Stirling to Aberfoyle; Mondays to Saturdays.

Postbus: Aberfoyle to Kinlochard and Inversnaid; Mondays to Saturdays.
Callander to Trossachs Pier; Mondays to Saturdays.
Callander to Aberfoyle via the Duke's Pass; Mondays to Fridays.
Callander to Strathyre and Kingshouse Hotel; Mondays to Fridays.

Ferry: Private ferry service operated by Inversnaid Hotel across Loch Lomond from Inversnaid to the Sloy Power Station.

Boat: The steamer service on Loch Katrine carries passengers between Trossachs Pier and Stronachlacher on some, but not all sailings. (Consult timetable locally or phone 041-355-5333).

ACCOMMODATION
Hotels in Aberfoyle, Callander, Strathyre, The Trossachs, Kingshouse Hotel (Balquhidder) and Inversnaid.
Youth hostels at Loch Ard and The Trossachs (Brig o' Turk).
Camp and caravan sites at Aberfoyle (2km south on A81) and Strathyre.

MAPS
Ordnance Survey 1:50,000, Sheets 56 and 57.
Bartholomew 1:100,000, Sheet 48.

by Dorothy in her *Recollections of a Tour Made in Scotland,* and William was inspired to write several poems. A few years later Sir Walter Scott published his poem *The Lady of the Lake,* followed shortly afterwards by his novel *Rob Roy,* and the fame of The Trossachs became established in literature. Since then no traveller's tour of Scotland has been complete without a visit to The Trossachs.

The whole area embraces a great variety of scenery from the pastoral to the very wild and rugged. Ben Venue and its neighbouring tops occupy the south-western corner between Loch Ard and Loch Katrine, and the Menteith Hills in the south-east corner overlook the Lake of Menteith and the flat expanse of Flanders Moss through which winds the River Forth. The road from Aberfoyle to The Trossachs crosses the Duke's Pass between Ben Venue and the Menteith Hills, and from the top of the pass the traveller gets a grand impression of The Trossachs as a whole, a region of forests, lochs and rugged hills with the central flat lands of Scotland to the south and east.

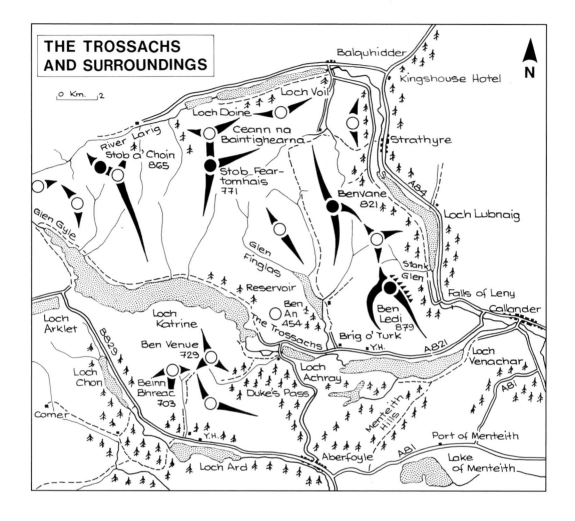

THE TROSSACHS
AND SURROUNDINGS

     The Trossachs, and in particular the glen between Loch Katrine and Loch Achray
which is the true heart of the area, is a fine example of Highland scenery in miniature.
The glen and the steep hillside of Ben An above it are beautifully wooded with birch
and oak, with darker and more regimented forests of larch and spruce on the slopes
of Ben Venue to the south. Sadly, the afforestation of the last two decades has seen
the encroachment of dense plantations of conifers into the existing natural wood-
lands. Nowhere is this more evident than on the approach to Ben An from Loch
Achray; at one time the path led upwards through lovely open birchwoods with
clear views of the hill ahead, now the path is enclosed by larch and spruce and the
hill is hidden until one is almost upon it.

Loch Katrine is the reservoir for Glasgow's water supply and has remained largely unspoiled. The road along the north shore is private and the lochside is free from motor traffic and its attendant crowds and noise. The steamer *Sir Walter Scott* still plies its waters and is a reminder of the more gracious and leisurely days of tourism of past years.

To the north of The Trossachs the country as far as Loch Voil is hilly, and the interior is wild and uninhabited. The two highest mountains in this area are Ben Ledi in the south-east corner and Stob a'Choin in the north-west. Between them is a rather desolate stretch of featureless hills of no great interest to the climber or walker. In the lower part of Glen Finglas the reservoir of the same name supplies additional water to Loch Katrine through a pipeline under Ben An. In the north-east corner of this area there is some attractive country round Loch Voil, Balquhidder, Strathyre and Loch Lubnaig, but the landscape of this corner, with the big mountains such as Stob Binnein and Ben Vorlich showing their peaks above the lower hills, is more akin to the Highlands than to The Trossachs.

If the hills of The Trossachs, with the exception of those already mentioned, lack outstanding character or interest, the same cannot be said of the lochs. There are, if one includes those just outside the perimeter of our area, twelve lochs (or to be more precise, eleven lochs and a lake). Each one has its own particular character and beauty, from the placid expanse of the Lake of Menteith among its fields and woods to the narrow, mountain-girt lochs Voil and Lubnaig.

The Trossachs have more to offer the hillwalker than the rock-climber, for whom there are only the small but very pleasant crags on Ben An and some boulders and pinnacles on Ben Ledi. For the winter climber there is practically nothing at all, although in a hard winter it might be possible to find some not too serious climbing on the east side of Ben Ledi or the north face of Stob a'Choin. For the ski-mountaineer, Ben Ledi is the only hill noted for its potential, although Benvane might also be worth a visit. There are, however, many good walks in the area, through the hills and forests and along the lochsides. It is worth emphasising that of the four seasons autumn is undoubtedly the best for the Trossachs; then the summer crowds have dwindled and the colours on the hillsides and in the woods add an extra dimension to the beauty of the region.

Part of the Queen Elizabeth Forest Park lies within the area covered by this chapter, and the Park Guide is a good source of information about the district and the recreational facilities, particularly the forest walks, within the park. The Forestry Commission publishes a very useful map which shows the principal footpaths in the Park, in particular those which are waymarked by the Commission. It is obtainable from the Commission's offices and visitor centres, and local shops.

Ben An

Looking west from the summit of Ben An to Loch Katrine

THE HILLS

Ben An (454m)

This is the conspicuous little hill which is well seen across Loch Achray from the north side of the Duke's Pass. Its sharp pointed summit and rocky front rise grandly above the birch woods of The Trossachs, and it is not apparent that it is just a spur of the higher and rather featureless hill Meall Gainmheich. However, such is its distinctive shape and character, Ben An is always regarded among climbers as being a distinct hill in its own right, and it is probably the most popular one in The Trossachs with both walkers and rock-climbers. Note that on the Ordnance Survey 1:50,000 map the placing of the name Ben An is rather misleading as it apparently refers to a point about half a kilometre east of the rocky summit of the hill.

The best approach is by the path which climbs steeply uphill from a car park at the edge of the woods a few hundred metres west of the Trossachs Hotel. Recent planting by the Forestry Commission has spoiled this approach, which no longer gives clear views of the hill on the way up through the woods. Just beyond the point where it emerges from the trees, the path branches. The left-hand branch goes to the foot of the rocky south face where a series of short rock climbs up the hill begins. The right-hand path climbs steeply beside a little stream to go round the east side of the hill and through a little notch to approach the summit from the north-east.

The summit of Ben An is formed by a pointed rock which commands a view out of all proportion to the modest height of the hill. To the south Ben Venue looks very impressive on the opposite side of Loch Katrine, and to the west looking towards the head of the loch there is a distant glimpse of the Arrochar hills.

An alternative route may be used for the descent, but it gives rough going. Drop down from the summit westwards for a few hundred metres, then turn south down the steep hillside between small crags and through deep heather, bracken and oakwoods to reach a stream which is followed down to the Loch Katrine road a short distance from the car park at the pier. There is a cafe at the pier, open in summer, which may be welcome before walking back along the road to the foot of the ascent path.

Ben Venue *(hill of the caves or hill of the stirks)* (729m)
This is a rugged hill, very much more of a mountain than its height would suggest. Its finest aspect is the north-east face as seen from Loch Achray, and this is one of the best-known views of The Trossachs. From the south the hill is not well seen, for the twin summits just appear above the long flat ridge of Beinn an Fhogharaidh. The two tops of Ben Venue are less than half a kilometre apart, the north-west one being 729m, and the south-east one 727m.

Low down on the north side of the hill the Bealach nam Bo *(pass of cattle)* is a little notch in the hillside through which the highlanders from Glen Gyle are said to have driven stolen cattle on their return from plundering raids on the lowlands. Just below the pass, in the crags above Loch Katrine, is the Coire na Urisgean *(goblin's cave)* from which the hill may take its name.

On the north side of Ben Venue three possible routes of ascent start at the Loch Achray Hotel and follow the Forestry Commission road westwards. One route, which is waymarked, bears left at the first junction and follows a road, then a path south-west through the forest in Gleann Riabhach. For part of the way through the forest this path has been well constructed, but there are several places where it is usually very wet and muddy, so much so in wet weather as to be almost impassable, so be prepared. In such conditions, this route can hardly be recommended.

Leave the path at the point where it emerges from the forest and climb north to the 727m top of Ben Venue. Descend steeply north-west for a short distance and cross the col to reach the summit.

The second route continues west (i.e. going straight ahead at the first junction after leaving the Loch Achray Hotel) to the edge of the forest and along a path past the Loch Katrine sluices below the steep and craggy north-east face of Ben Venue. About 300 metres past the sluices (at grid reference 486 069) leave the path and find another one which climbs uphill beside the most obvious of several streams which tumble down the craggy hillside. Climb steeply up the path through birchwoods and emerge into an open grassy corrie at whose head is the 727m top.

The third route goes further along the low path past the Loch Katrine sluices and climbs up among big boulders to the Bealach nam Bo. From there climb south up an ill-defined ridge, bearing right across a little stream to reach the summit directly.

From the south the normal route of ascent starts at Ledard farm near the west end of Loch Ard. The way follows a path first up the west side of the Ledard Burn, then on the east side to reach the col between two of Ben Venue's outliers, Beinn Bhreac and Creag a'Bhealaich. The path continues horizontally across the north side of the latter hill to the col marked by a very large cairn between it and Ben Venue, from where one branch of the path goes south-east down Gleann Riabhach towards Loch Achray. The route to Ben Venue continues up its south-west ridge, the path zigzag-ing upwards between little crags and rocky outcrops. The view from the summit gives a fine contrast between the forests and low hills to the south-east and the high mountains to the north-west, but its greatest charm is the nearer view of lochs and wooded shores on the north side of the hill.

Beinn Bhreac (703m) can easily be included in this route to Ben Venue as it lies close to the path at the head of the Ledard Burn. The best route to it is from the col between it and Creag a'Bhealaich, following a faint path along a line of fence posts to the 700m east top,then across a drop to the summit.

Ben Ledi *(hill of the gentle slope or God's hill)* (879m)
This is the highest of the Trossachs hills and it occupies a very prominent position on the southern edge of the Highlands between Loch Lubnaig and Loch Venachar. It is clearly seen from Stirling and other places in Central Scotland, and from Callander it dominates the view up the River Teith.

The main spine of the hill rises north-west as a broad grassy ridge above the east end of Loch Venachar. The ridge narrows at the summit and then turns north to a broad peaty col in which is situated Lochan nan Corp, so named after a funeral party which (so it is said) disappeared through the ice one winter's day on its way to St Bride's Chapel. To the north of the lochan there is a nameless top (c.710m) where the main ridge divides, the east branch going out over several knolls to Ardnandave Hill (715m), and the north-west branch dropping to the col (c.600m) which separates Ben Ledi from Benvane.

The western and southern slopes of Ben Ledi are for the most part rather featureless and uninteresting, but the east face overlooking the Pass of Leny and the south end of Loch Lubnaig is much grander, forested along its whole length and in places craggy above the tree-line. The east face of Ardnandave Hill in particular is very steep and rocky, with trees clinging to the hillside, but although it is impressive to look at it is not likely to entice the climber.

The Stank Glen is a fine forested corrie between Ben Ledi and Ardnandave Hill. High up on the Ben Ledi side of the corrie there is a group of pinnacles and boulders which give the only rock-climbing that the hill has to offer. However, it is not very popular, for there is quite a long uphill walk for some very short routes.

Ben Ledi from Auchineden Hill across the valley of the River Forth

The normal hillwalkers' route up Ben Ledi starts at a Forestry Commission car park (grid reference 586 093) on the narrow road from the A84 at the Pass of Leny to Stank. There is a signposted path which climbs westwards through the forest. Above the tree-line the path bears south-west below the craggy face of Ben Ledi to reach the south-east ridge just over one kilometre from the summit. The last part of the path up this ridge to the summit is well-defined.

The most interesting ascent of Ben Ledi is by the Stank Glen. Start up the forest road on the south side of the glen and in a few hundred metres, at the first bend in the road, look for a waymarker post. This indicates the start of a path (marked by more posts) uphill through the trees which leads up the Stank Glen on the south side of the Stank Burn. Once beyond the trees turn left (south-west) and climb steeply uphill, following a fairly distinct path towards the boulders and pinnacles higher up on the south side of the corrie. The most prominent of the pinnacles is the *Ben Ledi Pinnacle*, which was christened the *RIP Pinnacle* by early climbers, possibly by association with Lochan nan Corp at the head of the corrie. Once above the pinnacles, reach a narrow rocky ridge up which a path leads to gain the main ridge of the hill half a kilometre north-west of the summit.

From the south-west, starting at Brig o'Turk, there is an easy route. Take the private road on the east side of the Glen Finglas Reservoir to the farm at the foot of

Looking west along Loch Voil to Stob a'Choin

Gleann Casaig and continue along the track up this glen for about one and a half kilometres. Then climb more or less due east up grassy slopes to the summit.

The traverse northwards from Ben Ledi along the main ridge involves some fairly rough going over peat bogs and hummocks. From a point north of the 710m knoll a broad ridge leads east to Ardnandave Hill. A more direct ascent of this hill can be made from Stank, taking the route described above up the Stank Glen. Near the upper limit of the trees cross to the north side of the Stank Burn and climb north to Ardnandave Hill. There are three little boulder-strewn corries on the north side of the hill, and in the middle one there is a small pinnacle (rather like the Cioch in Skye) which can be seen from the road near the north end of Loch Lubnaig.

Benvane *(white hill)* (821m).
Five kilometres north-west of Ben Ledi is Benvane, the two hills being linked by a broad high ridge on the west side of Loch Lubnaig. Benvane is a rather featureless grassy hill whose west side falls steeply into Gleann nam Mean, while the east side drops more gradually towards the north end of Loch Lubnaig, the lower slopes being densely forested. The main spine of the hill is a south to north ridge which rises above the Glen Finglas Reservoir and drops north from the summit to Glen Buckie a few kilometres south of Balquhidder.

The shortest route to the hill is from Strathyre and it is possible to drive south to a point (grid reference 557 151) within half a kilometre of Laggan farm. From there walk up the forest road westwards, keeping to the road which leads west towards the head of Glen Buckie. Near the top of this road a path through a clearing in the forest leads to the col at the head of Glen Buckie. Continue north-west down the glen for barely a kilometre to clear the recently planted forest, then turn south-west past the remains of old shielings to reach the north ridge of Benvane one kilometre from the top.

A slightly longer, but probably easier route is from Ballimore farm at the end of the public road in Glen Buckie, reached from Balquhidder. The way goes up the long, easy-angled, grassy north ridge without any complications.

A similar, but rather longer route, is possible from the south starting from the end of the public road just north of Brig o'Turk. Walk up the private road on the east side of the Glen Finglas Reservoir to the farm at the foot of Gleann Casaig, and from there climb north past Creag na h-Airighe and up the south ridge of Benvane.

It is perfectly feasible to combine Ben Ledi and Benvane in a good traverse. The bus service along Loch Lubnaig between Callander and Strathyre makes this possible. The intervening ridge is five kilometres long and drops to 600m.

Beinn an t-Sidhein (572m) is a steep little hill between Strathyre and Glen Buckie, its east side above Strathyre being almost completely blanketed by forest, some of it recently felled. There is a waymarked path starting at Strathyre which leads up through the forest, west then south-west to emerge on the south ridge of the hill just over one kilometre from the summit. The walk up the ridge from there over a few knolls is easy, and the view from the top towards the mountains beyond Loch Voil is very fine.

Stob Fear-tomhais *(surveyors' peak)* (771m)
This name for the hill on the south side of Loch Voil does not appear on any map. It has been coined because the highest point of the hill, un-named on all existing maps, has a trig point and is apparently known locally as the surveyors' peak. In earlier guidebooks the name Ceann na Baintighearna has been applied to the hill, but it clearly refers to a 701m point over a kilometre north of the true summit.

It is possibly not surprising that the hill has gone un-named, for it has no great distinction. Its slopes are mainly grassy, with broad ridges and open corries. Only to the north, above Loch Voil, is the hillside steep and craggy, but it is also forested along the whole length of the loch.

The ascent may be easily made from Ballimore at the end of the public road in Glen Buckie. Take the path on the south side of the Calair Burn (it is a right of way) for almost two kilometres, and at the point where it turns south towards Glen Finglas descend west to cross the burn, which may be difficult in spate. (The hillside on the north of the Calair Burn is a deer farm, and is best avoided). Once across the burn climb due west up a featureless grassy slope to the east ridge of the hill which leads over a knoll (684m) to the summit.

Stob a'Choin *(peak of the dog)* (869m)

This is the dominating hill in the north-west corner of the area covered by this chapter, but in height, character and position it is more a part of the Crianlarich hills than The Trossachs. Its north side overlooking the River Larig is continuously steep for about 700m, while the south side of the hill drops very gradually in a long broad ridge towards Loch Katrine. The north-east corner of the hill above Glen Sgionie and Blaircreich has recently been planted with trees, and access up the north-east ridge (previously the best route) is no longer recommended.

Inverlochlarig farm at the foot of the north side of the hill is the site of the house where Rob Roy MacGregor lived for the last years of his life, and he was buried in the churchyard at Balquhidder.

The recommended ascent route for Stob a'Choin starts at the car park at the end of the public road half a kilometre east of Inverlochlarig. Walk west along the private road, which is a right of way, past Inverlochlarig to a bridge across the River Larig one and a half kilometres further. Go upstream on the south side of the river for a further half kilometre to a sheepfold and then climb south up the steep hillside to about 450m. There make a rising traverse south-west up a fairly obvious grassy rake below a line of broken crags to reach the steep north ridge of the hill at a level spot about 630m. Continue up this ridge over a false top and on to the slightly higher point of the true summit.

An alternative route which can be used for the descent to give a traverse of the hill goes south-east from the summit across the Bealach Coire an Laoigh and over a few lower knolls to the top of the north-east ridge. Go down this to about 550m and then leave the crest to descend the north-west flank of the ridge direct to the footbridge across the River Larig. It is probably advisable not to try to descend by any of the streams on the north side of the mountain, as they flow down quite steep and narrow gullies.

From the south Stob a'Choin can be climbed from Loch Katrine by the Allt a'Choin, or up the hillside to the east of this stream. Both routes are rather uninteresting, but a lot less steep than the one from the north. A bicycle would be useful to reach the foot of the Allt a'Choin from the car park at the east end of Loch Katrine.

To the west of Stob a'Choin a rather featureless ridge separates Glen Gyle from the head of the River Larig. At the west end of this ridge the Bealach nan Corp *(pass of the corpses)* is the pass that was once used by funeral parties between Loch Voil and Glen Gyle, and it is still possible to see cairns marking the route. Glen Gyle itself is on the line of an old drove road from Dalmally to the head of Loch Lomond, then south-east through the glen to The Trossachs and Falkirk. There was once a village near the head of Glen Gyle, but it is long since deserted and the glen is desolate beyond the west end of Loch Katrine.

Stob a'Choin from the north

PATHS AND WALKS

Aberfoyle to Callander by the Menteith Hills. Start from the A81 road two kilometres east of Aberfoyle and take the forest road and path which go north-east across the hills to Loch Venachar. (14 kilometres).

Aberfoyle to Brig o'Turk by the Menteith Hills. Follow the route described above as far as Loch Venachar, then turn west past Invertrossachs along a path to Loch Drunkie and then a road through the Achray Forest to Brig o'Turk. (15 kilometres). There are many other possible walks in the Achray Forest between Aberfoyle and The Trossachs; refer to the Forestry Commission map.

Trossachs Pier to Stronachlacher. The walk along the road on the north side of Loch Katrine to the west end and back along the south side to Stronachlacher is very pleasant, and might be combined with the steamer sailings on the loch. (21 kilometres). The complete circuit of Loch Katrine is about 32 kilometres, of which only about two kilometres, between Glasahoile and the Bealach nam Bo on Ben Venue, are trackless.

Brig o'Turk to Balquhidder. Take the road north from Brig o'Turk up the east side of the Glen Finglas Reservoir and follow the track north up Gleann nam Meann. The track almost reaches the col at the head of this glen. On the north side of the col

Climbing on Ben An; Ben Venue beyond

descend to Gleann Dubh and follow the path to Ballimore farm. From there walk down the public road in Glen Buckie to Balquhidder. This route is a right of way. (16 kilometres).

Circuit of Beinn an t-Sidhein from Strathyre. Most of this walk is along narrow and relatively unfrequented public roads. Take the forest path which climbs the east side of Beinn an t-Sidhein and circles round its south side. Descend to Ballimore farm and return to Strathyre by the road down Glen Buckie and past Stroneslaney. (11 kilometres).

Stronachlacher to Inverarnan. Take the private road to the west end of Loch Katrine and continue by a track up Glen Gyle. Cross the pass between Beinn Ducteach and Parlan Hill and descend across boggy ground to the Ben Glas Burn. Follow the path down the north side of the burn to Beinglas farm half a kilometre from Inverarnan. (15 kilometres). Beyond the head of Loch Katrine this route follows a right of way, the line of an old drove road; electricity transmission pylons along the whole way detract from any sense of wildness in what is otherwise a rather desolate stretch of country.

Loch Achray Hotel to Loch Ard. This waymarked route goes from the hotel up Gleann Riabhach, as described for Ben Venue. (Note in particular the remarks about the very wet and muddy condition of this path, particularly in wet weather). Above the forest the path continues to the head of the glen at the col, marked by a large cairn, between Ben Venue and Creag a'Bhealaich. From there follow the path south-west and down the Ledard Burn to Loch Ard. (10 kilometres).

CLIMBING

The most popular climbing in The Trossachs is on Ben An. The steep and rocky south face of the hill is formed by a series of little crags, one above another, with ledges and heathery slopes between them and trees growing here and there. The nature of the hill and the crags, and the wonderful views from them give a very relaxed atmosphere to climbing on Ben An. It is an excellent place for a carefree summer's afternoon or evening.

The climbs on Ben An are fully described in the *Climbers' Guide to Central and Southern Scotland*, edited by J.Handren and published by the Scottish Mountaineering Trust (1986). Here mention will be made only of four of the best routes which, if climbed in succession give a very pleasant ascent of the hill from the foot of the crags almost to the summit rock. Referring to the sketch opposite, the routes are: 1. *Ash Wall* (Severe); 2. *Birch Wall* (Severe); 3. *Rowan Rib* (Difficult); and 4. *The Last Eighty* (Severe). By these routes over 80m of excellent climbing lead to the top of this fine little hill.

Not far from the foot of Ben An, at the bridge which takes the Duke's Pass road over the Achray Water, there is a prominent roadside crag which has given several routes up to 25m long which are much harder than those on Ben An.

The climbs on Ben Ledi have already been mentioned. They are high up on the south side of the Stank Glen. There are some boulders, all of which have their routes. The *Ben Ledi Pinnacle* is not so much a pinnacle as a group of boulders on top of each other, the highest one forming a pillar leaning against the hillside. There are at least two distinct routes, partly subterranean, starting at a crack at the foot of the pinnacle and ending on its summit (30m, Severe). From the top a 4m descent, which is not entirely easy, is needed to regain terra firma.

Ben An

CHAPTER 4

Ben Lomond and Surroundings

Ben Lomond	974m	367 029
Beinn a'Choin	770m	354 130
Conic Hill	358m	430 922

ACCESS

Two minor roads give access to the area described in this chapter. One is the B837 road from Drymen to Balmaha, and from there to Rowardennan, and the other is the B829 road from Aberfoyle to Inversnaid.

TRANSPORT

Bus: Glasgow to Drymen and Aberfoyle; daily. Drymen to Balmaha; daily.

Postbus: Aberfoyle to Kinlochard and Inversnaid; Mondays to Saturdays.

Passenger ferry: Inversnaid to the Sloy Power Station. (Private ferry operated by Inversnaid Hotel). Summer pleasure boat sailings on Loch Lomond between Balloch, Balmaha, Luss, Rowardennan, Tarbet and Inversnaid.

ACCOMMODATION

Hotels at Drymen, Rowardennan, Inversnaid, Aberfoyle and Loch Ard. Youth hostels at Rowardennan and Loch Ard. Camping and caravan site at Milarrochy on the east side of Loch Lomond two kilometres north of Balmaha. Bothy at Rowchoish on the east side of Loch Lomond opposite Tarbet.

MAPS

Ordnance Survey 1:50,000, Sheets 56 and 57
Bartholomew 1:100,000, Sheets 44 and 48

Ben Lomond is the most southerly of Scotland's high mountains, and with the possible exception of Ben Nevis and Cairn Gorm it is the most popular and frequently ascended of them. Its height and position at the southern edge of the Highlands make it a prominent feature of the landscape of west-central Scotland, and contributes to the wonderful views from its summit on a clear day, views that can include much of the Highlands to the north and the Lowlands to the south.

Another factor which contributes to the character of Ben Lomond is its relative isolation on the east side of Loch Lomond; it completely dominates the surrounding

Ben Lomond from Beinn Ime

hills, moorland and forest. To the south-east an extensive undulating moor stretches towards Drymen. There is little of interest for the climber or walker in this area except possibly the picturesque little Conic Hill (358m) which lies on the Highland Boundary Fault near Balmaha, and repays the short ascent with fine views over the south end of Loch Lomond. To the north-east of this rather uninteresting moorland is the extensive Loch Ard Forest on the south side of Loch Ard. This is part of the Queen Elizabeth Forest Park. The southern part of Ben Lomond, from the summit down to Blairvokie, is now in the ownership of the National Trust for Scotland. North of Ben Lomond there is a stretch of rough country extending to Loch Arklet, and on the north side of this loch there is a small group of hills, of which Beinn a'Choin is the highest, in the area between Glen Gyle and Loch Lomond.

The references to Ben Lomond in literature show that its fascination is not just of recent date, but that the mountain excercised its spell on many who passed along the shore of Loch Lomond in years gone by. One of the earliest narrated attempts to climb the mountain appeared in a poem, dated 1785, inscribed on a pane of glass in the old inn at Tarbet. Unfortunately the pane is no longer there.

In most early references to Ben Lomond there is a tendency to magnify the difficulties of the ascent, due no doubt to the impression of mystery and lurking danger that surrounded the mountains over two hundred years ago. Thus John

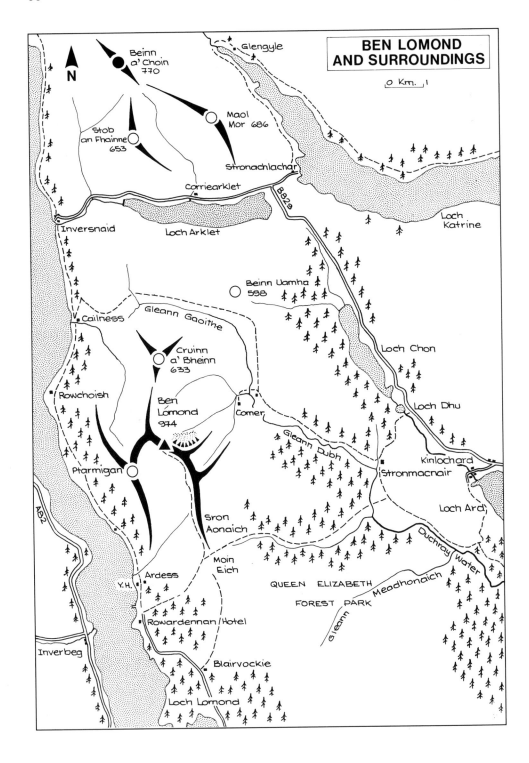

BEN LOMOND AND SURROUNDINGS

0 Km. 1

N

Beinn a' Choin 770

Glengyle

Maol Mor 686

Stob an Fhainne 653

Stronachlachar

Corriearklet

B829

Loch Katrine

Inversnaid

Loch Arklet

Beinn Uamha 598

Cailness

Gleann Gaoithe

Loch Chon

Cruinn a' Bheinn 633

Rowchoish

Ben Lomond 974

Comer

Loch Dhu

Gleann Dubh

Kinlochard

Ptarmigan

Stronmacnair

Loch Ard

A82

Sron Aonaich

Duchray Water

Moin Eich

Ardess

Y.H.

QUEEN ELIZABETH

Meadhonaich

Rowardennan Hotel

FOREST PARK

Gleann

Inverbeg

Blairvockie

Loch Lomond

Stoddart in 1799 wrote of the ascent: 'That which you look toward as an unbroken surface, upon your approach becomes divided by impossible valleys: an unheard rill becomes a roaring torrent, and a gentle slope is found to be an unscalable cliff.' He went on to describe the north side of Ben Lomond as 'exciting a degree of surprise, arising almost to terror: this mighty mass which hitherto had appeared to be an irregular cone placed on a spreading base, suddenly presents itself as an imperfect crater, with one side forcibly torn off, leaving a stupendous precipice of two thousand feet to the bottom.' One may question the accuracy of Stoddart's estimate of the height of the northern cliffs, but no one would quarrel with his feelings on reaching the summit 'far above the clouds of the vale. . . it seemed as if I had been suddenly transported into a new state of existence, cut off from every meaner association and invisibly united with the surrounding purity and bright-ness.'

There is a good account in *SMC Journal Volume 1* of an early ascent of Ben Lomond by William and Mary Howitt, and they too were mightily impressed by the dangers - trembling bogs and impetuous torrents. However, as far as the usual route from Rowardennan is concerned, John MacCulloch very truly described it in 1811 as 'an ascent without toil or difficulty: a mere walk of pleasure.'

No description of Ben Lomond and its surroundings would be complete without a mention of Loch Lomond, which is undoubtedly the best known of Scotland's lochs, and also one of the most beautiful. The entire 34 kilometre length of the loch encompasses some grand and contrasting scenery. The southern end is broad and open, dotted with islands and backed by low hills and parkland; but the north end is narrow, steep-sided and enclosed by mountains. Almost the entire shoreline, except where recent road works on the west side have encroached on it, is beautifully wooded with oak, birch, rowan, hazel and alder, as well as more recent coniferous plantations. The west side of the loch carries the very busy A82 road on its way north from Glasgow to Fort William, and the recent 'improvement' of this road has in some places virtually destroyed the natural shoreline. In other places where the road has been re-aligned higher up the hillside above the loch there are now some relatively tranquil corners at the lochside. The east side of the loch is much more peaceful. There is a narrow public road from Drymen to Rowardennan, but beyond that point the road is private, although it forms part of the popular West Highland Way. Walkers can enjoy this side of the loch in comparative peace, disturbed only by the distant rumble of traffic on the other side of the loch.

THE HILLS

Ben Lomond *(beacon hill)* (974m)
The name Lomond may well be derived from an old Brittonic word 'Llumnan' meaning beacon, and this would certainly be an apt description of the mountain. It is interesting to note that the Lomond Hills in Fife are of the same shape and there also the name 'beacon hill' seems appropriate. It may also be significant that Loch

Ben Lomond from Inveruglas on the west side of Loch Lomond

Leven lies at the foot of West Lomond in Fife, and that Loch Lomond was once called Loch Leven and the River Leven flows from its south end. It seems likely that the name of the hill has been applied to the loch.

Geologically, Ben Lomond consists of a hard mass of mica-schist dipping steeply to the south-east. The summit appears from many viewpoints to be a conical peak set on a broadly spreading base, but it is in fact a short level ridge enclosing the north-facing corrie, the actual summit being at the north-west end of this ridge. The corrie is ringed by crags, below which scree and grassy slopes drop steeply towards Comer farm at the head of Gleann Dubh.

The mountain has three principal ridges or spurs. The long and broad south ridge rises on the east side of Loch Lomond above Rowardennan and leads gradually over Sron Aonaich to its final steepening just below the summit. On the other side of the mountain a well-defined and quite rocky ridge drops north-west from the summit for three quarters of a kilometre and then, turning northwards it becomes broader and grassy and leads across a col (c.450m) to the outlying hill Cruinn a'Bheinn (633m). At the point where this ridge turns north, a third ridge runs out south-west to the subsidiary top called Ptarmigan (731m). This hill stands out prominently in views of Ben Lomond from the south as a long flat shoulder from which steep wooded slopes drop to Loch Lomond.

Ben Lomond from the Kelty Water at Gartmore

Loch Arklet, looking west to the Arrochar Alps

It is interesting to recall that in the 1970s the shallow grassy corrie on the north-west side of Ben Lomond which is the source of the Cailness Burn was considered as the site of a proposed pumped storage hydro-electric scheme which luckily never came to fruition. Had it done so, there would now be an artificial reservoir in this corrie and a power station on the side of Loch Lomond not far from Rowchoish bothy.

The most popular route of ascent of Ben Lomond is from Rowardennan, starting at the car park a few hundred metres north of the hotel. From the east side of the car park a signposted path leads east then north-east through the forest to reach open slopes at the foot of the south ridge of the mountain. The path is much trodden and eroded, and a great deal of effort has been made to repair it on the grassy lower slopes of the south ridge. At Sron Aonaich (577m) the ridge becomes more level and very broad and the path continues along its crest for one and a half kilometres to the final steepening where a few zigzags lead up to the fairly level summit ridge. This leads over a few bumps, with a very steep drop on the right side, to the summit.

An alternative route from Rowardennan goes north from the car park for one kilometre along the private road, past the youth hostel and one or two small cottages at Ardess. Climb the wooded slopes on the north side of the Ardess burn by a fairly well-marked path and continue above the trees up a grassy slope to about 300m (just level with the waterfall of the Ardess burn). There turn north and follow sheep tracks and an intermittent path along the knolly ridge to Ptarmigan. Bear north-east across a fairly level col and reach the north-west ridge of Ben Lomond at the foot of its uper rocky section, and climb this to the summit.

The approach from the east provides a much wilder and less-frequented route to Ben Lomond, leading naturally up into its northern corrie. Leave the B829 road nine kilometres north-west of Aberfoyle at Loch Dhu and follow the private road round the foot of this little loch and south-west through the forest over a low pass into Gleann Dubh. Continue up the glen to the isolated farm of Comer at the foot of Ben Lomond. (It is quite possible to cycle as far as this point). From the farm climb south-west up the burn which flows from the main corrie of Ben Lomond and continue right up into the corrie, with steep cliffs on one's left, to reach the summit ridge a short distance south of the top. In summer this route will give no difficulty. In winter, with hard snow conditions, the final climb at the head of the corrie may require a little step-cutting, or crampons.

Note that there is another adjacent corrie, Coire a'Bhathaich, from which the Allt Mor flows down to Comer farm. If this burn is followed to the head of the corrie, the path of the normal route is reached just below its zigzags near the summit.

From the north the ascent of Ben Lomond starts at Cailness on the side of Loch Lomond, two and a half kilomteres south of Inversnaid. Climb the steep hillside on the north of the Cailness Burn to reach level ground above 300m and continue south-east up the burn to the col between Cruinn a'Bheinn and Ben Lomond. (This col can also be reached from Comer farm to its east). From the col climb the north ridge to the summit.

Beinn a'Choin *(hill of the dog)* (770m)

This summit is at the centre of a small area of rough hilly ground between Loch Lomond and Glen Gyle, to the north of Loch Arklet. The south-west corner of the area forms a steep craggy hillside above Loch Lomond and is a nature reserve owned by the Royal Society for the Protection of Birds.

The ascent of Beinn a'Choin can be conveniently combined with two of its lower neighbours in a short circular traverse starting and ending at Corriearklet farm on the north side of Loch Arklet. From the farm climb north-east onto the south ridge of Maol Mor (686m) and up it to the top. Continue north-west down a long knolly ridge to the Bealach a'Mhaim, the pass on the south-east side of Beinn a'Choin, and climb this hill, a Corbett and the second highest hill on the east side of Loch Lomond. The continuation of the traverse southwards to Stob an Fhainne (653m) follows a fence all the way to this top, from where a descent south-east leads back to Corriearklet.

Conic Hill (358m)

This little hill lies on the Highland Boundary Fault. Its name may be appropriate for the appearance of the hill as seen from the south-west, but from the south-east it appears as a long knolly ridge. Conic Hill may be climbed by paths either from the car park at Balmaha, or from a point of the road just north of the Pass of Balmaha. The two paths join half way up the south-west ridge and the ascent goes up this ridge, which towards the summit becomes quite bare and rocky, with outcrops of knobbly conglomerate rocks. The path of the West Highland Way takes a lower line along a natural shelf round the north side of the hill, passing close below the summit and providing an easy route to it.

The panorama from the summit of Conic Hill is very fine. Of particular interest is the view south-westwards where the line of islands in Loch Lomond - Inchcailloch, Torrinch, Creinch and Inchmurrin - and the more distant Ben Bowie above Helensburgh mark the line of the Highland Boundary Fault. Much further away in the same direction is Arran, also on the line of the Fault.

PATHS AND WALKS

Rowardennan to Kinlochard. This is a fine cross-country walk through the Queen Elizabeth Forest park. From Rowardennan follow the Ben Lomond path for two and a half kilometres to a point half way up the grassy slope below Sron Aonaich where another path leads east over a wide col, the Moin Eich. Follow this path down into the Loch Ard Forest along the north side of the Bruach Caorainn Burn. A forest road is reached and leads across the Duchray Water. There either turn north to the ruined cottage at Stronmacnair and over the pass to Loch Dhu on the B829 road (12 kilometres), or turn south-east and follow the forest road to Couligartan and Kinlochard (15 kilometres).

On the West Highland Way near the north end of Loch Lomond

Rowardennan to Inverarnan. This path along the east side of Loch Lomond is part of the West Highland Way; probably its most scenic part. From Rowardennan the route follows the private road beyond Ptarmigan Lodge to a point just north of Rowchoish bothy. Thereafter the path, narrow in places and crossing the remains of two landslides caused by exceptionally wet weather in 1985, continues along the lochside past Cailness, Inversnaid and Doune bothy to Beinglas farm and the bridge over the River Falloch near Inverarnan. (22 kilometres).

CLIMBING

Serious climbing on Ben Lomond is confined to the high north-facing corrie which has cliffs on its south wall which reach 100m high. The rocks are not suited for summer climbing, but there are some pleasant short winter routes. The corrie can be reached either directly from Comer, or from Rowardennan by going almost to the summit of the mountain and descending into the corrie from a little col before the top.

Features of the crag are three parallel narrow gullies separated by ribs. The easternmost gully is very narrow at its foot and quite easy (Grade I). The central gully has a small chockstone pitch which may be difficult, but it is possible to traverse

Approaching the summit of Ben Lomond at the top of the south ridge

out of the gully across the rib on its right and into the western gully which is easier (Grade II). The lower half of the western gully is not well defined.

Further east the crag is higher but very vegetatious, and crossed by a grass ledge. A few climbs have been done in summer many years ago, but records are not precise and the climbing cannot be recommended at that time of year. It is, however, surprising that there have been so few reports of winter routes in this corrie.

SKI MOUNTAINEERING

Given good snow cover low down, Ben Lomond is a very good ascent on skis, following the summer route up the south ridge. Alternative starts which avoid the forested lower slopes are either Blairvokie farm from where there is a track which leads easily to the foot of the south ridge, or Ardess from where one can climb fairly easy slopes to the north of the Rowardennan Forest. The final climb of the summit cone may best be made by a rising traverse across its south-west side rather than by following the line of the footpath.

CHAPTER 5

The Luss Hills

Beinn Chaorach	713m	288 924
Beinn a'Mhanaich	710m	269 947
Creag an Leinibh	658m	311 919
Beinn Eich	702m	302 947
Doune Hill	734m	290 971
Cruach an t-Sidhein	684m	275 965
Mid Hill	655m	322 963
Beinn Dubh	643m	336 954
Beinn Bhreac	681m	322 000

This group of hills is situated between Loch Lomond and Loch Long, and is bounded on the south by Glen Fruin. The group is roughly sixteen kilometres in extent from north to south and eleven kilometres from east to west at its widest point.

The highest point in this group, Doune Hill, is 734m high and there are about a dozen distinct hills over 600m. Generally they are smooth and grassy in character,particularly in the southern half of the group, however the hills have a certain amount of individuality as they are separated from each other by low cols and deep glens. Because of their very grassy character, these hills have nothing to offer the rock climber, and it is very unlikely that any good winter climbing can be found among them. On the other hand, the very smooth grassy slopes, particularly of the southern hills, makes them suitable for ski touring, and only a comparatively thin covering of snow is needed to make skiing possible.

The main attraction of the Luss hills, however, is the very pleasant hillwalking that they offer within easy reach of Glasgow and its neighbouring towns, and their position between the Firth of Clyde, Loch Lomond and the Arrochar Alps gives some grand views from their tops. Despite their proximity to industrial Clydeside, there is a remarkable feeling of peace and tranquility in their interior, and it is surprising how quickly the traffic noise and crowds of Loch Lomond-side are left behind as one goes up Glen Luss or Glen Douglas.

ACCESS
The A82 road from Glasgow to Luss, Inverbeg and Tarbet. The A814 road from Helensburgh to Garelochhead and Arrochar. Minor roads from Arden (Loch Lomond) to Garelochhead through Glen Fruin, from Luss up Glen Luss and from Inverbeg to Loch Long
through Glen Douglas.

TRANSPORT
Bus: Glasgow to Luss, Inverbeg, Tarbet and Arrochar; daily.
Helensburgh to Garelochhead and Arrochar; daily.

Train: Glasgow to Helensburgh, Garelochhead and Arrochar and Tarbet; daily.

ACCOMMODATION
Hotels at Luss, Inverbeg, Arrochar and Tarbet. Youth hostel at Inverbeg. Camp and
caravan site at Luss. Caravan and cabin site at Inverbeg.

MAPS
Ordnance Survey 1:50,000, Sheet 56
Bartholomew 1:100,000, Sheet 44

The south and east sides of the Luss hills are very much easier as regards access than the west side, where there are military firing ranges at the south end near Garelochhead, extensive forestry plantations along the east side of Loch Long and at the head of Glen Douglas a storage site for nuclear weapons, most of it fortunately out of sight in deep tunnels under Doune Hill. It is quite surprising, in view of the military presence in the Luss hills, that they retain such a peaceful and relatively unspoilt character.

The principal activity in these hills is sheep farming, and care should be taken, particularly in the lambing season, not to disturb animals on the hills. Many notices, particularly in Glen Luss, ask walkers not to take their dogs onto these hills.

THE HILLS

The southern area of the Luss hills between Glen Fruin and Glen Luss is more extensive than the other two groups, and it consists for the most part of smooth grassy hills with broad ridges. The southern hillsides in particular drop towards Glen Fruin in long easy-angled shoulders, although there are some steeper, and in places almost craggy slopes above Glen Luss. The recently constructed military road through Glen Fruin runs between the narrow public road and the higher hillsides, but there are several places where access across it is possible.

Beinn Chaorach *(sheep hill)* (713m)
This is the highest of the hills on the south side of Glen Luss. It is fairly steep and grassy on all sides, with well-defined ridges dropping north-west, east and south-east, the last one connecting with Beinn Tharsuinn.

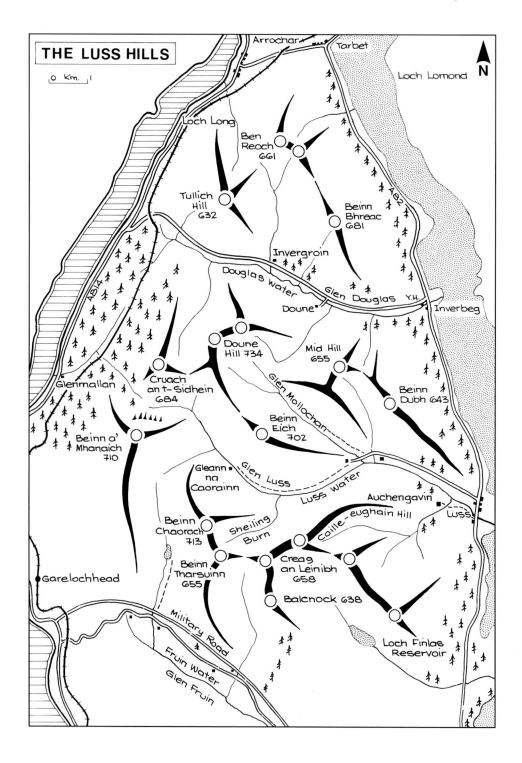

THE LUSS HILLS

0 Km. 1

N

Arrochar
Tarbet
Loch Lomond

Loch Long

Ben
Reoch
661

Tullich
Hill
632

Beinn
Bhreac
681

A82

Invergroin

Douglas water   Glen Douglas Y.H.

Doune   Inverbeg

A814

Doune
Hill 734

Mid Hill
655

Cruach
an t-Sidhein
684

Glen Mollochan

Beinn
Dubh 643

Glenmallan

Beinn
Eich
702

Beinn a'
Mhanaich
710

Gleann
na
Caorainn

Glen Luss

Luss water

Auchengavin

Coille-eughain Hill

Luss

Beinn
Chaorach
713

Sheiling
Burn

Beinn
Tharsuinn
655

Creag
an Leinibh
658

Garelochhead

Balcnock 638

Loch Finlas
Reservoir

Military Road

Fruin Water

Glen Fruin

The quickest ascent of Beinn Chaorach is from Glen Fruin, starting near Auchengaich and walking a short distance up the private road on the east side of the Auchengaich Burn before striking north-east up the grassy hillside to Beinn Tharsuinn, from where a broad ridge leads to Beinn Chaorach.

The approach up Glen Luss starts from the end of the public road in the glen near Glenmollochan farm and goes for over two kilometres past Edentaggart farm. Cross the Luss Water near the Shieling Burn (or by a footbridge downstream if the river is in spate) and climb the east ridge of Beinn Chaorach, which joins the north-west ridge a short distance north of the summit.

Longer traverses can be made. One which may be recommended starts from Luss on the south side of the Luss Water and goes past Auchengavin farm and west from there up the long ridge of Coille-eughain Hill, a broad peaty ridge, then steeply up to Creag an Leinibh. From there follow the main ridge which gives easy grassy going for most of the way over Pt.693m and Beinn Tharsuinn to Beinn Chaorach. To return to Luss, go north for a few hundred metres and descend the east ridge to cross the Luss Water and walk down the road in Glen Luss.

Beinn a'Mhanaich (710m)

This hill is isolated from the other Luss hills by fairly low cols, and its north face is one of the few places in the area that is steep and craggy. The long south ridge which rises above the head of Glen Fruin certainly gives a very easy ascent, but it is at the edge of a military firing area and is probably best avoided, particularly if warning flags are flying. A safer route from Glen Fruin goes up the Auchengaich Burn past the little reservoir to the col (c.350m) at the head of the glen, from where a fairly steep climb north-west leads to the summit.

From Glen Luss a much longer approach goes to the end of the track up the glen at the shepherd's cottage of Gleann na Caorainn, then one kilometre further up the glen before climbing the east ridge of Beinn a'Mhanaich.

On the north side of Glen Luss there are two groups of hills, separated by the smaller Glen Mollochan. To the west are Doune Hill and Beinn Eich, both well seen from Luss village, and to the east are Mid Hill and Beinn Dubh, the latter rising in a long smooth ridge directly above the village. To the west of Doune Hill is the rather isolated Cruach an t-Sidhein, which alone among the Luss hills may be more easily approached from the west than from the east.

Doune Hill (734m)
Beinn Eich *(horse hill)* (702m)

These two hills form a long ridge between the head of Glen Luss and Glen Mollochan. Beinn Eich is the prominent pointed hill which is the most obvious feature of the view up Glen Luss from the village at its foot. Doune Hill has a flatter summit, with the slight bump of Beinn Lochain to its south-west and its north-east top (700m) barely visible from Luss, but prominent above Glen Douglas.

Beinn Eich from the ridge to Doune Hill

The most straightforward route to traverse both these hills is up Glen Luss. From Edentaggart farm climb west up the broad grassy ridge of Beinn Eich directly to its top. Continue north-west across a broad peaty col and up the gradual ascent to Beinn Lochain, then north to Doune Hill. The return can be varied by going north-east across a col at about 620m to the 700m north-east top, and descending south-east from there to the head of Glen Mollochan. The walk down this glen is rather boggy in places, but a track is reached on the north side of the stream which leads back to the road in Glen Luss.

A shorter approach to Doune Hill can be made from Glen Douglas, starting from the bridge over the Douglas Water at Doune and climbing the east ridge of the 700m north-east top. The north-east side of the hill is seamed by several tree-filled gullies.

Cruach an t-Sidhein *(stack of the fairy hill)* (684m)
This is a fine little peak, lying one and a half kilometres south-west of Doune Hill. With its steep flanks all round and its small grassy summit table it is possibly the shapliest of the Luss hills.

Cruach an t-Sidhein can be climbed by making a diversion from Beinn Lochain on the way to or from Doune Hill, or by walking the long way up Glen Luss and climbing to the col on its east side.

At the head of Glen Luss looking towards Cruach an t-Sidhein

The shortest route to the hill, however, is from the A814 road along Loch Long at Glenmallan. Start on the north side of the bridge over the stream coming down Gleann Culanach and go uphill at first through overgrown rhododendrons, then up a narrow path beside the forest high on the north-west bank of the stream which flows through a deep and narrow gorge. After about one kilometre cross the stream and continue up to and then along the south side of the Allt Derigan, under the West Highland Railway, and up the south-west side of this stream, following traces of a path between it and the forest to the col at its head. There turn north and climb a steep grassy slope to Cruach an t-Sidhein.

Mid Hill (655m)
Beinn Dubh (*black hill*) (643m)
These two hills form a horseshoe ridge on the north side of Glen Luss, enclosing Glen Striddle. A pleasant circuit can be made by climbing directly from Luss up the long easy-angled south-east ridge of Beinn Dubh, and continuing round the head of Glen Striddle to Mid Hill. The cairn on top of this hill is about 150 metres north-east of the highest point, which is no more than a slight rise in the broad grassy ridge. Continue south-south-west, then south-east down the grassy ridge between Glen Striddle and Glen Mollochan to return to the road in Glen Luss.

Looking up Glen Luss to Beinn Eich, Doune Hill and Mid Hill

Beinn Bhreac *(speckled hill)* (681m)
The hills on the north side of Glen Douglas are rather more rugged than those further south. The three hills, of which Beinn Bhreac is the highest, form a big horseshoe to the north of Invergroin farm. The other two are Ben Reoch (661m) and Tullich Hill (632m). The three hills can be climbed in a circular traverse starting and finishing at Invergroin. On a clear day the view of the Arrochar Alps from Ben Reoch is particularly fine.

Although the Luss hills have been described in three groups according to the glens through them, it is quite possible to make longer traverses from north to south or vice versa. For example, the use of bus services along the A82 road enables a traverse to be made over the hills from Tarbet to Luss.

PATHS AND WALKS

Luss to Glenmallan (Loch Long). The first part of this cross-country walk up Glen Luss needs no description, there being a road, then a track almost to the cottage at Gleann na Caorainn. Continue up the glen along the bank of the river to the col at its head. Enter the forest and go down the Allt Derigan; the south-west bank of the stream gives rather dryer going than the other side. Reach the stream in Gleann Culanach, go down its left bank for a few hundred metres, then cross to the right bank and follow a faint path above the deep and narrow gorge of the stream down to the A814 road at the side of Loch Long. (13 kilometres).

Doune Hill from Mid Hill

SKI TOURING

As noted earlier in this chapter, the smooth contours and grassy slopes of many of the Luss hills make them suitable for ski touring. Only a modest covering of snow is necessary to make skiing perfectly feasible.

The traverse of Beinn Eich and Doune Hill from Edentaggart farm is a fine tour, with good slopes for downhill skiing on the descent from Beinn Eich. Further south, the slopes above Glen Fruin are very smooth and suitable for skiing. For example, a good circuit can be made starting and finishing at Ballevoulin farm over Balcnock, Pt.693m, Beinn Tharsuinn and Auchengaich Hill.

CHAPTER 6

Cowal and Ardgoil

Beinn an Lochain	901m	218 079
Ben Donich	847m	218 044
The Brack	787m	245 031
Cnoc Coinnich	761m	233 008
Beinn Lochain	703m	161 007
Beinn Bheula	779m	155 983
Sgurr a'Choinnich	661m	159 957
Beinn Mhor	741m	108 908
Clach Bheinn	643m	126 886
Creag Tharsuinn	641m	086 913

The area covered by this chapter is the large peninsula bounded by Loch Long and the Firth of Clyde on the east, and Loch Fyne on the west. It is about 56 kilometres long from north to south, and 25 kilometres from east to west at its widest point, and the southern tip facing the Island of Bute is divided into three prongs by Loch Striven and Loch Riddon.

Ardgoil is the district at the northern end of the peninsula, and it is enclosed by Glen Kinglas, Glen Croe, Loch Long, Loch Goil, Hell's Glen and Loch Fyne. It is rugged and entirely mountainous, and includes the three highest peaks in the area covered by this chapter - namely Beinn an Lochain, Ben Donich and The Brack. In many ways the character of Ardgoil is similar to that of the Arrochar Alps just to the north; the mountains are steep, rocky and rugged, and are defended along many of their flanks by dense plantations of coniferous trees.

Cowal is much more extensive. In its northern part adjacent to Ardgoil it is rugged and mountainous, but gradually as one goes south the hills become lower, and the western and south-western parts of Cowal are mainly moorland and forest, with farms on the lower ground near Loch Fyne. Forestry is an important industry in Cowal, and Glenbranter is an example of a fair-sized village which has grown up round this industry.

Cowal was at one time part of the Kingdom of Dalriada which was colonised by the Irish Gaels between the third and sixth centuries AD, and the name Cowal is

ACCESS
The A83 road from Arrochar over the Rest and be Thankful to Loch Fyne, followed by the A815 road south from there by Loch Eck to Dunoon. The B828 from the Rest and be Thankful and the B839 from Loch Fyne to Lochgoilhead and Carrick Castle, and a minor road from Whistlefield on Loch Eck to Ardentinny on the west shore of Loch Long.

TRANSPORT
Bus: Glasgow to Arrochar, Inveraray and Campbeltown; daily.
Arrochar to Rest and be Thankful, Lochgoilhead and Carrick; Mondays to Saturdays. Dunoon to Strachur and St. Catherines; Mondays to Saturdays. (Goes to Cairndow on schooldays).
Ferry: (vehicles and passengers): Gourock to Dunoon; daily.

ACCOMMODATION
Hotels at Arrochar, Cairndow, Strachur, Lochgoilhead, St.Catherine's and Dunoon. Youth hostel at Ardgartan. Camp and caravan sites at Ardgartan, Arrochar, Lochgoilhead, south end of Loch Eck and head of the Holy Loch. Climbers' hut in Glen Croe.

MAPS
Ordnance Survey 1:50,000, Sheets 55,56,62 and 63.
Bartholomew 1:100,000, Sheets 44 and 48.

derived from Comghall, one of the Irish chieftains of that time. Following the arrival of Columba at Iona in 563, Celtic priests established Christian outposts at several places in Cowal, including St.Catherine's, Strachur and Strathlachlan on the shores of Loch Fyne. The Norsemen were not attracted to Cowal, which was much less fertile than the neighbouring lands, and only at the end of their occupation of the western coast did they sail up Loch Long. After the departure of the Norsemen, Cowal and Ardgoil came under the power of the leading clans of the area, and gradually the Campbells gained control of the whole area.

Ardgoil and Cowal are the only parts of the Southern Highlands in which the sea and sea-lochs form a significant part of the landscape, and the combination of mountains, loch and forest makes this area one of great beauty, embodying in miniature many of the finest aspects of Highland scenery. Despite this, the area is surprisingly neglected by hillwalkers, presumably because of the more obvious attractions of the neighbouring Arrochar Alps.

The Argyll Forest Park lies within Ardgoil and the north-eastern part of Cowal, and includes nearly all the higher mountains of these districts. The Park is administered by the Forestry Commission, and the Forest Park Guide (published by HM Stationery Office) is invaluable for the visitor wishing to gain a full understanding of the area. In addition to the extensive forests of larch, fir and spruce, there are some fine groups of native Scots pines near Loch Eck and the Holy Loch, and in the same area the Younger Botanic Garden, the Benmore Pinetum, the Kilmun Arboretum and Puck's Glen are all worth visiting. The Younger Botanic Garden is said to have the largest collection of rhododendrons in the country.

Beinn an Lochain

THE HILLS

Beinn an Lochain *(hill of the little loch)* (901m)
This is the highest hill in Ardgoil, and it rises at the northern edge of the district overlooking Glen Kinglas. It is well seen as one approaches up the A83 road in Glen Croe towards the Rest and be Thankful, and from the pass its steep and rocky east face is seen to overlook the dark waters of Loch Restil. The north side of the hill is also very steep and has some fine crags high up under the summit. Between the east and north faces the north-east ridge is a fine feature of the hill, dropping from the summit to the road near Butterbridge.

To the south the hill drops quite steeply to the forest in Gleann Mor while to the west it is linked by a low col to two lesser tops, Beinn an t-Seilich (719m) and Stob an Eas (732m). These two hills, largely surrounded by forestry plantations, are not of much interest and are seldom climbed.

The summit ridge of Beinn an Lochain is about 600 metres long and connects the lower south top (834m) to the summit. At the wide col between the two tops there are a few tiny lochans.

The best route of ascent is the north-east ridge as it is in places steep and narrow enough to give the impression of a real mountain ridge. The foot of the ridge at

Looking from Beinn an Lochain towards Ben Donich

Butterbridge has been planted with trees, and the best start is from the road just north of the north end of Loch Restil. Cross the stream flowing from the loch and bear north-west across level ground for a short distance then up a wide grassy gully to the right of the crags overlooking the loch. The ridge is reached at about 350m and followed easily to the first knoll (637m). Beyond a short drop, the ridge rises very steeply and the path makes a rising traverse rightwards across steep grass to reach the crest again at a level section. Beyond this the final rise to the summit is climbed just to the left of the crest, whose right hand side at that point falls steeply into the northern corrie. The summit cairn is reached suddenly at the top of the ridge.

A rather shorter, but less attractive route can be made from the Rest and be Thankful, starting from a car park a short distance along the B828 Gleann Mor road. Climb due west up steepening slopes which form the east shoulder of the 834m south top. There are many small rock outcrops and cliffs, but they can be easily avoided. Towards the top of this slope one can bear slightly towards the right to reach the col between the two tops of the hill.

Ascents by the east and north faces are reserved for serious climbers. There are some interesting climbs on these sides of the hill in good winter conditions, but summer rock climbs are less attractive.

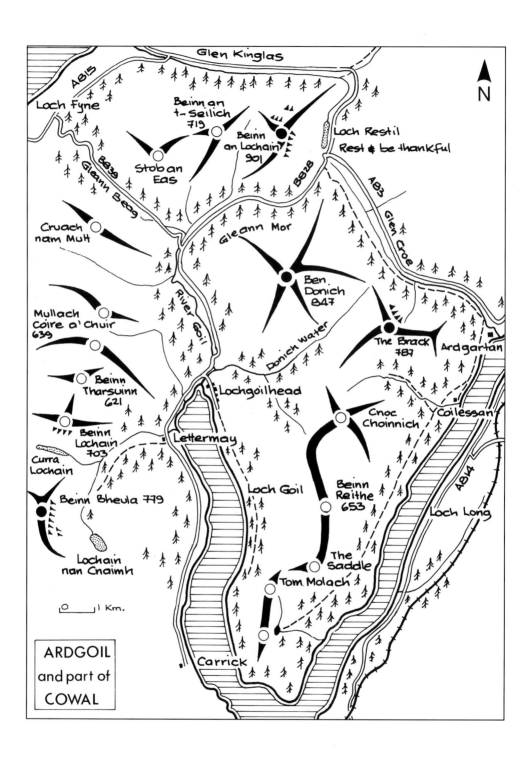

Glen Kinglas

A815

Loch Fyne

Beinn an t-Seilich 719

Beinn an Lochain 901

Loch Restil

Rest & be thankful

B839

Gleann Beag

Stob an Eas

B828

A83

Glen Croe

Cruach nam Mult

Gleann Mor

Ben Donich 847

River Goil

Donich water

The Brack 787

Ardgartan

Mullach Coire a' Chuir 639

Beinn Tharsuinn 621

Lochgoilhead

Cnoc Choinnich

Coilessan

Curra Lochain

Beinn Lochain 703

Lettermay

Beinn Bheula 779

Loch Goil

Beinn Reithe 653

A814

Loch Long

Lochain nan Cnaimh

0   1 Km.

The Saddle

Tom Molach

ARDGOIL and part of COWAL

Carrick

N

Ben Donich *(brown hill)* (847m)
This is a very bulky hill between Glen Croe and Lochgoilhead, just south of the Rest and be Thankful. It is connected to The Brack by a low col, the Bealach Dubh-lic (384m), but otherwise is almost completely surrounded by forestry plantations. Some of these forests are now mature and are being felled, which may temporarily complicate access to the hill.

There are three broad ridges radiating from the summit towards the north, east and south, and each one provides a route of ascent.

The shortest route is the north ridge which starts at almost 300m from the B828 road at the head of Gleann Mor, less than half a kilometre from the Rest and be Thankful. Leave this road by a forest road which in a short distance reaches a junction. Turn left and continue for a few hundred metres to a point where the hillside above has been clear-felled. Climb uphill through the felled area where a few white posts mark a rough way through the remains of the forest to reach a fence above it. Cross the fence at a stile and climb a steep grassy slope to reach the north ridge which is followed along a faint path. At one point there are some quite deep fissures across the ridge and higher up the way goes close to the edge of the ridge above its precipitous west face where the rock scenery is spectacular. The ridge ends at the flat summit area and a false top is passed before the trig point is reached.

The route from Glen Croe by the east ridge is much longer, but it does enable Ben Donich to be traversed with The Brack. Near the foot of Glen Croe are the former offices of the Forestry Commission at a bridge across the Croe Water (grid reference 270 037). Start from there and walk along the road up the glen through the forest on the south side of the river. In about three kilometres a path leaves the road and climbs through scattered trees towards the Bealach Dubh-lic. From the bealach climb the broad east ridge of Ben Donich.

The ascent of the south ridge from the B828 road near the bridge across the River Goil near Lochgoilhead has little to recommend it, being devoid of any interesting features.

The Brack *(possibly from breac, meaning speckled)* (787m)
This is a fine, rugged mountain, rising steeply above the lower part of Glen Croe. The north face of the mountain above the glen has a rocky corrie high up, backed by steep cliffs, features of which are the dark slits of *Great Central Groove* and *Elephant Gully*. A long shoulder of the mountain extends eastwards to end above Ardgartan, and on three sides (north, east and south) its slopes are forested up to about 300m. Only to the west is The Brack clear of forest, and at the foot of its north-west ridge it is connected to Ben Donich at the Bealach Dubh-lic.

The Brack is usually climbed from Ardgartan, and two routes are possible which can be combined to give a good circular traverse of the mountain. Both routes start at the former Forestry Commission offices (grid reference 270 037) near the foot of Glen Croe.

Ben Donich from Loch Goil

The more direct route goes up the forest road on the south side of the Croe Water for about one and a half kilometres until, just beyond a double bend in the road, a bridge is reached over the stream flowing down from The Brack's northern corrie. On the east side of this stream a narrow path climbs steeply uphill along a clearing between forest and stream. Cross the fence at the top of the forest and follow the right-hand stream uphill towards the cliffs above, at whose foot is a large pointed boulder. Above and to the right is the dark vertical wall which is the most impressive feature of The Brack, but the walkers' route continues uphill to the left (east) of the cliffs into the upper corrie in which there are several small pinnacles and crags. Avoid these by climbing a steep grassy gully on the right side of the corrie ending a short distance north of the summit, or alternatively bear further left below the crags to reach the east ridge, and finish easily up this.

The other route from Glen Croe goes south along the private road past Ardgartan towards Coilessan, then up a forest road into the Coilessan Glen. From the end of this road a path continues up the glen and emerges from the forest. Continue up it for a short distance then turn north below the east side of Pt.579m to reach the broad south-west ridge of The Brack, which is followed to the summit.

The traverse from The Brack to Ben Donich is made by descending the north-west ridge to the Bealach Dubh-lic, from where the east ridge of the latter rises. A footpath from Glen Croe to Lochgoilhead crosses this bealach.

The Brack beyond Lochgoilhead from the path to the Curra Lochain

Cnoc Coinnich *(mossy knoll)* (761m)

To the south of The Brack the Ardgoil peninsula between Loch Long and Loch Goil forms a line of small rugged hills rising above the lochside forests. Cnoc Coinnich is the highest of these hills, and to its south are Beinn Reidhe (653m) and The Saddle (519m). The traverse of these three hills along the knobbly skyline of the peninsula is a fine undulating walk with splendid views.

The area close to the Corran Lochan to the south of The Saddle was named on some early maps as Argyll's Bowling Green, a strange name for such a rough uneven place. The lochan is beside the old drovers' path from Lochgoilhead to a ferry crossing of Loch Long, and cattle may have rested there. The name is derived from the Gaelic buaile a'ghrianain *(cattlefold of the sunny hillock)*, which has been corrupted by English-speaking mapmakers with the addition of the Duke of Argyll's name, for he owned the whole area.

The traverse of Cnoc Coinnich and the other hills of the Ardgoil peninsula is best done from north to south, and Lochgoilhead is the best starting and finishing point. Follow the path from there eastwards on the south side of the Donich Water, through the forest and towards the pass between The Brack and Cnoc Coinnich. From the pass climb the north-west ridge of Cnoc Coinnich. The route to Beinn Reidhe follows the crest of the rather broad and rough connecting ridge, but there are sheep tracks here and there along the way. The south side of Beinn Reidhe drops steeply and it is probably best to keep to the west side of the ridge which drops to the heathery hollow below The Saddle, which is reached by a short steep climb. Once again a steep descent south-westwards leads to rough boggy ground near the original Bowling Green. From there follow the path north into the Ardgoil Forest to reach a road leading back to Lochgoilhead.

The traverse can also be done from Ardgartan, but it is much longer that way. The start of the ridge can be reached by the road and path up the Coilessan Glen to the col at its head as for The Brack. From the end of the traverse at the Corran Lochan there is a long walk back to Ardgartan along a forest road.

Beinn Lochain (*hill of the little loch*) (703m)

To the west of Lochgoilhead there is a small group of hills bounded on the north by Hell's Glen (Gleann Beag) and on the south by the pass holding the Curra Lochain. The lower eastern slopes above the River Goil are densely forested, but to the west there is an expanse of featureless undulating moorland. The finest and highest of these hills is Beinn Lochain, which rises very steeply on the north side of the Curra Lochain, and it is also the most accessible of them. The ascent is a pleasant short climb from Lettermay on the west side of Loch Goil near its head.

Follow the forest road which starts a very short distance south of the houses at Lettermay and climbs westwards into the forest. In just over one kilometre take a right fork and descend to the Lettermay Burn. Cross the burn by a footbridge and climb uphill through the forest for about 100 metres to reach a horizontal firebreak. Follow a path along this firebreak south-westwards almost to the burn which cascades from the Curra Lochain and then go more steeply uphill to emerge from the forest close to the lochan. The hillside of Beinn Lochain above is very steep and there are many huge boulders which have fallen from the cliffs above. Climb northwards to aim for the crest at a little col a short distance south-east of the summit, and finish up the ridge to the top.

The traverse can be continued north-eastwards by going to Beinn Tharsuinn (621m) and Stob na Boine Druim-fhinn (658m). From there it is possible to return to Lettermay by descending south-east along a knolly ridge which eventually drops towards the forest and a very obvious break in the trees leading straight down to Corrow, just north of Lettermay.

A longer traverse can be made by going north-west from Stob na Boine Druim-fhinn, then north across a 500m col to reach Mullach Coire a'Chuir (639m). Its summit ridge is cut away sharply on the north side to leave a large, partially

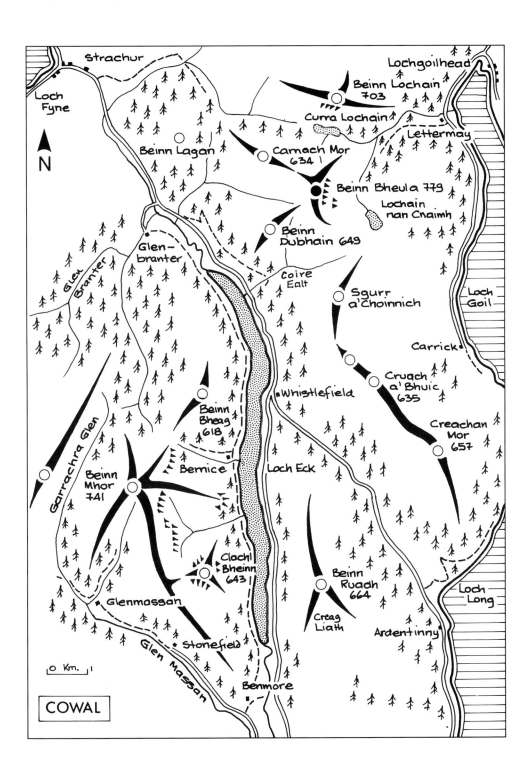

N

Strachur

Loch Fyne

Lochgoilhead

Beinn Lochain 703

Curra Lochain

Lettermay

Beinn Lagan

Carnach Mor 634

Beinn Bheula 779

Lochain nan Cnaimh

Glen Branter

Glen- branter

Beinn Dubhain 649

Coire Ealt

Sgurr a'Choinnich

Loch Goil

Carrick

Cruach a'Bhuic 635

Whistlefield

Creachan Mor 657

Garrachra Glen

Beinn Bheag 618

Bernice

Loch Eck

Beinn Mhor 741

Clach Bheinn 643

Beinn Ruadh 664

Creag Liath

Loch Long

Ardentinny

Glenmassan

Stonefield

Glen Massan

0 Km. 1

Benmore

COWAL

detached flake which gives the summit its characteristic cleft appearance when seen from the east. The continuation involves a traverse along the ridge north-west for almost one kilometre to a 578m knoll, and then a descent north to a col at about 320m followed by a steep climb to the grassy top of Cruach nam Mult (610m). To complete the traverse, descend east down rather steep craggy slopes and reach the road in Hell's Glen.

Beinn Bheula *(from the Gaelic beul, meaning mouth)* (779m)

This hill, the highest in Cowal, stands to the west of Loch Goil. Its east face above the Lettermay Burn is steep and craggy, and has the name Caisteal Dubh *(black castle)*. It gives the hill a fine appearance as seen from Lochgoilhead. The west side of the hill is much less impressive, dropping towards the forest above the River Cur in the featureless grassy slopes of Coire Aodainn.

The best route of ascent for Beinn Bheula is from Lettermay on the west side of Loch Goil, and it follows the same way as described above for Beinn Lochain as far as the stream flowing from the Curra Lochain. Cross this stream below the lochan and climb south-west up the grassy slopes of Beinn Bheula; the route is not well defined and there are several knolls which may be confusing in mist. There is a discontinuous line of broken crags high up, but in clear weather there is no difficulty in seeing and climbing a grassy gully which slants up to the left through them to reach the summit ridge a few hundred metres north of the top. The final climb up this ridge is very easy going up a smooth grassy slope.

The descent can be varied by going south to the flat twin tops of Creag Sgoilte (764m). There is a steep drop to the south of these, so go south-west at first then south-east down grassy slopes to a broad col. A path is reached and followed north-east down to the outflow of Lochain nan Cnaimh, then down through the forest on a long descending traverse to rejoin the forest road of the uphill route.

Beinn Bheula may also be climbed from the west, but the routes are less interesting. The most direct way is by a zigzag forest road starting a few hundred metres south-east of Invernoaden. This road leads to the upper edge of the forest at the foot of Coire Aodainn, and one can continue up this corrie to the summit.

Sgurr a'Choinnich *(peak of moss)* (661m)

This is the highest point of the undulating line of hills between Loch Eck and Loch Goil, and it lies less than a kilometre from the path which crosses the hills between these two lochs. This path provides the easiest way to reach the hill. The shortest approach is from Invernoaden in Glen Branter. From there follow the forest road south-east through the Loch Eck Forest climbing gradually to almost 300m at the foot of Coire Ealt, then follow the path up the south side of the corrie to a point less than one kilometre north of Sgurr a'Choinnich. It is quite feasible to continue south-east over the lower tops of Beinn Bhreac (623m) and Cruach a'Bhuic (635m) and descend south-west from there to the road one kilometre south-east of Whistle-field Inn.

Looking north along Loch Eck

Beinn Mhor *(big hill)* (741m)
Clach Bheinn *(stone hill)* (643m)

The road from Strachur on Loch Fyne to Dunoon passes along the east side of Loch Eck, a narrow fiord-like loch with steep forested slopes on both sides. The west side of the loch is particularly craggy, and its south end is dominated by Clach Bheinn, a rocky peak which is the outlier of the higher, flatter mass of Beinn Mhor, which lies three kilometres back from the lochside. High up on the north-east side of Clach Bheinn there is a small corrie in which there are some pinnacles and huge boulders.

The forest road along the west side of Loch Eck is private and not accessible to cars, but there seems no reason why one cannot cycle along it and reach Bernice. From there Beinn Mhor can be climbed by taking the road up the Bernice Glen and a path beyond its furthest point through the forest to reach the pass at the head of the glen. This path is now very indistinct and overgrown in places. From the pass climb the north-east ridge of Beinn Mhor direct to its summit plateau. The trig point is on a rocky knoll at the south-west edge of this flat area of grass and small rocky outcrops.

To continue the traverse to Clach Bheinn, go south-east along a wide grassy ridge towards the edge overlooking Coire an t-Sith and reach the col below Clach Bheinn. A short grassy slope with rock outcrops leads to the summit cairn of this hill. The

Clach Bheinn from Loch Eck

shortest descent to the road along the side of Loch Eck is south-east. Alternatively, the descent towards Bernice goes north-east not far from the boulders mentioned above to reach the forest at the foot of Coire an t-Sith where a road leads down to Bernice.

The Paper Cave in the forest on the east side of Clach Bheinn is close to the descent route described above. It is just below the upper forest road about half a kilometre south of the stream flowing down Coire an t-Sith, and is worth a visit with a torch and rope. According to tradition, the deeds and documents of the Campbell family were hidden in the cave during the troubled times at the end of the 17th century when Cowal was plundered by highlanders from Atholl.

A shorter traverse of Beinn Mhor and Clach Bheinn if one does not have a bicycle starts from Glen Massan. From the end of the public road near Stonefield walk up the glen to Glenmassan farm and continue up the forest road on the west side of the Allt Coire Mheasain. This road narrows to a grassy track which goes beyond the forest up the hillside almost to the summit of Beinn Mhor, and gives a very easy ascent. From Clach Bheinn the return to Glen Massan goes south-west over the flat top of Creachan Mor, then south-east down a narrowing ridge towards Creachan Beag. From the first col on this ridge make a descending traverse south down the steep grassy hillside and drop down to the glen through a gap between two blocks of forestry.

Creag Tharsuinn *(transverse crag)* (641m)
This hill forms a long ridge running from south to north on the west side of Garrachra Glen, the higher continuation of Glen Massan. On its east side above this glen it is quite steep, but to the west it is much less so, dropping in long forested slopes towards Srath nan Lub near the head of Glendaruel.

The most pleasant approach is from Glen Massan, starting from the end of the public road near Stonefield. Continue up the glen past Glenmassan farm until just beyond Garrachra it is possible to climb north-west up the hillside between two blocks of forest. Reach the main ridge of the hill just north of Meall Dubh, drop slightly to the Bealach nan Sac and finally climb to the summit of Creag Tharsuinn.

PATHS AND WALKS

Ardgartan to Lochgoilhead (1). Walk up the forest road on the south side of the Croe Water for about three kilometres and take the footpath which branches uphill through scattered trees to the Bealach Dubh-lic. Continue south-west from this pass along the path down into the forest and along the south side of the Donich Water to Lochgoilhead. (10 kilometres).

Ardgartan to Lochgoilhead (2). From Ardgartan follow the road south towards Coilessan and take the branch up the Coilessan Glen. From the end of the road continue west by the footpath which crosses the col between The Brack and Cnoc Coinnich and descend into the forest above Lochgoilhead to join the preceding route. (10 kilometres).

Ardgartan to Lochgoilhead (3). This is a longer and very indirect route, but a worthwhile low-level expedition to explore the Ardgoil peninsula, with splendid views across Loch Long and Loch Goil. From Ardgartan go south along the road towards Coilessan, but keep above this lochside house and continue along the road which contours along the wooded hillside above Loch Long at about 150m and eventually reaches the Corran Lochan. From there go north by a path across Argyll's Bowling Green and descend into the Ardgoil Forest to reach a forest road which leads to Lochgoilhead. (18 kilometres).

Lochgoilhead to Strachur. This route crosses the hills between the head of Loch Goil and Loch Fyne by the splendid pass at the foot of Beinn Lochain. It starts from Lettermay, two kilometres from Lochgoilhead village. Follow the route described earlier in this chapter for Beinn Lochain and Beinn Bheula as far as the Curra Lochain. Continue west by the path on the north side of the lochan, over the Bealach an Lochain and down the Leavanin Burn to the forest road which goes round the north side of Beinn Lagan to reach Strachurmore, not far from Strachur itself. (11 kilometres).

Lochgoilhead to Invernoaden. This route also starts at Lettermay. Follow the forest road west and keep left at the junction to reach and continue along the path which makes a rising traverse through the forest on the south-east side of the Lettermay Burn.

Reach the outflow of Lochain nan Cnaimh and after going round the west end of the lochan continue along the path up the grassy hillside to cross the watershed just east of the bealach below Beinn Bheula. Descend south-west into the upper part of Coire Ealt to enter the forest just south of the stream in this corrie. Once in the forest a road is reached which may be followed north-west to reach Invernoaden. (11 kilometres).

Carrick Castle to Ardentinny. Carrick Castle is at the end of the public road on the west side of Loch Goil. Go south from there by a narrow road then a path for about two kilometres to the start of the forest and continue uphill along the path through it to reach the tall pylon which carries the electricity transmission line across Loch Long. At that point a forest road is joined which continues south to Stronvochlan, one kilometre north of Ardentinny. (9 kilometres).

Gairletter (Loch Long) to Benmore or Puck's Glen. From Gairletter take the forest road west on the south side of the stream to reach the upper edge of the forest at about 300m. Follow a path south-west parallel to the electricity transmission line over a col and down to the forest above Strath Eachaig. Having reached a forest road, either turn north to descend to Benmore, or go down Puck's Glen. The latter gives a delightful walk down a beautiful gorge where the path has in places been cut out of the cliff which overhangs the cascading stream. (6 kilometres).

CLIMBING

The east face of Beinn an Lochain above Loch Restil is over 600m high and the upper half is steep and craggy, but the rocks are very broken and vegetatious and quite unsuitable for summer climbing. A number of winter climbs have been done on this face and considerable variation is possible at about Grade II to III. The obvious shelf which rises across the face from left to right is Grade I.

The north face of Beinn an Lochain has two lines of cliffs. The lower one, named Kinglas Crag, is about 60m high and has four winter routes of Grade III/IV. The upper crag, which is just below the summit of the mountain, has several winter routes of Grade II to V. Some of these routes are rather complex in their topography, and the earliest of them, *Raeburn's Route*, has probably seldom been repeated in summer, although winter variants have been done.

Low down on the south face of Beinn an Lochain above the forest in Gleann Mor is Slabby Crag on which three routes of up to 40m and from Severe to Hard Very Severe have been done. The approach to this crag is rather impeded by recent afforestation.

On Ben Donich the west side of the north ridge forms a number of small but very steep crags high up near the summit. The best approach is up the ridge until a traverse across its west side leads above a boulder field to the foot of the crags. Five routes from Severe to E1 have been done on the first and third crags (counting from the north), the longest being 60m.

The Brack gives the best and certainly the most serious climbing in Ardgoil on the great dark cliff at the head of its north corrie. The prominent gully near the right of the cliff is *Elephant Gully* (90m, Difficult), an entertaining but very grassy climb mainly on the right wall and ending up a subterranean passage. To its left in the centre of the cliff is *Great Central Groove* (90m, Hard Very Severe), a classic climb in the best Scottish tradition. In winter it has given an excellent Grade V route. There are E grade routes to the right and left of Great Central Groove. Much further left there are several scrappy routes, better in winter than summer, and round the corner in the north-east facing corrie there are some small crags and pinnacles which have given short rock-climbs up to Difficult standard.

The largest of the low-level crags in Cowal is Creag Liath on the steep hillside above the south end of Loch Eck on its east side at grid reference 145 873. The crag is steep and rather scruffy, and the strata of its rock lies at an unfriendly angle. Of about a dozen routes recorded, only one is less than Severe. On the opposite side of Loch Eck there are two crags beside the forest road just north of Benmore Home Farm. One of them is extensively bolted and is evidently used as a practice crag by the Benmore Adventure Centre.

CHAPTER 7

The Arrochar Alps

The Cobbler	884m	259 059
Beinn Narnain	926m	272 067
A'Chrois	849m	289 078
Beinn Ime	1011m	255 085
Beinn Luibhean	858m	243 079
Ben Vane	915m	278 098
Ben Vorlich	943m	295 124
Stob Coire Creagach	817m	231 109

ACCESS
The A82 road from Glasgow northwards goes along the west side of Loch Lomond through Tarbet, Inveruglas and Ardlui. The A83 road branches off the A82 at Tarbet and goes through Arrochar and Glen Croe and over the Rest and be Thankful pass to Glen Kinglas and Loch Fyne. The A814 road goes from Helensburgh to Arrochar along the side of Loch Long.

TRANSPORT
Bus: Glasgow to Tarbet, Arrochar, Inveruglas and Ardlui and over the Rest and be Thankful pass; daily.
Helensburgh to Garelochhead and Arrochar, daily.
Train: Glasgow to Arrochar and Tarbet and Ardlui. (West Highland Line); daily.

ACCOMMODATION
Hotels at Arrochar, Tarbet, Ardlui and Cairndow. Youth hostel at Ardgartan (head of Loch Long). Caravan and camp sites at Arrochar, Ardgartan and Ardlui.

MAPS
Ordnance Survey 1:50,000, Sheet 56
Bartholomew 1:100,000, Sheet 48

The mountains to the north and west of Arrochar at the head of Loch Long are among the best-known and most popular not only in the Southern Highlands, but in the whole of Scotland. The six principal peaks are Beinn Ime (the highest), Beinn

The Cobbler from the Narnain Boulders

Narnain, A'Chrois, The Cobbler, Ben Vane and Ben Vorlich, and they have from the earliest days of climbing in Scotland been known collectively as The Arrochar Alps.

Of these six peaks The Cobbler is undoubtedly the finest, although not by any means the highest, and the extraordinary outline of its three rocky summits is equalled in Scotland only by some of the Torridonian mountains and the Cuillin of Skye. The names Cobbler and Arrochar are almost synonymous, signifying the best rock-climbing in the Southern Highlands and one of the earliest centres of the development of climbing in Scotland. The Cobbler has been a focal point in the development of rock-climbing three times during the last century. In the early days of Scottish climbing, when trains and not cars were the normal form of transport to the mountains, Arrochar with its station on the West Highland Railway was one of the most accessible mountain centres in Scotland, and much rock-climbing exploration was done on The Cobbler in the eighteen-nineties. Almost forty years later, in the days of the depression on Clydeside, young climbers from Glasgow inspired by J.B.Nimlin carried out the second wave of climbing exploration on The Cobbler and many fine routes, some still classics, were done. Then in the late nineteen-forties and early nineteen-fifties yet another group of young climbers, mainly from the Creag Dhu Mountaineering Club and the natural successors of Nimlin, pioneered many new routes which were at the time among the hardest rock climbs in Scotland and have only recently been exceeded by the modern climbers with their greatly improved equipment.

The other mountains of the Arrochar Alps may suffer somewhat by comparison with The Cobbler, few mountains in Scotland do not, but they are all fine peaks in their own right. They are a good deal steeper and rockier than most other peaks of the Southern Highlands, and although none of them can offer rock-climbing to compare with The Cobbler, there are some fair-sized buttresses on Beinn Ime and Creag Tharsuinn (on the ridge between Beinn Narnain and A'Chrois) and some smaller crags elsewhere, including low-level crags in Glen Croe which give hard modern climbing.

The Arrochar Alps are enclosed by Loch Lomond and the head of Loch Long on the east, Glen Croe on the south, and Glen Kinglas and Srath Duibh-uisge on the west and north. The area covered by this chapter also includes the featureless expanse of hills and moor to the north of Glen Kinglas, but the only hill of interest in this area is Stob Coire Creagach and its westward extension Binnein an Fhidhleir on the north side of lower Glen Kinglas.

Arrochar has the reputation, probably deservedly, of a rather wet climate, and climbers are warned that Arrochar rock, which is mainly mica-schist with a coating of lichen, becomes as slippery as soap when wet. For this reason The Cobbler and its neighbours tend to be out of condition for serious rock-climbing during the all-too-frequent spells of wet weather. However, it is well worth waiting for good weather and dry rock.

Although the Arrochar Alps are not noted as a winter climbing centre, there is no doubt that in the right conditions there are some excellent snow and ice routes of all standards of difficulty. Unfortunately, because of the proximity to the west coast and the modest height of the mountains, the right conditions for winter climbing tend to be rather rare and not infrequently the winter passes with little or no accumulation of snow or ice.

Details of all rock, snow and ice routes are contained in the Scottish Mountaineering Club's *Climbers Guide to Arran, Arrochar and the Southern Highlands* by K.V.Crocket and A.Walker, published in 1989.

The Arrochar Alps lie partly within the Argyll National Forest Park, and the Forestry Commission has extensive forests along the lower slopes of the hills above Glen Croe, Loch Long, Coiregrogain and Glen Loin, as well as on the low hill Cruach Tairbeirt between Glen Loin and Loch Lomond. Coiregrogain is a fine wild glen enclosed by the steep crags of A'Chrois, Ben Vane and Beinn Ime; it is the true heart of the Arrochar Alps, but its lower reaches are rather spoiled by electricity transmission pylons.

North of Coiregrogain, Loch Sloy lies in a deep glen between Ben Vorlich and Ben Vane and is the reservoir for the generating station at Inveruglas beside Loch Lomond. Much of the area described in this chapter is within the catchment area of this scheme, and many of the mountain streams are dammed just above the 300m contour to provide their share of water for Loch Sloy.

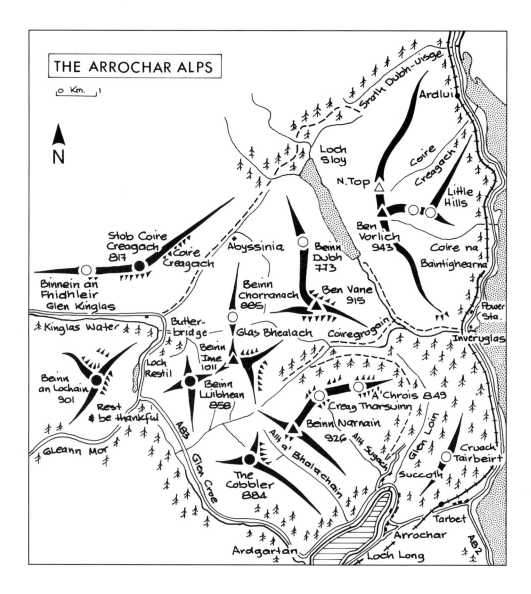

THE ARROCHAR ALPS

0 Km. 1

N

Srath Dubh-uisge

Ardlui

Loch
Sloy

Coire
Creagach

N. Top

Little
Hills

Stob Coire
Creagach
817

Coire
Creagach

Abyssinia

Beinn
Dubh
773

Ben
Vorlich
943

Coire na
Baintighearna

Binnein an
Fhidhleir
Glen Kinglas

Beinn
Chorranach
885

Ben Vane
915

Kinglas Water

Butter-
bridge

Glas Bhealach

Coiregrogain

Power
Sta.

Inveruglas

Beinn
Ime
1011

Beinn
an Lochain
901

Loch
Restil

Beinn
Luibhean
858

A'Chrois 849

Creag Tharsuinn

Beinn Narnain
926

Glen Loin

Cruach
Tairbeirt

Rest
& be thankful

Gleann Mor

A83

Glen Croe

Alt a' Bhalachain

Alt Sugach

Succoth

The
Cobbler
884

Tarbet

Arrochar

A82

Ardgartan

Loch Long

THE HILLS

The Cobbler (884m)

Although not by any means the highest, The Cobbler is certainly the best-known and most interesting mountain of the Arrochar Alps. The extraordinary outline of its three rocky peaks is one of the strangest and most impressive sights in the Scottish mountains, and it is well seen by travellers passing in the train along the West Highland Line near Arrochar. Its position at the southern edge of the Arrochar Alps makes The Cobbler prominent in views from the south and south-east, and from its

The South Peak of The Cobbler.   The climber is on Nimlin's Direct Route

The North Peak of The Cobbler

summit the climber has grand views towards Ben Lomond, the Luss Hills and the Firth of Clyde. Northwards, however, the view is rather restricted by The Cobbler's higher neighbours.

The origin of the name Cobbler is obscure, but it is much more commonly used than the alternative name Ben Arthur. It is hard to find anything in the shape of the mountain which resembles a cobbler, but it is interesting to note that some of the peaks of the Eastern Alps whose shapes are just as spectacular have the name *schuster* or *cobbler* attached to them. John Stoddart in his Local Scenery and Manners in Scotland, 1799-1800 writes: 'This terrific rock forms the summit of a huge mountain, and its nodding top so far overhangs the base as to assume the appearance of a cobbler sitting at work, from whence the country people call it an greasaiche crom, the crooked shoemaker.'

There has been considerable confusion over the years as to which of the three peaks is the true cobbler, although the name is commonly applied to the whole mountain. This confusion is increased by the fact that there are also the cobbler's last and his wife Jean to fit into the picture. Different writers, seeing the mountain in different lights, have come up with different ideas. Suffice to say that climbers regard the South Peak as Jean, for example J.B.Nimlin's classic direct route on the peak is often referred to as 'Jean Direct'.

The summit of The Cobbler is formed by a huge block of rock about four metres high at the south-west end of the broad grassy ridge which forms the backbone of the Centre Peak. Were it not for this block of rock, which is sheer on all sides, the summit would be as easy to reach as any in the Southern Highlands. However, there are many who reach the foot of the summit rock and go no further. Although the last few metres are no more than a scramble in rock-climbing terms, there is sufficient exposure to worry anyone with a bad head for heights, and a slip might result in a long fall. The route onto the topmost point goes through the window or gap at the north-west end of the summit rock, along a broad (but outward sloping) ledge on its south-west side and up its south-east end. The rocks tend to be slippery when wet, and if a high wind is blowing the situation can be distinctly unnerving.

The North Peak is probably the most spectacular of the three as it is formed by two huge overhanging beaks of rock. The small summit cairn is close to the edge of the higher of these beaks. The east face of the peak is entirely rocky, and there are many excellent climbs on it. The other three sides are much less steep, and the ascent from the col between the Centre and North peaks is short and easy.

The South Peak is steep on all sides and is the most difficult of the three peaks for the 'non-climber' to reach. The north-east and south-west faces are particularly formidable and give rock-climbers many interesting routes. The north-west face drops to the col between the South and Centre peaks and is only about 30m high, but it is quite steep and a little awkward to climb or descend when wet. The south-east ridge is probably the easiest route to the top of the peak; it is easy-angled and gives a good scramble with a few short steep sections.

The summit of The Cobbler

The most popular approach to The Cobbler is from the head of Loch Long up the Allt a'Bhalachain *(the buttermilk burn)*. The traditional way starts from the old torpedo station opposite Arrochar village, and there is a path, now rather overgrown by trees and bushes, on the south-west side of the burn which leads to a dam at about 340m. The alternative and more used path to reach this point starts near the head of Loch Long at the road to Succoth. A path leads uphill through the forest for a short distance and continues along an old concrete staircase built in the days of construction of the Loch Sloy hydro-electric scheme. At the top of this staircase a horizontal path is reached which is followed to the left to reach the dam on the Allt a'Bhalachain.

From the dam continue up the north-east side of the burn by a well-made path to the Narnain Boulders which have for many years provided spartan shelter under the lower one and some rock-climbing practice on the higher one. A short distance beyond the boulders cross the burn and follow the path, wet and boggy in places, up into the corrie enclosed by the three peaks of The Cobbler. The path, becoming steeper and narrower, leads to the col between the Centre and North peaks. The North Peak is a few minutes walk up a rocky path to the right; the Centre Peak is further away to the left along a broad ridge which leads to the foot of the summit rock.

The Cobbler traverse at the foot of the South Peak

From Ardgartan the ascent of The Cobbler goes up a path from the foot of Glen Croe along the edge of the forest to reach the south-east ridge , which is followed to the foot of the South Peak. If one is not going to traverse over this peak, go round its south side below the impressively steep south-west face to reach the col between the South and Centre peaks. Continue up the ridge to the Centre Peak, avoiding a steep pitch on the left. Above this pitch one can stay on the crest of the ridge and with a little easy scrambling reach the highest point of the mountain.

The traverse of the three peaks of The Cobbler is a classic scramble which calls for a modest degree of rock-climbing ability and a good head for heights. In dry weather there are no great difficulties although the pitch on the north-west side of the South Peak is steep and a little exposed. In wet and windy weather the difficulties are greater and care is needed on the rather slippery rock.

The shortest ascent to The Cobbler, but one which completely misses the fine views of the mountain that one gets on the ascent by the Allt a'Bhalachain, is from Glen Croe. Leave the A83 road at a car park at grid reference 243 060 and climb up beside a fence on the south side of the stream flowing down from the Bealach a'Mhaim. In just over a kilometre bear south-east up a tributary to the col between the Centre and North peaks.

Beinn Narnain (926m)
A'Chrois *(the cross)* (849m)
In views of the Arrochar Alps from the south and east, Beinn Narnain appears prominently standing in front of Beinn Ime and higher than its two neighbours The Cobbler and A'Chrois. It stands directly above the forested slopes at the head of Loch Long, the south-east ridge rising over the knoll of Cruach nam Miseag to the rocky prow of The Spearhead and the little level plateau of the summit. The other principal ridge of Beinn Narnain runs north-east from the summit over the rocky ridge of Creag Tharsuinn (781m) to the prominent little peak of A'Chrois which has a fine position above Coiregrogain. The two ridges of Beinn Narnain enclose a big grassy corrie down which the Allt Sugach flows to the head of Loch Long. This corrie is unnamed on the 1:50,000 map and is named Coire Feorline on the 1:25,000 map, but it has always been known to climbers as Coire Sugach, and that name persists.

A'Chrois is also a prominent peak despite it modest height. From Inveruglas on the A82 road along Loch Lomond it is seen to rise very steeply and impressively above the forest and it appears to be almost the twin of Ben Vane on the opposite side of Coiregrogain. The south-east face of A'Chrois high up under the summit is steep and rocky, with a prominent gully, the Chrois Gully, splitting the face. It is well seen from the A82 road south of Tarbet.

The north-west side of Beinn Narnain and A'Chrois and the ridge between them drops very steeply into the head of Coiregrogain, and that side of the two peaks is relatively unfrequented.

The ascent of Beinn Narnain is best made up the south-east ridge from the head of Loch Long. Follow the path through the forest and up the concrete staircase (as

Recess Route on the North Peak of The Cobbler

Chimney Arête on the North Peak of The Cobbler

for The Cobbler) to the horizontal path. From there continue uphill more or less on the crest of the ridge, avoiding rocky outcrops and crags to reach the knoll of Cruach nam Miseag. Descend slightly and climb rockier slopes to the foot of The Spearhead. Go up the stony gully on the right (north-east) of this prominent buttress and reach the summit plateau; the cairn is a short distance away to the west.

As an alternative, one can follow The Cobbler path as far as the Narnain Boulders and climb due north from there to reach the foot of The Spearhead where the previous route is joined.

The north-west ridge of Beinn Narnain is not well defined. It drops from the summit plateau as a broad stony slope , grassy lower down, to the Bealach a'Mhaim (637m). This ridge is climbed or descended if one is making a traverse between Beinn Narnain and The Cobbler or Beinn Ime.

The traverse from Beinn Narnain to A'Chrois is very straightforward and gives a good walk along the broad ridge over Creag Tharsuinn. The summit of A'Chrois is an excellent viewpoint, particularly towards Ben Vane and Ben Vorlich, with Loch Sloy lying in the deep glen between them. To descend from A'Chrois to Succoth at the head of Loch Long go south down grassy slopes into Coire Sugach and follow the Allt Sugach downhill past several fine little waterfalls to the glen.

The northern and eastern slopes of A'Chrois are steep, rocky and forested, and routes on that side of the peak are rough going. There is a forest road starting above Succoth in Glen Loin and ending high up in Coiregrogain. If one continues beyond its end up to the Bealach a'Mhaim and down the Allt a'Bhalachain back to Succoth, one gets a good low-level circumnavigation of Beinn Narnain and A'Chrois.

Beinn Ime *(butter hill)* 1011m
This is the highest mountain of the Arrochar Alps, and in most views of the group it rises clearly above its neighbours.The summit ridge is at the head of the north-eastern corrie, and there is a little top a few hundred metres south-east of the summit. The northern and eastern sides of the mountain are very steep and rugged, and the north-east ridge between them is a fine feature of the mountain. The west face above Glen Kinglas is also steep, but less rocky. By contrast the southern slopes are uniformly grassy and the broad south-south-east ridge drops to the Bealach a'Mhaim, the col which separates Beinn Ime from Beinn Narnain and The Cobbler.

The north ridge drops to the Glas Bhealaich (c.750m) and rises to Beinn Chorranach, a rather neglected hill and probably the least often climbed of the Arrochar Alps.

There are four possible routes of ascent of Beinn Ime, some very short and others a good deal longer. The shortest route is from the A83 road a short distance south of the bridge over the Kinglas Water near Butterbridge. This point gives the best roadside view of Beinn Ime, which rises steeply above the glen to a symmetrical cone. Start at a ruined house and go up a path, muddy in places, on the south side of the stream coming down from the Bealach a'Mhargaidh, the col between Beinn

Beinn Narnain from Beinn Ime

Beinn Ime from The Cobbler

Ime and Beinn Luibhean. Go to the col and from it climb the south-west face of Beinn Ime direct to the summit where the cairn and trig point are on top of a small crag.

A similar route starts from the A83 road in Glen Croe at grid reference 243 060. Go north-east up the stream (paths on both sides) for about a kilometre and then bear north up easy grassy slopes to the summit.

The approach from the head of Loch Long follows the well-worn path to The Cobbler past the Narnain Boulders and right up the Allt a'Bhalachain to its source. Then go north for a short distance to the Bealach a'Mhaim where there is a fence across the wide col. Beyond the fence climb north-west up easy grassy slopes to the summit ridge a short distance south-east of the top.

The longest, but probably the most interesting approach to Beinn Ime is from Inveruglas up Coiregrogain. (Note that cars should be parked near the power station and not at the foot of the private road up Coiregrogain). From the A82 road along Loch Lomond walk up the private road on the north side of the Inveruglas Water for two kilometres and continue left across a bridge and up the road beside the Allt Coiregrogain to the point where it enters the forest. From there climb the fine north-east ridge of Beinn Ime; it becomes rocky high up, but there are no difficulties and the ridge leads to the lower south-east top.

Beinn Luibhean *(hill of the little plant)* (858m)
This rather undistinguished hill is little more than an outlier of Beinn Ime, separated from it by the Bealach a'Mhargaidh. All round its western perimeter there are steep grassy slopes with rock outcrops above Glen Croe and the Rest and be Thankful pass.

Two routes of ascent are possible. One, which can be combined with the ascent of Beinn Ime, is from Butterbridge to the Bealach a'Mhargaidh (see above) and up the east ridge of Beinn Luibhean. The other is from Glen Croe up the south ridge of the hill.

Ben Vane *(middle hill)* (915m)
This is an isolated and imposing little mountain on the north side of Coiregrogain. Its south face overlooking the corrie is very steep for a height of over 600m and there are considerable rock outcrops near the summit. The other sides of the mountain are not nearly so steep, and northwards a ridge leads out to Beinn Dubh (773m). The col between Ben Vane and its nearest big neighbour, Beinn Ime, is about 500m, so although the two mountains can be traversed together, there is a lot of climbing between them.

The best and most frequented ascent route on Ben Vane is the south-east ridge. The start is from Inveruglas on the A82 road up the private road on the north side of the Inveruglas Water. (Note that cars should not be parked at the foot of this road). In two kilometres cross the bridge and go a further few hundred metres before leaving the road. Climb west-north-west up easy grassy slopes which become steeper, with many rock outcrops and small crags higher up; however, there is no difficulty in finding a way through them to the little plateau which forms the summit of Ben Vane. The cairn is at the south edge of this plateau.

The return may be varied by going north along the ridge to Beinn Dubh and descending from there to the Loch Sloy dam. It is also possible to descend west from the summit to the col between Ben Vane and Beinn Chorranach. From there the latter hill may be climbed, or its southern slopes traversed to reach the Glas Bhealach and Beinn Ime.

Although there is no recorded rock-climbing on Ben Vane, there is the possibility for many short climbs on the crags south of the summit. In hard winter conditions the direct ascent of the south face might give an interesting route, similar to the east face of Beinn an Lochain above Loch Restil. The steepness and character of the two mountains are similar.

Ben Vorlich *(hill of the bay)* (943m)
This, the northernmost of the Arrochar Alps, is rather a sprawling mountain on the west side of Loch Lomond at its north end. In plan it is crescent-shaped with a central spur running east from the summit over the Little Hills to end above Loch Lomond. The east side of Ben Vorlich above the loch has two large corries, Coire na Baintig-hearna and Coire Creagach, which are wooded with birch and oak along their lower slopes as well as having innumerable small crags. The impression of Ben Vorlich from the Loch Lomond road between Inveruglas and Ardlui is of a rather rocky, wooded hill with no obvious routes of ascent. The west side is very different, being much steeper and treeless, and dropping in a single plunge of over 600m to the waters of Loch Sloy.

Several different routes of ascent for Ben Vorlich are possible, all of similar length and character, and most of them involving a good deal more effort than might be expected considering the accessibility of the mountain. This is because the three main ridges, the south ridge above Inveruglas, the north ridge above Ardlui and the Little Hills are all very knolly with many ups and downs. The only routes that are continuously uphill are Coire Creagach and the steep and direct ascent from the Loch Sloy dam.

The traverse of the Little Hills is probably the most attractive route of ascent. The start is at Stuckendroin farm and the climb goes south-west up a well-defined ridge overlooking Coire Creagach to two little tops, 793m and 808m, before dropping to a col at 763m and climbing west to the summit of Ben Vorlich. The Ordnance Survey trig point is at the south end of the level summit ridge, but the true top is about 200 metres north on a little crag.

The route up Coire Creagach may be quicker, but it is less attractive and the going is likely to be wetter underfoot. Start under the railway at a 'cattle-creep' about 400 metres south of Ardlui and bear south-west up the corrie to reach the ridge of Ben Vorlich a little north of the summit. Another route from Ardlui starts past Garristuck cottage and goes west onto the north ridge which is followed over Stob nan Coinnich Bhacain and the North Top (931m).

From the south Ben Vorlich can be climbed up its south ridge, starting from the private road on the north side of the Inveruglas Water. The ascent is quite long with many ups and downs. It is also possible to make the ascent from the Loch Sloy dam; the climb is steep and there are many crags on the hillside, but they can be easily avoided and a bearing north-east leads to the main ridge of the hill not far from the trig point.

Stob Coire Creagach *(peak of the craggy corrie)* (817m)
This is the highest point of the steep-sided ridge which forms the north wall of Glen Kinglas. It is not really one of the Arrochar Alps, being separated from them by Glen Kinglas, and it is not even named on the Ordnance Survey maps. One and a half kilometres west its lower neighbour Binnein an Fhidhleir *(fiddler's peak)* (811m) is the second highest point on the eight-kilometre long ridge which stretches from Loch Fyne almost to the head of Loch Sloy.

The name Stob Coire Creagach has been given to this hill as the summit is close to the craggy headwall of Coire Creagach. This corrie, which is only named on the 1:25,000 map, overlooks the upper part of Glen Kinglas to the north-east of Butterbridge. Although the south side of the hill rises with impressive steepness from the glen, the north side is an extensive and totally featureless expanse of moorland.

The hill is climbed from Glen Kinglas starting near the bridge which takes the A83 road over the Kinglas Water. Bear north-north-west directly up the steep grassy hillside. Higher up the angle eases, but there is no respite until the summit is reached. A good high-level walk leads west to Binnein an Fhidhleir and down towards Loch Fyne and the village of Cairndow where the Strone Garden is worth a visit. However, there is a long walk back up the road in Glen Kinglas to the day's starting point.

No description of the Arrochar Alps would be complete without mention of the many howffs among these mountains. For many years these caves, shelter stones and holes in the ground have provided rude shelter for climbers and cave-dwellers, and they have become part of the folklore of the Arrochar Alps. The most famous are probably the A'Chrois caves which are located low down in the forest on the west side of Glen Loin. For many years their exact position was a closely guarded secret, but now they are marked on the Ordnance Survey 1:25,000 map. They are reached along the low-level track on the west side of Glen Loin as far as the point where it enters the forest, from where a path uphill through the trees leads to the caves, which provide accommodation in the bowels of the earth and some rock-climbing on the outside of the crags and huge fallen boulders.

On The Cobbler the best-known howff is under the lower of the two Narnain Boulders, but it is a draughty and a muddy place, less attractive nowadays than it was in 1926 when it was the site of the inaugural meet of the Junior Mountaineering Club of Scotland. Just over half a kilometre further up the path towards The Cobbler there is a fine shelter under an overhanging crag a few metres to the right of the path. Higher still, there are some good caves under the huge boulders which litter the upper corrie under the three peaks of the mountain.

Beinn Ime from Butterbridge in Glen Kinglas

Elsewhere there is a howff in Coire Sugach at about 600m just below the Beinn Narnain - Creag Tharsuinn col, and another one beside the Allt Sugach just above the upper Forestry Commission road. On The Brack (just outside the area covered by this chapter) there is a good howff, romantically named 'Cobbler View', at about 450m below the main crags and to the right of the approach path from Glen Croe, and on the north face of Beinn an Lochain above Glen Kinglas two huge boulders leaning against each other form the howff known as 'Sunset Arch', but access to it is impeded by recent forestry plantings along the lower slopes of the hill on the south side of the Kinglas Water. Finally, high up on Ben Vorlich above the Loch Sloy dam the Vorlich Fissures are the most remote and least visited of Arrochar's natural mountain refuges.

PATHS AND WALKS

Butterbridge (Glen Kinglas) to Ardlui. This walk follows a rough private road up Glen Kinglas past the curiously named and ruined Abyssinia cottage, into an area of forest at the head of Loch Sloy and out of it to the end of the road near the head of Srath Dubh-uisge. From there continue along the south side of the stream to descend steeply through woodland to the Loch Lomond road one kilometre north of Ardlui. (12 kilometres). The walk can be shortened and some wet going in Srath Dubh-uisge avoided by climbing less than 100m to cross the northern extremity of Ben Vorlich's north ridge just south of Stob an Fhithich.

Butterbridge (Glen Kinglas) to Inveruglas. Start from the A83 road in Glen Kinglas near the bridge over the Kinglas Water and climb steeply east to the Glas Bhealach. Descend on the east side of the bealach and reach the road on the north side of the Allt Coiregrogain. As far as this point the walk is over rough country with no path. Continue down the road to Inveruglas on the Loch Lomond road. (9 kilometres).

Butterbridge (Glen Kinglas) to Arrochar. This variation of the previous walk has the same start and follows the same way over the Glas Bhealach to the road in Coiregrogain. There go south-west along the road up the corrie for half a kilometre, cross the Allt Coiregrogain and return east along the road down the corrie below the north and east sides of A'Chrois to reach Succoth half a kilometre from Arrochar. (12 kilometres).

CLIMBING

It is not possible within the scope of this guidebook to describe in detail the wealth of excellent rock-climbing on The Cobbler, and the other climbing possibilities in the Arrochar Alps. This is done in the Scottish Mountaineering Club's *Climbers Guide to Arran, Arrochar and the Southern Highlands* by K.V.Crocket and A.Walker (1989). In the following paragraphs some of the most notable climbs on The Cobbler and its neighbouring peaks will be mentioned.

The North Peak of The Cobbler gives the best selection of routes on the mountain, and the peak is particularly noted for several excellent Severes. The classic climb is *Recess Route* (110m, Very Difficult) which starts near the lowest rocks below the Ramshead (the name given by climbers to the overhanging summit of the peak) and leads up by a series of short varied pitches to end up *Ramshead Wall* at the summit. The exposed right-hand edge of the Ramshead is the line of *Whither Wether* (54m, Very Severe), one of the most exposed and sensational of Cobbler climbs. To the left of the overhanging prow of the Ramshead there is a steep wall bounded on its left by *Right-angled Gully* (36m, Very Difficult) which forms the angle between the two prows of the North Peak. On this wall *Club Crack* (40m, E2) and *Rest and be Thankful* (45m, E5) are two of the hardest routes on The Cobbler.

On the steep wall to the left of Right-angled Gully is *Punster's Crack* (48m, Severe), one of the best Severes in the country, steep and exposed in a superb situation and the epitome of Cobbler climbing. To its left *Wild Country* (48m, E5) and *The Nook* (57m, E2 with aid) are two more extreme routes which are on the exposed left-hand prow. The left-hand rocks of the North Peak just above the path to the col between it and the Centre Peak have five shorter routes of which *Right-angled Chimney* (30m, Difficult) is the most obvious.

The Centre Peak has few climbing possibilities. In winter the narrow *Centre Gully* (Grade I/II) in the middle of the east face is a pleasant climb, and to its left an easier gully leads up to the crest of the ridge close to the summit rocks. The *Centre Peak Arête*, which is the ridge leading up to the peak from the South Peak, has one

The final pitch of Punster's Crack

awkward pitch if climbed directly as the rock is becoming increasingly smooth with the passage of many climbers.

The South Peak has two principal faces, north-east and south-west. The former gets little sunshine, and tends to be vegetatious and damp. Although there are several good routes, some very hard, they lack the quality and popularity of the North Peak routes. One exception is the classic *Nimlin's Direct Route* (75m, Very Difficult) which goes up the exposed edge between the north-east and north-west faces to end dramatically at the summit of the peak. This route traverses onto the edge about 30m above its foot, and a direct and more difficult start is provided by *Slack's Route* (69m, Hard Severe) which starts from the base of the rocks. The north-east face has given some good hard winter ascents of the rather grassy summer routes, for example *Sesame Groove* and *North Wall Traverse* (105m, Grade IV) to the left of Nimlin's Direct Route.

The south-west face of the South Peak gets plenty of sunshine, but the rock is very steep and the routes are mostly E1. The right-hand edge of the wall is at an easier angle and is the line of *Ardgartan Arête* (60m, Severe). To its right is the narrow south face,bounded on its right by the *South-East Ridge. Ardgartan Wall* (60m, Very Difficult) is the classic route up the centre of the south face.

Beinn Narnain is best known among rock-climbers for the small but prominent Spearhead Ridge just below the summit of the mountain. The classic routes are the obvious *Jamblock Chimney* (40m, Very Difficult) on the south face and *Spearhead Arête* (40m, Very Difficult) which is the fine and exposed terminal end of the Ridge. There are also some underground routes, for example *Engine Room Crack* (30m, Difficult), which is entered by a hole in the ground a few metres left of Jamblock Chimney. A torch is useful.

To the south of the summit of Beinn Narnain at about 750m, facing The Cobbler across the Allt a'Bhalachain, is Yawning Crag which is identifiable by a deep chimney splitting it. There are three routes of Difficult and Very Difficult standard up to 33m long.

Creag Tharsuinn, though not a very distinguished summit itself, has a considerable crag on its south-east face overlooking Coire Sugach. The main mass of rock is Sugach Buttress on which *Garrick's Route* (120m, Very Difficult) is the classic trade route. Above and to the right is *Maclay's Gully*, an old-fashioned climb only worth doing in good winter conditions (60m, Grade III). There are four much more modern and much harder climbs on the sides of Maclay's Gully, for example *Terminal Wall* (60m, Very Severe) high on the right wall of the gully. Low down in the gully a chimney breaches the right wall; this is *McLaren's Chimney* (60m, Very Difficult), a rather messy and complex climb.

Elsewhere on the face of Creag Tharsuinn to the right of Maclay's Gully and at a higher level there are several minor buttresses and grassy gullies which are probably better suited for winter rather than summer climbing.

A fine route on Creag Tharsuinn that gives about 250m of varied and interesting climbing is Garrick's Route to the foot of a knife-edge pitch from where a descending traverse rightwards across the slab of *Slab and Groove* route leads into Maclay's Gully. Descend this to the foot of McLaren's Chimney, climb it to a broad rake above which a fine 30m pitch (Very Difficult) leads to the top of the crag.

The south face of A'Chrois is cleft by a prominent gully, *Chrois Gully* (Grade I), with the narrower *Pinnacle Gully* to its right (Grade I/II).

The big crag on the south-east face of Beinn Ime is Fan Gully Buttress. Although it faces down Coiregrogain, it is best approached by the Allt a'Bhalachain, or from Glen Croe, to the Bealach a'Mhaim followed by a traverse to the foot of the crag. The buttress is about 150m high, with a big grassy recess in the centre. This is the line of the original route, *Ben's Fault* (120m, Difficult). There are several variations of this route and others of a similar nature on the buttress which on the whole is very vegetatious with many grass ledges. Winter ascents have given better, but much harder climbs, up to Grade IV. The classic winter route is *Fan Gully* (100m, Grade II/III) on the right of the buttress.

Creag Coire an Creagach above Glen Kinglas is reached from the A83 road near Butterbridge by a long rising traverse north-north-east. The crags are high up not far below the crest of the north-east ridge of Stob Coire Creagach, and just over one kilometre north-east of that peak. There is a mixture of climbing, some in grassy gullies and chimneys and some on excellent clean rock.

Finally in the Arrochar Alps there are some low-level crags which have been developed in recent years. The most popular of these are the Glen Croe outcrops on the north side of the glen about two kilometres up from Ardgartan. As befits such short climbs on steep and overhanging crags, the standard is extremely high, many of the climbs being in the E grades. Many early routes which originally required aid have now been climbed free.

Near Loch Sloy power station there is another recently discovered outcrop, Sub-Station Crag. It is reached in about 15 minutes walking up the private road into Coiregrogain on the north side of the Inveruglas Water, and six routes have been recorded, Hard Very Severe to E3. Above Sub-Station Crag on the south ridge of Ben Vorlich there are three or four more small crags, all of which have their quota of short hard climbs.

SKI MOUNTAINEERING

The Arrochar Alps do not provide good terrain for ski mountaineering and their position near the west coast does not result in a suitable climate. However, if the snowline is fairly low the ascent of Beinn Ime on skis from Succoth at the head of Loch Long is an interesting tour, seldom done. Once the lowest slopes have been climbed, there is good terrain up the Allt a'Bhalachain to the Bealach a'Mhaim and from there up the smooth south-south-east ridge of Beinn Ime.

CHAPTER 8

Loch Fyne to Strath Fillan

Beinn Bhuidhe	948m	204 187
Meall an Fhudair	764m	271 192
Ben Lui	1130m	266 263
Beinn a' Chleibh	916m	251 256
Ben Oss	1029m	288 253
Beinn Dubhchraig	978m	308 255
Beinn Chuirn	880m	281 292

ACCESS
The A82 road from Glasgow to Crianlarich and Tyndrum gives access to the east side of this area. From Tyndrum the A85 to Dalmally goes along the north side. Branching off the A82 at Tarbet, the A83 over the Rest and be Thankful to Inveraray, followed by the A819 from there to Dalmally complete the ring of roads around the area described in this chapter. There are no public roads into the interior, those up Glen Fyne and Glen Shira being private.

TRANSPORT
Bus: Glasgow to Arrochar, Cairndow and Inveraray; daily.
Glasgow to Ardlui, Crianlarich, Tyndrum and Dalmally; daily.
Postbus: Inveraray to Dalmally; Mondays to Saturdays.
Train: Glasgow to Ardlui, Crianlarich, Tyndrum (Lower) and Dalmally; daily.

ACCOMMODATION
Hotels at Ardlui, Inverarnan, Crianlarich, Tyndrum, Dalmally, Inveraray and Cairndow.
Youth hostels at Ardgartan,Crianlarich and Inveraray.
Camp and caravan sites at Ardgartan, Ardlui and Tyndrum.

MAPS
Ordnance Survey 1:50,000, Sheets 50 and 56.
Bartholomew 1:100,000, Sheet 48.

The area described in this chapter lies to the west and north-west of the head of Loch Lomond. The northern corner of this area, close to the village of Tyndrum, has one of the finest groups of mountains in the Southern Highlands, dominated by Ben Lui. Further south-west the hills, with the exception of the isolated ridge of Beinn Bhuidhe, are much lower and to the west of Glen Shira the country is best described as rough undulating moorland with some quite large areas of afforestation in Glen Aray.

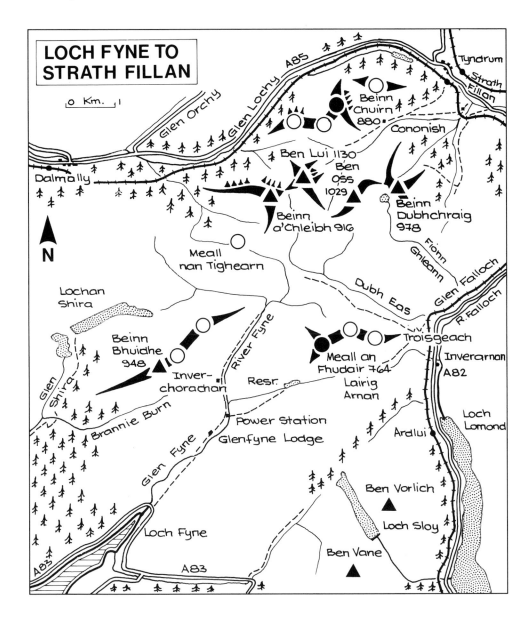

The eastern and northern boundary of the area is formed by Glen Falloch, Strath Fillan and Glen Lochy. The southern boundary goes from Inverarnan at the foot of Glen Falloch through the Lairig Arnan westwards to Glen Fyne, down that glen and along Loch Fyne to Inveraray. The western boundary is Glen Aray and the north-east end of Loch Awe. This boundary omits parts of south-west Argyll and the land between Loch Awe and Oban. There are no hills of any great interest in these parts, but there are two low-lying crags and some cross-country walks which will be mentioned in the relevant sections at the end of this chapter.

Almost all the mountaineering interest in this area is concentrated in the northern corner where Ben Lui is at the centre of a fine group of mountains several kilometres south of Tyndrum. To the south of these peaks there is a rather featureless tract of country at the head of Glen Fyne, and to its south-west the high ground between Glen Fyne and Glen Shira is dominated by the lonely mass of Beinn Bhuidhe. These two glens run down to the head of Loch Fyne not far from Inveraray, and this corner shows some of the characteristic features of Scottish west coast scenery - long narrow sea-lochs penetrating far inland towards the mountains. At its north-west corner, the area of this chapter reaches the head of Loch Awe, and there are fine views across it to Ben Cruachan and its neighbours, but these peaks are part of the Central Highlands and are described in a companion volume to this guidebook.

THE HILLS

Beinn Bhuidhe *(yellow hill)* (948m)

Probably the most isolated mountain in the Southern Highlands, solitary Beinn Bhuidhe rises between Glen Fyne and Glen Shira, whose rivers and streams surround it on three sides. To its south-west long forested ridges drop towards the head of Loch Fyne.

Although it has only a single top over 914m, the mountain is a long and well-defined ridge with three tops, the highest point being near the middle of the ridge. To the north-east of the summit the main ridge, which is quite narrow at that point, drops to a broad col before rising to the north-east top (c.900m). Beyond there the ridge continues to Ceann Garbh (803m), and as this name (meaning rough head) implies, the north-east end of the mountain above the headwaters of the River Fyne is quite rough. By contrast the ridge which runs out south-west from the summit is broad and grassy, and its lower end is surrounded by densely planted trees at the confluence of the Brannie Burn and the River Shira.

Despite its isolated position, it is not easy to get a good impression of Beinn Bhuidhe from the south-west , for it is hidden by lower hills at the head of Loch Fyne. The best views of the mountain are to be had from the east and north-east. From Ben Oss, for instance, the long ridge of Beinn Bhuidhe is seen end on, and the mountain appears to be quite steep and isolated.

The best approach to Beinn Bhuidhe is up Glen Fyne; the road up the glen from the head of Loch Fyne is private, but it is a right of way as far as the small power station just beyond Glenfyne Lodge. A bicycle would be very useful for the first few kilometres up this road as far as the power station, or possibly two kilometres further to Inverchorachan. The ascent of the mountain starts from there up the burn which flows down a steep wooded gully above the cottage. If the burn is dry, the ascent of the gully itself is an entertaining scramble, but the easier ascent is up the steep grass and bracken slope on its north side. At about 550m the grassy upper corrie is reached, and one can either climb straight ahead to the col between Beinn Bhuidhe and its north-east top, or by bearing right one can climb the east ridge of the north-east top.

Beinn Bhuidhe from the east

This ridge is quite rocky and gives some pleasant scrambling high up. The final ascent along the summit ridge from the col is straightforward as there is a distinct path to the trig point.

The alternative ascent by Glen Shira is a good deal longer; the glen is wooded in its lower reaches with deciduous as well as coniferous trees and is worth a visit. The private road up the glen leads to the Lochan Shira Reservoir, where it crosses the dam to continue along the north side of the reservoir and end in the remote hinterland north of Beinn Bhuidhe. A bicycle might be used to reach the point well up the Brannie Burn where a firebreak in the forest gives access to the foot of the south-west ridge of Beinn Bhuidhe. The ascent of this long grassy ridge over Tom a'Phiobaire and Stac a'Chuirn is long and rather tedious.

Meall an Fhudair *(hill of gunpowder)* (764m)
This is the highest point of a sprawling hill between the head of Glen Fyne and the foot of Glen Falloch. The Lairig Arnan, which is a right of way between these two glens, is just to the south of the hill. Meall an Fhudair is at the west end of a high lochan-studded plateau, at whose eastern end is Troisgeach (734m), which by virtue of its accessibility from Glen Falloch is a more popular summit than its higher neighbour.

The ascent begins in Glen Falloch opposite Glen Falloch farm. Follow a hydro road up the lower slopes of Troisgeach Bheag to the junction with a higher horizontal road and from there climb west up the ridge to Troisgeach. Continue along the highest and driest ground by following the broad ridge past some little lochans to Meall nan Caora (722m) and there turn south-west to descend to a col with several more lochans and climb to Meall an Fhudair.

Although not a particularly distinguished hill itself, Meall an Fhudair gives good views of the surrounding hills, particularly Beinn Bhuidhe and the Ben Lui group, and far to the south-west down Glen Fyne to Loch Fyne.

Ben Lui (Beinn Laoigh) *(calf hill)* (1130m)
This is a magnificent mountain which many would consider to be the finest in the Southern Highlands. It may lack the height of Ben Lawers and the symmetrical simplicity of Ben More and Stob Binnein, but it more than makes amends by its classical mountain form and the splendid north-east corrie, the Coire Gaothaich, which holds snow in early summer long after the other mountains of the Southern Highlands are bare.

Ben Lui has four corries, facing west, north, north-east and south-east, and five ridges radiate outwards from the summit between these corries. The western, northern and eastern slopes are all steep and in places craggy, and the southern side of the mountain drops in long easy-angled slopes towards the desolate country at the head of Glen Fyne. The level summit ridge of the mountain is just over a hundred metres long and connects the summit to the slightly lower North-west Top (1127m).

The best-known view of the mountain, and one which captures its character exactly, is from the east, looking up the glen of the River Cononish directly towards the great north-east corrie. In winter and spring the snow-laden headwall of this corrie falls like a great white curtain below the summit ridge of the mountain, and it looks remarkably steep. However, the appearance is deceptive and only the uppermost slopes just below the cornice exceed about 45 degrees.

The western view of the mountain from the head of Loch Awe or Strath Orchy is also impressive. From that side Ben Lui is seen to tower above its neighbour Beinn a'Chleibh and its north-west ridge rises above the forested slopes of Glen Lochy in a series of rocky knolls, the Ciochan Beinn Laoigh.

Two routes of ascent of Ben Lui are popular, one from Strath Fillan or Tyndrum up the River Cononish and the other from Glen Lochy up the Fionn Choirein between Ben Lui and Beinn a'Chleibh. The former is much longer, but has the benefit of fine views of the mountain on the approach. The latter is short and direct and can be used also for the ascent of Beinn a'Chleibh.

The Cononish approach starts either at Dailrigh just north-west of the A82 bridge over the River Fillan or at Tyndrum Lower Station. Both ways follow private roads which join a kilometre east of Cononish farm. Continue west along the track past the farm. The hillside to the west of the farm on the lower slopes of Beinn Chuirn is now the site of a recently developed gold mine, and the scarring of the ground is particularly ugly. Go to the end of the track at the Allt an Rund and cross this stream. Follow a path uphill on the north side of the stream flowing down from Coire Gaothaich to reach more level ground in the foot of the corrie. From there the climbers' route in winter or spring to the *Central Gully* and other climbs lies straight ahead up the corrie, but the hillwalkers' routes go up either of the corrie's bounding ridges.

To climb the north-east ridge, bear west up steep grassy slopes, following a faint path, to reach the ridge at a level shoulder and continue up it, following a path. In summer the route is well-defined and not difficult, though quite steep near the top. In winter it may be a serious enough climb to call for ice-axe and crampons, and the ascent by this route calls for winter climbing skill. The climb ends at the North-west Top.

The ridge which bounds Coire Gaothaich on its south side gives a route of similar character ending right at the summit.

The approach from Glen Lochy starts at a car park off the A85 road near the foot of the Eas Daimh. The first problem may be to cross the River Lochy if it is in spate. The easiest place is near the outflow of the Eas Daimh, but if this is not possible there is a footbridge about a kilometre downstream. Follow a path on the north side of the Eas Daimh, crossing to the south side after a few hundred metres and then bearing south through the forest beside the main stream flowing down from Fionn Choirein. At the upper edge of the forest cross the fence by a stile to reach the open corrie.

From there two routes are possible; either bear east up the grassy hillside to reach the north-west ridge high above the Ciochan Beinn Laoigh and follow it to the top, or continue up Fionn Choirein to the bealach at its head and from there climb the broad south-west ridge of the mountain. The last short climb up to the bealach is steep, but there are no difficulties in summer. In winter there may be a steep snow slope.

It is possible to reach Coire Gaothaich and the unnamed north corrie of Ben Lui from Glen Lochy by starting as described above and continuing up the path beside the Eas Daimh to the end of the forest. From there the col on the north side of Ben Lui is less than a kilometre further. Having crossed it one can traverse upwards below the Ciochan Beinn Laoigh to reach the relatively unfrequented north corrie, or the north-east ridge at its rocky lower end called Stob Garbh. By continuing further south-east, Coire Gaothaich is reached. This is a much shorter approach to the corrie than from either Dailrigh or Tyndrum.

The headwall of Coire Gaothaich is often liable to avalanche in springtime, particularly if there is still a lot of melting snow with big cornices overhanging the upper edge of the snowfield. It is not unknown for collapsing cornices to trigger huge avalanches which send masses of snow and ice crashing down to the foot of the corrie.

Ben Lui from the road to Cononish

Beinn a'Chleibh *(hill of the creel or chest)* (916m)
This hill is the small western neighbour of Ben Lui. Its north-east face above Fionn
Choirein is very steep and rocky, and to the west a long broad ridge drops towards
the forest in Glen Lochy. The south side of the hill is quite featureless above the
headwaters of the River Fyne.

The best and shortest ascent of Beinn a'Chleibh is from the car park in Glen Lochy
as described above for the ascent of Ben Lui. The route follows the Ben Lui route to
the bealach at the head of Fionn Choirein, and at that point turns west-south-west
up the broad ridge to the summit. It is very easy to combine the ascent of both
mountains by this route.

The north-west side of Beinn a'Chleibh is best avoided as it is steep and the lower
slopes are densely forested above the railway line in Glen Lochy. Any approach from
the west involves a long walk through the forest from Strath Orchy to Succoth Lodge
and some distance further along the line of the electricity transmission pylons to
reach the open hillside south-west of the summit.

The summit of Ben Lui

Ben Oss *(loch-outlet hill)* (1029m)
Beinn Dubhchraig *(black-rock hill)* (978m)

These two hills, lying between the head of Loch Lomond and Strath Fillan, are usually climbed together, and can be conveniently described together. They form the extension eastwards of the Ben Lui range, to which Ben Oss is connected by a ridge which drops to about 690m at the head of Coire Laoigh.

The two mountains are well seen from several points along Loch Lomond, and although they are not usually climbed from the south, the view from that direction gives a good impression of their character. Ben Oss has a rounded whale-back ridge running from south-west to north-east, and from the north end of Loch Lomond near Ardlui it appears as rather a pointed peak. To its east Beinn Dubhchraig has a steep south face of broken crags below the more level summit ridge.

The usual approach to these two mountains is from Strath Fillan to their north-east. On that side Ben Oss has a rather steep flank above Coire Buidhe and the headwaters of the River Cononish. The north-east side of Beinn Dubhchraig is a wide open corrie, the Coire Dubhchraig, which drops from the summit in grassy slopes forming a great bowl above the recent forestry plantations at the foot of the corrie. Below these plantations is a fine remnant of the Old Caledonian Forest, the Coille Coire Chuilc, at the confluence of the River Cononish and the Allt Gleann Auchreoch.

The normal route for the traverse of these two mountains starts at Dailrigh in Strath Fillan. Cross the River Fillan and follow a track west parallel to the railway, which is crossed by a bridge. Just beyond this bridge leave the track and go west for a hundred metres to cross the Allt Gleann Auchreoch by a footbridge.

Continue south-west through the Coille Coire Chuilc by a footpath under the fine old pine trees, and cross two stiles to reach the recently forested area of the Coire Dubhchraig. Continue south-west by a path between the trees and the Allt Coire Dubhchraig and beyond the upper forest fence climb up the corrie by steepening grassy slopes to reach the summit of Beinn Dubhchraig.

Two variations of this route may be noted. One is to avoid the plantings in Coire Dubhchraig by going west from the Coille Coire Chuilc along the top of Creag Bhocan and up the north ridge of Beinn Dubhchraig; this route gives good views of Ben Lui. The other is to continue up the track in Gleann Auchreoch to a point in the forest high on the north-east ridge of Beinn Dubhchraig and climb this ridge; this route may become impracticable as the trees grow.

From Beinn Dubhchraig traverse north-west along the broad summit ridge, past a little lochan and down a steeper drop to the col. Continue west over a knoll (which may be bypassed easily by a rising traverse on its south side) and finally climb south-west up the rounded ridge of Ben Oss to its summit.

The shortest return from Ben Oss to Dailrigh is back along the ridge to the little lochan on Beinn Dubhchraig, and from there down Coire Dubhchraig by the uphill

Beinn Chuirn from the pinewood of Coille Coire Chuilc

route. Any attempt to descend directly from Ben Oss towards Cononish down Coire Buidhe should only be undertaken with care, for the ground is steep and rocky.

The traverse from Ben Oss to Ben Lui makes possible a fine long day, which can be extended to Beinn a'Chleibh with a final descent to Glen Lochy. The return to Dailrigh may be made by the late afternoon bus from Oban. The south-west ridge of Ben Oss is broad and rocky in places, and one must gradually bear round west to reach the 690m col between Ben Oss and Ben Lui. In thick weather careful route-finding is needed as the ridge is rather featureless and any deviation southwards from it could lead one a long way astray. From the wide grassy col the ascent of the south ridge of Ben Lui is very straightforward.

The route to Ben Oss and Beinn Dubhchraig from Glen Falloch is not as popular as the one described above, but is perfectly feasible. The ascent goes up the Fionn Ghleann by discontinuous paths and sheep tracks for several kilometres to Loch Oss, from where the ascent of either hill can be made.

Beinn Chuirn *(cairn hill)* (880m)
This hill is the northern outlier of the Ben Lui group, lying between Cononish and Glen Lochy. Its long west ridge ends at Beinn Dubh, a craggy hill directly above Glen Lochy. When seen from the east, the shape of Beinn Chuirn is rather similar to Ben Lui, on a much smaller scale, as there is a steep eastern corrie with snow clinging to its high gullies in winter and spring.

The lower slopes of Beinn Chuirn above Cononish are the site of a recently developed gold mine which has created a very ugly scar on the hillside. It remains to be seen whether the mine will prosper or, like so many other similar ventures, close down prematurely leaving rusting machinery and piles of debris.

Beinn Chuirn may be easily climbed from Cononish, reached from Dailrigh or Tyndrum as described for Ben Lui on page 117. Continue west beyond the farm along the track for half a kilometre and then climb west up the hillside to the south of the deep rocky ravine of Eas Anie. Higher up, bear north-west across open slopes to reach the summit ridge at the south end of Coire na Saobhaidhe. Pass the top of a steep gully and 200 metres further reach the summit. The remains of an old fence cross the summit a short distance north of the cairn.

A much shorter route starts in Glen Lochy half a kilometre down the glen from Arrivain. Cross the river and climb uphill through scattered trees on the east side of the Allt Garbh Choirean for several hundred metres, then climb east up a steep ridge past a tiny lochan to reach the summit of Beinn Chuirn from the north-west.

PATHS AND WALKS

Glen Fyne to Glen Falloch (Inverarnan). Walk up Glen Fyne to the little power station and continue up the road on the south side of the Allt na Lairige to the reservoir. Go along the south side of the reservoir and across wet pathless ground towards the Lairig Arnan. On the east side of this pass a road is reached on the north side of the Allt Arnan. Either follow this road down to Glen Falloch farm or descend directly down the north side of the Allt Arnan to Inverarnan. (16 kilometres).

Strath Orchy to Glen Falloch (Inverarnan). This is the line of an important old drove road from Dalmally to Inverarnan and the cattle markets of central Scotland. Inverarnan was a resting place for the drovers.

Leave the A85 road in Strath Orchy just west of the B8074 road up Glen Orchy. Follow the private road through the forest to Succoth Lodge and continue for a further one and a half kilometres along the track through the forest to the clearing for the electricity transmission line. Follow this clearing east-south-east to reach open ground. Continue for four kilometres across featureless country along the line of pylons or just to their south to reach the end of a road on the south side of the Allt nan Caorainn and follow this road for several kilometres on the south side of Gleann nan Caorann to Glen Falloch farm, one kilometre north of Inverarnan. (20 kilometres).

Glen Fyne to Glen Shira. It is possible to make a long circular walk starting and finishing on the A83 road beside Loch Fyne. Walk up Glen Fyne past Inverchorachan; the path ends about three kilometres beyond. Follow the headwaters of the River Fyne westwards past Meall Reamhar to reach the end of a hydro-electric road which comes up from the Lochan Shira Reservoir. Follow this road west over a pass to reach the reservoir, cross the dam and continue right down Glen Shira to the road beside Loch Fyne. (35 kilometres).

Climbing the Central Gully of Ben Lui

Glen Fyne to Strath Orchy. Follow the route described above up Glen Fyne to the end of the path and continue north-east up the Allt Chaluim across very featureless terrain to the Allt a'Mhinn. From there go north-west between Meall nan Tighearn and Beinn a'Chleibh to reach Succoth Lodge and Strath Orchy by the old drove road from Dalmally. (20 kilometres).

The district between Oban and Loch Awe, known as Lorne, is not mountainous. Rather it is an extensive tract of rough undulating moorland with many little hills and lochans and some areas of forestry, particularly in the north in Glen Lonan. There are many narrow roads, tracks and paths through this area which give cross-country walks. Various possibilities exist between Kilmore and Kilninver in the west and Kilchrennan and Barnaline Lodge (near Dalavich) on the north-west side of Loch Awe.

Further south in the district of Argyll between Loch Fyne and the south-west end of Loch Awe there is a similar tract of country, much afforested and having a number of tracks and paths across it. Cross-country routes along them can be made from Loch Fyne, starting two kilometres north of Furnace, and aiming for Ford and Durran on the side of Loch Awe, and to Kilmichael. Some of the paths shown on pre-metric Ordnance Survey maps may have disappeared as a result of afforestation.

CLIMBING

The most popular climbs in the area of this chapter are on Ben Lui. In the early years of Scottish mountaineering the existence of two stations at Tyndrum, one on the Edinburgh to Oban line and the other on the Glasgow to Fort William line, made the mountains round Tyndrum among the most accessible in the Highlands. Early climbers were attracted to the great north-east corrie of Ben Lui, the Coire Gaothaich, and for the last hundred years the winter climbs in this corrie have been among the most popular in Scotland. By modern standards these climbs are regarded as easy, but their character and situation high on this fine mountain more than compensate for any lack of technical difficulty.

Central Gully (Grade I) is the obvious gully which goes up the headwall of the corrie, ending a few metres north of the summit. It is a long climb, easy-angled for most of its length, but steepening below the cornice, which may be very large and overhanging in snowy winters. At the end of such winters the spring thaw may produce an avalanche hazard as the cornice melts and collapses down the gully.

There are other climbs of similar character and difficulty to the left and right of Central Gully, but they are little more than variations of the classic route. The one exception is the *South Rib* (Grade II), a curving ridge on the left of Central Gully which ends high up on the south-bounding ridge of Coire Gaothaich. The ascent of the lowest part of the rib may be difficult, but can be avoided by climbing round to the left and traversing back onto the crest higher up. The upper part of the Rib is a pleasant scramble up the crest.

On Beinn Chuirn the best climb, and technically the best winter climb in the whole Ben Lui group, is the Eas Anie, the waterfall not far above Cononish farm and now immediately above the gold mine workings. Prolonged hard frost is sufficient to convert the waterfall into a fine cascade of ice which gives an excellent climb (Grade

III/IV). High up in Coire na Saobhaidhe, the east-facing corrie of Beinn Chuirn, there are some steep but relatively short gullies, one of which has been described as similar to the Central Gully of Ben Lui, but much shorter.

The western spur of Beinn Chuirn is Beinn Dubh, c.700m. The north-west face of this hill overlooking Glen Lochy is steep and rocky, and has three gullies. All have been climbed in summer and winter, but they are probably more suited as winter climbs. The central gully, *Sickle Gully*, is the longest and hardest (Very Difficult; Grade III).

Far to the south-west of the high mountains described in this chapter are two low-lying crags of considerable rock-climbing interest. Full details of routes on both these crags are contained in the Scottish Mountaineering Club's *Climbers Guide to Arran, Arrochar and the Southern Highlands* by K.V.Crocket and A.Walker.

Dun Leacainn (grid reference 034 014) is a steep crag almost 100m high, one and a half kilometres north-east of Furnace on the west side of Loch Fyne. The approach is through conifer plantations which extend right up to the foot of the crag. Seven routes have been recorded from Hard Severe to E1 standard.

Creag nam Fitheach (grid reference 782 848) is in Knapdale not far from the road from Bellanoch on the Crinan Canal to Castle Sween. The approach is from Kilmichael of Inverlussa up the Lussa Water, and the crag is on the south side of Kilmichael Hill. There are about twenty routes of all grades from Very Difficult up to E5, the longest being about 30m and the best being the hard ones.

SKI MOUNTAINEERING

The most popular mountains for skiing in this area are Ben Oss and Beinn Dubhchraig. The north-east corrie of Beinn Dubhchraig holds snow well and gives a very easy ascent and descent of this hill, although the growth of the forest in the lower part of the corrie will in years to come adversely affect the skiing there. The traverse from Beinn Dubhchraig to Ben Oss is easy, with the exception of the steep descent to the col between the two hills which needs a good snow cover to be readily skiable, otherwise it is rather rocky. The best ascent from the col towards Ben Oss is on the south-east side of the first knoll to reach the ridge beyond it.

The continuation of the traverse to Ben Lui involves no difficulty in good conditions, but this is a long expedition for short winter days. The descent from Ben Lui is best made down the south-west ridge and the Fionn Choirein to reach Glen Lochy.

It is also possible to approach Ben Oss and Beinn Dubhchraig from Glen Falloch up the Fionn Ghleann and Sput Ban to Loch Oss, from where the col between the two mountains is easily reached. This route can be recommended if there is good snow cover well down towards Glen Falloch. In midwinter it gets more sunshine on a good day than does Coire Dubhchraig.

CHAPTER 9

The Crianlarich and Balquhidder Hills

Beinn Chabhair	933m	368 180
An Caisteal	995m	379 193
Beinn a'Chroin	940m	394 186
Beinn Tulaichean	946m	416 196
Cruach Ardrain	1046m	409 212
Ben More	1174m	433 244
Stob Binnein	1165m	435 227
Meall an t-Seallaidh	852m	542 234
Creag Mac Ranaich	809m	546 256

This very fine group of mountains is in the heart of the Southern Highlands, and contains some of their best-known and most frequently climbed peaks. The area is well defined geographically by Loch Voil, Loch Doine and the River Larig on the south, Glen Ogle on the east, Glen Dochart on the north and Glen Falloch on the west. It is about 28 kilometres from east to west and 11 kilometres from south to north.

These mountains are for the most part formed of massive grits and crumpled mica-schists belonging to the Highland Metamorphic Series, and there are also many small intrusive dykes of basalt and other basic igneous rocks. The whole group has been weathered evenly to give grass-covered hills with many small outcrops of rock, but no large crags, and consequently the area is not of much interest to the rock-climber. However, there is much excellent hillwalking and the position of these mountains, remote from the sea, ensures that the highest of them carry snow until late in springtime.

The mountains are separated into several groups by glens which run from south to north between them. At the centre are the grand twin peaks of Ben More and Stob Binnein, which are the highest in the area described in this chapter and are exceeded in height in the Southern Highlands only by Ben Lawers. South-east and east of Stob Binnein, and linked to it by a high ridge, are the subsidiary tops of Stob Coire an Lochain, Meall na Dige and Stob Creagach. To the east of these hills, between the

ACCESS
From the east by the A84 and A85 roads from Stirling to Callander, Lochearnhead and
Crianlarich. From the west by the A82 road up Loch Lomond to Crianlarich. The public
road which goes west from the A84 at Kingshouse Hotel through Balquhidder and along
Loch Voil ends about one kilometre beyond the west end of Loch Doine.

TRANSPORT
Bus: Stirling to Callander, Strathyre, Kingshouse Hotel and Lochearnhead; Mondays to
Fridays.
Glasgow to Ardlui and Crianlarich; daily.
  Postbus: Callander to Strathyre, Kingshouse Hotel, Lochearnhead and Crianlarich;
Saturdays.
Train: Glasgow to Ardlui and Crianlarich; daily

ACCOMMODATION
Hotels at Callander, Strathyre, Lochearnhead, Killin, Luib (Glen Dochart), Crianlarich,
Inverarnan and Ardlui.
Youth hostels at Crianlarich and Killin.
Camp and caravan sites at Strathyre, Luib and Killin.
Climbers hut at Crianlarich, for details see Introduction.

MAPS
Ordnance Survey 1:50,000, Sheets 50,51,56 and 57.
Bartholomew 1:100,000, Sheet 48.

Monachyle and Kirkton glens, there is a lower and rather featureless tract of hill
country, and to the north-east of the Kirkton Glen the highest hills are Meall an
t-Seallaidh and Creag MacRanaich. A fine feature of this corner of the hills is the
imposing crag called Leum am Eireannaich *(the Irishmman's leap)* and the lonely
Lochan an Eireannaich near its foot. The southern slopes of the hills above Loch Voil
and Loch Doine are called the Braes of Balquhidder.

To the west of Ben More and Stob Binnein is the deep glen of the Benmore and
Inverlochlarig burns which provides the most feasible south to north route through
the hills and is an old right of way. Next, going westwards, are the three peaks of
Cruach Ardrain, Stob Garbh and Beinn Tulaichean which form a Y-shaped ridge to
the south of Crianlarich, and to their south-west, across the headwaters of the River
Falloch are An Caisteal, Beinn a'Chroin and Beinn Chabhair in a triangular group,
the last-named peak overlooking Glen Falloch at the head of Loch Lomond.

Ben More and Stob Binnein are the dominant mountains in this group, and they
are among the finest in the Southern Highlands. They are prominent in the views
from many places as far apart as Glasgow and Ben Nevis, and their very symmetrical
twin peaks of almost equal height are easily recognised from afar. Probably the best
view of them is from the north-west, looking down Strath Fillan; the combination
of foreground river winding through fields and trees with the three high mountains
Ben More, Stob Binnein and Cruach Ardrain at the end of the strath make this one
of the finest of Highland landscapes.

Loch Voil on the southern edge of the area described in this chapter is relatively quiet and secluded for the narrow public road along its north side leads only to its head; there is no through route for cars. The view along the whole length of this loch from the hillside above Balquhidder to the distant Stob a'Choin is particularly fine. Loch Doine, which is separated from Loch Voil by only a few hundred metres of sluggish river, is rather more bleak. Beyond it the River Larig, which has its source on the slopes of Beinn Chabhair, winds down a treeless and rather barren glen in which stands the farm of Inverlochlarig on the site of the house where Rob Roy lived in his later settled years.

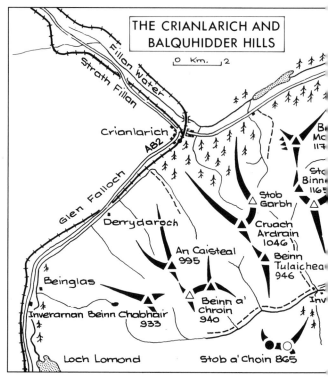

On the other side of Beinn Chabhair is Glen Falloch which is well wooded in its lower reaches near Loch Lomond where the River Falloch plunges down a series of falls and cascades. Higher up, the glen is rather treeless and barren near its head where only a few remnants of the Old Caledonian Forest survive on the lower slopes of An Caisteal, in marked contrast to the densely planted rows of conifers along the foot of Cruach Ardrain.

THE HILLS

The three hills at the west end of the area described in this chapter, Beinn Chabhair, An Caisteal and Beinn a'Chroin, are most easily accessible from Glen Falloch. However, they can equally well be climbed from the end of the public road which goes west from Balquhidder to a point beyond Loch Doine, especially if one has a bicycle to cycle the few kilometres along the right of way past Inverlochlarig to the end of the track up the River Larig.

Beinn Chabhair *(hill of the hawk)* (933m)
Despite its nearness to the road at the head of Loch Lomond, Beinn Chabhair is rather a retiring mountain when viewed from there, its summit and upper slopes being completely hidden above and beyond the steep lower ground. From further up Glen Falloch there is a good view of its north-west ridge, but the summit is just out of

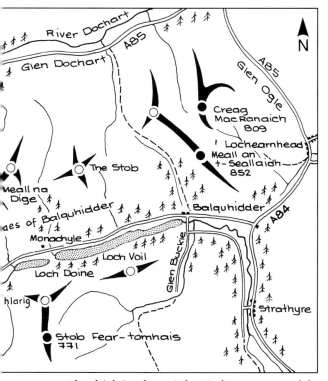

sight. Nevertheless, it is from Beinglas farm, near Inverarnan at the foot of Glen Falloch, that the ascent is usually made.

After crossing the bridge over the River Falloch, follow the West Highland Way signs round, not through, the farm-yard and reach the start of a steep path behind the farm. It ascends through open wood-land of birch and hawthorn, and traverses upward towards the falls of the Ben Glas Burn, which are a fine sight when the burn is in spate. Above the falls more level ground is reached, and two possible routes to Beinn Chab-hair diverge.

The quickest and most direct route continues up the north side of the Ben Glas Burn along a path which in places is lost in boggy ground, but leads quite easily to Lochan Beinn Chabhair. From there the west face of Beinn Chabhair is in full view and one could climb to the summit by almost any route, but the best way is probably to climb north-east up a wide grassy gully to reach the north-west ridge of the hill at a well-defined col. From there follow a path up the ridge; if the crest is adhered to, a small cairn is passed before reaching the top, where the summit cairn is perched on a small crag.

The alternative route is up the long undulating north-west ridge to the north of the Ben Glas Burn. Climb Meall Mor nan Eag and reach Lochan a'Chaisteil, go round the south side of this beautifully situated little loch and traverse upwards along sheep tracks on the south side of Stob Creag an Fhithich to the next col on this 'up-and-down' ridge. Climb over the knoll of Meall nan Tarmachan to reach the col of the direct route and continue up the ridge to the summit. This is a surprisingly strenuous route with its many ups and downs, and in thick weather it is likely to give a few navigational problems.

Beinn Chabhair can also be climbed quite easily by its south-east slopes above the head of the River Larig. The track westwards from the end of the public road near Loch Doine follows a right of way and goes for six kilometres almost to the foot of the mountain, and it is possible to cycle along it.

The Ben Lui group from the summit of Beinn Chabhair

The north-eastern slopes of Beinn Chabhair which link it to An Caisteal are steep and rocky, and care should be taken when descending them, particularly in winter.

An Caisteal *(the castle)* (995m)
Beinn a'Chroin *(hill of harm or danger)* (940m)
These two hills stand side by side at the head of the River Falloch, and can be very easily climbed together. An Caisteal is very prominent in views from Glen Falloch, the summit standing at the junction of the two broad ridges which rise from the glen above Derrydaroch. High up on the more easterly of these ridges is the prominent rocky knoll which may give the hill its name. To the south of its summit a third ridge drops quite steeply to the col between An Caisteal and Beinn a'Chroin. The latter hill has a fairly level summit ridge running from west to east, with the summit at the east end and two lower points near the west end. Beinn a'Chroin can be seen from the head of Glen Falloch, looking up Coire Earb in which rise the headwaters of the River Falloch.

The traverse of these two mountains is best made from Glen Falloch at the point where the River Falloch flows down from Coire Earb and makes a sudden turn to continue down the glen. Follow a track under the railway and over the river, and up its west side towards Coire Earb. To climb An Caisteal first, leave the track in less than a kilometre and climb south up broad grassy slopes which steepen to the top

Cruach Ardrain from Beinn Tulaichean

of Sron Gharbh. The ridge from there is level, then rises again along Twistin Hill towards the prominent rocky knoll. The summit of An Caisteal is a short distance beyond the knoll.

To continue the traverse, descend the south ridge which becomes rocky lower down and leads to a flat col. From there a path zigzags upward, first left, then right to avoid crags on the steep western end of Beinn a'Chroin's summit ridge. Continue along this undulating ridge past two cairned points to reach the summit at the eastern end. The descent goes north down a grassy ridge to reach the junction of streams at the head of Coire Earb. From there continue down the west side of the stream to join the track lower down the corrie, and follow it to Glen Falloch.

Beinn a'Chroin can be easily climbed from the east, starting from the end of the public road beyond Loch Doine and going west by the right of way past Inverloch-larig and the track up the River Larig. Leave this track about half a kilometre beyond the crossing of the Ishag Burn and climb north-west up the grassy hillside, keeping below the rockier crest of the south-east ridge. Beyond a knoll at about 760m the final rise to the summit is steeper with some rocky outcrops to be avoided.

The traverse of the three mountains just described can be done either from the River Larig or from Glen Falloch. In the latter case, Derrydaroch is the best starting and finishing point.

Cruach Ardrain *(stack of the high part)* (1046m)
Beinn Tulaichean *(hill of the hillocks)* (946m)
These two hills form a long north to south ridge between Crianlarich and Inverloch-larig. Cruach Ardrain is near the middle of this ridge and is its dominant feature. To its north two ridges extend towards Crianlarich and enclose Coire Ardrain, whose lower slopes are extensively forested. To the south a broad ridge drops to a col at 810m and rises to Beinn Tulaichean which is more the southern peak of Cruach Ardrain than a separate mountain in its own right.

From the north-west Cruach Ardrain appears as a fine pointed peak, a worthy companion to its two higher neighbours Ben More and Stob Binnein, and in winter and spring snow lies long in its high northern corrie and marks the lines of the Y-Gully. To the north-east of Cruach Ardrain is the lower top of Stob Garbh, a prominent rocky knoll which well lives up to its name - *rough peak*.

Beinn Tulaichean rises steeply to the north-west of Inverlochlarig, mostly grassy slopes round its southern perimeter. High up on the east flank there is an area of crags and huge fallen boulders forming many caves and fissures not far below the summit. The west and south-west flanks of the hill are quite steep and rocky.

The ascent of Cruach Ardrain from the north starts from the head of Glen Falloch about half a kilometre south of Crianlarich where there is a bridge over the West Highland Railway a short distance from the A82 road. After crossing the bridge go along a path through a clearing in the forest, first towards the right then left to reach a broken fence. Turn uphill along a narrow gap in the closely planted trees which leads south-south-east to the treeline half a kilometre north-west of Grey Height (685m). A path leads up the ridge over Grey Height and on to Meall Dhaimh (814m). From there descend to a wide col from which the north-west shoulder of Cruach Ardrain rises. Climb this shoulder, still following a path, to reach a false summit with two small cairns. The true summit is a short distance north-east of these cairns, across a little col, and is marked by a large cairn which stands close to the steep drop at the top of the north-east ridge.

As an alternative to returning by the same route, one can descend the north-east ridge, but care is needed (particularly in winter) for the slope directly below the cairn is steep and rocky for some distance. At its foot a wide col is reached with some tiny lochans in it, and the ridge rises northwards to Stob Garbh (960m). There are many little rocky knolls, and the place can be very confusing in misty weather.

From Stob Garbh go down the ridge north-north-west to the col below Stob Coire Bhuidhe and turn west to descend steep grassy slopes into the head of Coire Ardrain. Bear north-west across the corrie and continue through the forest along a firebreak which joins the route of ascent.

Beinn Tulaichean is most easily climbed from Inverlochlarig, and the continuation along the ridge to Cruach Ardrain is easy. From the farm climb the long grassy slopes north-westwards. The route can be made more interesting by bearing up

Ben More and Stob Binnein from Strath Fillan

through the area of fallen boulders and small crags; otherwise keep a little further south to reach the ridge at a fairly level point half a kilometre south of the summit.

The continuation northwards to Cruach Ardrain across the 810m col is perfectly straightforward, although in thick weather some careful route-finding may be needed as the connecting ridge leads slightly to the west of Cruach Ardrain's summit, not directly to it. The return to Inverlochlarig from Cruach Ardrain can be shortened by descending east from the col to reach a track on the west side of the Inverlochlarig Burn.

Ben More *(big hill)* (1174m)
Stob Binnein *(either from the Gaelic binnein meaning peak or from innean meaning anvil)* (1165m)
These are the two highest peaks south of Strath Tay, and they are among the best known of all Scotland's mountains. From most viewpoints they appear as almost identical twin summits. However, Stob Binnein has a rather more elegant outline with well-defined ridges sweeping up from north and south to the little plateau of its summit, while Ben More appears bulkier because of the very long drop of its northern slopes for over 1000m to Glen Dochart.

Because of their height and appearance, Ben More and Stob Binnein are easily recognised from many viewpoints far and near, and the view from their summits

Stob Binnein from Ben More

on a clear day embraces half of Scotland from the Cairngorms to Galloway, and from Edinburgh to the Western Isles.

The appearance of these two mountains does not at first sight suggest that they conceal any unexpected mountain dangers, but in winter they must both be treated with great respect. Ben More has on its north-west side a high hanging corrie (not clearly shown on the 1:50,000 Ordnance Survey map) whose headwall is surprisingly steep. In winter this corrie presents hazards to the unwary, hazards of hard steep snow and ice and of avalanche-prone slopes, which have been the cause of several fatal accidents on the mountain.

The usual route of ascent to Ben More starts at Benmore farm, three kilometres east of Crianlarich, and goes up the north-west shoulder of the mountain. It is a long and unrelenting climb. A stile at the roadside a short distance east of the farm gives access to a bulldozed track which zigzags up the lower hillside before going south towards the Benmore Glen. Just above the zigzags leave this track and climb directly up the grassy hillside. There is no well-defined route, but higher up a drystone dyke is a useful guide; it is on the north side of the hanging corrie mentioned in the preceding paragraph. A few small crags are passed and above them the angle eases and the summit is reached, where the cairn stands on a big crag.

Stob Binnein and Ben More from the south

An alternative route to Ben More from Glen Dochart, longer but more varied, starts four kilometres east of Benmore farm at the foot of the Allt Coire Chaorach. Follow a track on the east side of this stream up into the forest, and in about one kilometre cross the stream. On the west bank a path leads up through firebreaks in the forest to reach the open hillside at grid reference 458 254. From there bear west up rough ground to reach the north-east ridge of Ben More at about 750m. Continue up the ridge; at one or two points it becomes narrow and rocky, but not at all difficult, and it gives a pleasant ascent.

The third ridge of Ben More, the south ridge, drops 310m to the Bealach-eadar-dha Beinn *(pass between two hills)*, a broad flat col at the foot of the north ridge of Stob Binnein. The traverse of the two mountains from Benmore farm can best be done by descending the south ridge of Ben More, ascending and descending the north ridge of Stob Binnein and finally dropping down westwards from the Bealach-eadar-dha Beinn to reach the end of the bulldozed track on the east side of the Benmore Burn.

The ascent of Stob Binnein by itself (or the traverse of the two mountains from south to north) is best made from the car park at the end of the public road beyond Loch Doine. Climb due north up steep grassy slopes, with a few small crags high up, to reach the more level ridge at Stob Invercarnaig. Continue along the very easy grassy ridge, first to Stob Coire an Lochain (1066m) and then to Stob Binnein up its south ridge.

Meall na Dige (966m) is another top of Stob Binnein which is just over one kilometre north-east of Stob Coire an Lochain, and linked to it by a ridge which drops to 890m at the head of Glen Carnaig. It can easily be traversed going to or from Stob Binnein. From Monachylemore two routes are possible to Meall na Dige; one up the forest road in the Monachyle Glen to the foot of the Allt Coire Cheathaich and up this burn, the other up the steep slopes of Meall Monachyle and along the grassy ridge of Am Mam.

To the east of the Monachyle Glen the hills are lower and much less impressive than those to the west. The two highest, Meall an t-Seallaidh and Creag Mac Ranaich, lie to the north of Balquhidder and east of the Kirkton Glen. One of the most prominent features of this corner of the Braes of Balquhidder is the steep, almost overhanging crag called Leum an Eireannaich *(the Irishman's leap)* at the head of the Kirkton Glen. It is well seen from the south-east.

Meall an t-Seallaidh *(hill of the sight)* (852m)
This is a massive grassy hill, well seen from the south as one approaches from Strathyre; its southern slopes above the River Balvag look discouragingly steep and there is a good deal of afforestation on them. The hill is most easily climbed from Balquhidder; although the direct ascent up its southern slopes from the road east of the village is forbiddingly steep, at least this route has the merit of directness. Above the initial climb the ridge of the hill is reached and leads over a knoll to the summit which is on the edge of a little line of cliffs above Glen Kendrum.

Rob Roy's Putting Stone at the head of the Kirkton Glen

A less direct, but probably pleasanter route is up the Kirkton Glen, starting just behind Balquhidder Church and following a forest road to the upper limit of the trees in the glen. A short distance further along the path one passes a huge boulder, appropriately called Rob Roy's Putting Stone. Above it is the steep crag of Leum an Eireannaich, and a short distance further north-west, and rather hidden in the hollow of the pass, is the beautiful secluded Lochan an Eireannaich. Leave the path before the pass and climb east to reach a broad ridge between Meall an Fhiodhain and the 817m knoll, and continue south-east over this top and the next one called Cam Chreag to Meall an t-Seallaidh.

Creag Mac Ranaich *(MacRanaich's crag)* (809m)
This is a fine craggy hill, as the name suggests, but the crags which are a feature of its south-east face are broken and discontinuous, although there are a few walls and buttresses that are impressively steep. Below them are innumerable boulders, many of considerable size, that have fallen from the higher crags.

The shortest approach to the hill is from a point on the A85 road just south of Lochan Lairig Cheile at the top of Glen Ogle. Cross the old railway track by a footbridge and climb beside the forest to its upper edge, then continue south-west to Creag Mac Ranaich. A tall, finely built cairn is passed just before reaching the summit which has two tops, the northern one being slightly the higher of the two.

The approach from Lochearnhead up Glen Kendrum is rather longer, but more interesting. Walk up the narrow road past the Episcopal church and reach the track up the east side of the glen. Follow this track to its end and continue westwards up the rough heathery corrie along the traces of vehicle tracks which lead to the bealach south-west of Creag Mac Ranaich. From there climb the steep final slopes between small rock outcrops, following sheep paths in places.

This route can also be used as an approach to Meall an t-Seallaidh and makes possible the ascent of both hills in a single day. From the bealach climb a short steep slope south-west to the ridge just north of Cam Chreag and go one kilometre south to Meall an t-Seallaidh. It is quite possible to descend from this hill east into Glen Kendrum once the line of crags immediately below the summit have been negotiated. In winter the edge of these crags is likely to be corniced.

The northern approach to these two hills from Glen Dochart is possible, either up Gleann Dubh or the Ledcharrie Burn. There are paths up both glens, but the routes are less interesting than those from the south described above.

PATHS AND WALKS

Inverarnan to Inverlochlarig. This is an old right of way. From Beinglas farm just north of Inverarnan follow the route to Lochan Beinn Chabhair described for the ascent of Beinn Chabhair. Go south-east from the loch, climbing a little to cross the pass between Beinn Chabhair and Parlan Hill, and continue east down the glen of the River Larig. In three kilometres from the pass a track is reached which leads to Inverlochlarig. The car park at the end of the public road is half a kilometre further. (15 kilometres).

Inverlochlarig to Benmore farm (Glen Dochart). This route is a right of way. From Inverlochlarig go north along the track on the west side of the Inverlochlarig Burn. Continue beyond the end of the track over the pass on the west side of Stob Binnein and descend the east side of the Benmore Burn to reach the track going down to Glen Dochart at Benmore farm. (10 kilometres).

Balquhidder to Ledcharrie (Glen Dochart). From Balquhidder Church go north by a road through the forest in Kirkton Glen and then by a path over the pass beside Lochan an Eireannaich to descend to Glen Dochart along the east side of the Ledcharrie Burn. This route follows a right of way. (9 kilometres).

SKI MOUNTAINEERING

Stob Binnein gives the best ski ascent in these hills, and the continuation from there to Ben More makes a fine, but not easy traverse. The easiest approach is from the south up the west side of Glen Carnaig. After going up the glen for about one and a half kilometres, make a rising traverse north-west to reach the south ridge of Stob Binnein one kilometre south of Stob Coire an Lochain. The ridge gives an easy ascent if there is adequate snow cover. The continuation of the traverse north to Ben

Remnant of the Old Caledonian Forest at the head of Glen Falloch

The approach to Stob Binnein along the south ridge

Ski run down the north-west face of Stob Binnein

More involves steep skiing down the west side of the north ridge of Stob Binnein and should only be attempted in good conditions.

The return from Ben More to Glen Carnaig can be most easily done by skiing back down to the Bealach-eadar-dha Beinn, descending east from there for a short distance and traversing round the foot of the east side of Stob Binnein to reach the col at the head of Glen Carnaig. This glen gives a long easy downhill run. The descent of the north-east ridge of Ben More is a good run, calling for care at the rocky sections of the ridge and good route finding through the forest at its foot. Go down by the ascent route described on page 136.

Beinn Tulaichean is an easy, though continuously steep ascent from Inverloch-larig. Bear west-north-west up the south side of the hill, keeping below the crags, to reach the south ridge and finish the ascent up it. The traverse to Cruach Ardrain along the broad connecting ridge is easy. On the return it is probably best to ski east from the col between the two hills down fairly easy slopes to reach the bulldozed road on the west side of the Inverlochlarig Burn.

CLIMBING

The best known winter climb in these mountains is the *Y-Gully* on the north face of Cruach Ardrain at the head of Coire Ardrain. It is fairly easy-angled and does not normally have a cornice, so by modern standards it is regarded as very easy. (Grade I).

One kilometre south-south-west of Cruach Ardrain, at the head of the Ishag Glen, is the rocky spur of Stob Glas (833m). It is reached from Inverlochlarig along the track beside the River Larig and up the Ishag Burn. In summer the rock is not steep enough to offer any worthwhile climbing, but in winter the most obvious gully, *Hollow Gully,* has given a Grade II climb. In view of the southern exposure and low altitude of this crag, it is not likely that good conditions for winter climbing are common.

Leum an Eireannaich is a steep and impressive crag, reaching a height of 45m at its highest. There are seven routes recorded on the crag from Very Difficult to Very Severe. Rob Roy's Putting Stone below the crag was first climbed as long ago as 1899. There is a good Severe crack on its west face. A detailed description of these climbs will appear in the Scottish Mountaineering Club's *Climbers Guide to Central and Southern Scotland;* new edition to be published in 1992.

CHAPTER 10

The Loch Earn Group

Ben Vorlich	985m	629 189
Stuc a'Chroin	975m	617 175
Beinn Each	813m	602 158
Meall na Fearna	809m	651 186
Uamh Bheag	665m	691 119
Am Bioran	613m	694 221
Ben Halton	621m	720 203

ACCESS
The A84 road from Callander to Lochearnhead and the minor road on the south side of Loch Earn give access to most of the hills in this area. In addition there is a public road up Glen Artney as far as Glenartney Church, two and a half kilometres below Glenartney Lodge, and there is a narrow road from Callander, signposted to the Bracklinn Falls, which is public as far as a parking place just before Braeleny farm.

TRANSPORT
Bus: Stirling to Callander, Lochearnhead and Killin; Mondays to Fridays.
Stirling to Callander, connects with postbus from Callander to Killin; Saturdays.
Postbus: Callander to Strathyre, Kingshouse Hotel and Lochearnhead; Saturdays.

ACCOMMODATION
Hotels at Callander, Strathyre, Lochearnhead, St Fillans and Comrie.
Camp and caravan site at Strathyre. Caravan sites at St Fillans and Comrie.

MAPS
Ordnance Survey 1:50,000, Sheets 51 and 57.
Bartholomew 1:100,000, Sheet 48.

The area covered by this chapter is enclosed by the ring of roads through Dunblane, Comrie, Lochearnhead, Callander and back to Dunblane. More than half of this area, namely that part to the south of the line from Callander to Comrie, is high moorland of little interest to climbers and walkers, and nearly all the climbing interest is concentrated in the north-west corner of the area. There Ben Vorlich and Stuc a'Chroin are the two highest and most prominent mountains. To their east the country between Glen Artney and Loch Earn, the Forest of Glenartney, is rugged with some afforestation and woodland on the north side, but it is not an area of particular interest for climbers or walkers.

Ben Vorlich and Stuc a'Chroin from Meall an t-Seallaidh

Ben Vorlich and Stuc a'Chroin are two of Scotland's best known and most popular mountains. They are prominently seen from many viewpoints in Central Scotland. From Stirling and other points to their south-east the two mountains, particularly Ben Vorlich, appear as well-defined peaks, but from the south-west (for example from the Queen's View on the Glasgow to Drymen road) they appear more like two long whaleback ridges. They have always been popular by virtue of their accessibility, and in the days when trains and not private cars were the standard form of transport, the traverse of the two peaks between Callander and Lochearnhead stations was one of the few high mountain expeditions that could be done in a day from Edinburgh.

THE HILLS

Ben Vorlich (*most probably hill of the bay*) (985m)
Stuc a'Chroin (*peak of harm or danger, but possibly peak of the sheepfold from the Gaelic chroan*) (975m)
Although these two mountains are quite separate, the bealach between them being about 700m, they can conveniently be described together as they share the same approaches and are often traversed together.

The main ridge of Ben Vorlich runs from south-east to north-west, the actual summit being a level ridge about a hundred metres long, with the Ordnance Survey

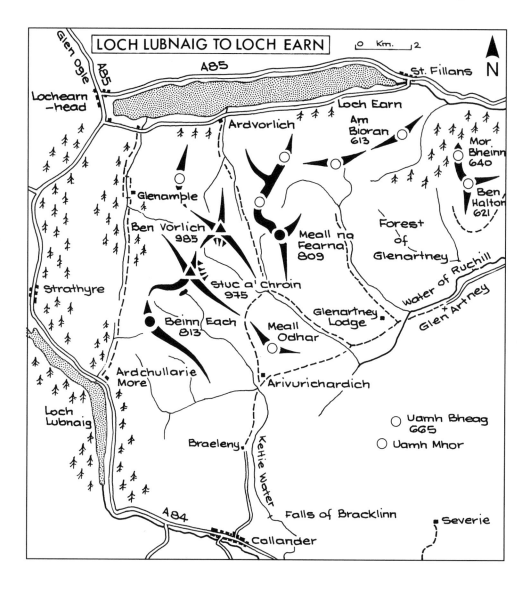

trig point at its north-west end, and a cairn (983m) at the other end. A short distance down the north-west ridge from the summit, two more ridges branch off, one to the north and the other to the south-west, so that the plan of the mountain is rather X-shaped. The south-west ridge drops to the Bealach an Dubh Choirein which separates Ben Vorlich from Stuc a'Chroin. High up on the south face of the mountain, not far below the summit, there are some quite steep rocky ribs.

The main feature of Stuc a'Chroin is its steep north-east face and in particular the rocky buttress that rises above the Bealach an Dubh Choirein to a cairned point about half a kilometre north of the summit. This buttress forms the characteristic profile of the mountain in views from the south or north. From its summit, in addition to the short steep north-east buttress, three ridges radiate: the south-east ridge is long and grassy and drops towards the head of the Keltie Water, the south-west ridge is twisting and hummocky and goes to Beinn Each above Loch Lubnaig, and the north-west ridge drops, steeply in its lower part, to Glen Ample.

Ben Vorlich and Stuc a'Chroin are usually climbed together, and there are five points where the traverse can start or finish, so several combinations of routes are possible. Some may require two cars or use of the bus service between Callander and Lochearnhead.

The approach from Ardvorlich on the south side of Loch Earn is the shortest route to Ben Vorlich. Start at the east gate of Ardvorlich House and take the right of way south up Glen Vorlich. In just over a kilometre leave the right of way, which continues towards Glen Artney and Callander, and follow a path marked by posts up the grassy lower slopes of the north ridge of Ben Vorlich. The path continues up the crest of the ridge (which steepens towards its top and may be icy in winter) and leads directly to the summit trig point.

The traverse to Stuc a'Chroin is simplified in misty weather by the fence which goes from Ben Vorlich down its south-west ridge to the Bealach an Dubh Choirein. (Note that there is another subsidiary ridge leading south which, if followed, leads into the head of Gleann an Dubh Choirein). From the bealach climb south-west up a steepening slope, boulder-strewn in its upper part, to the foot of the north-east buttress. The direct ascent of the buttress gives a very good scramble on sound rock, with some difficulties if one looks for them. On the other hand, all difficulties can be avoided by traversing about 50 metres right (north-west) and climbing a steep path up the broken rocks. At the top of the buttress a cairn is reached and the summit of Stuc a'Chroin is half a kilometre south along a line of fence posts.

To return from Stuc a'Chroin to Ardvorlich, descend to the Bealach an Dubh Choirein and from there traverse horizontally north across a grassy hillside to reach the col at the head of the Coire Buidhe. Go down this corrie on its east side to regain the path in Glen Vorlich.

The other possible starting point on the south side of Loch Earn is at the Falls of Edinample at the foot of Glen Ample. Follow the road up the glen to the bridge where a signpost indicates the right of way along a path on the west side of the stream. Half a kilometre further the right of way crosses the burn by a footbridge. Once on the east side of the burn climb east uphill for a short distance (follow the red arrows on some wooden waymarkers) and reach the start of a track, marked as a path on the OS 1:50,000 map, which climbs diagonally uphill through newly planted trees on the east side of Glen Ample. (The full extent of the new forest on the east side of the glen is not shown on the 1988 edition of this map). The track emerges from the forest and goes for a further kilometre high above the Allt a'Choire Fhuadaraich. Beyond its end continue up the grassy corrie to the Bealach an Dubh Choirein, where the preceding route is joined.

Ben Vorlich from the north-east buttress of Stuc a'Chroin

The return from Stuc a'Chroin to Glen Ample may most easily be made down the north-west ridge for about a kilometre, then north-east down grassy slopes into Coire Fhuadaraich to rejoin the uphill route.

Stuc a'Chroin may be climbed from Ardchullarie More on the east side of Loch Lubnaig. Follow the right of way north towards Glen Ample, and from its highest point climb diagonally north-east to the Bealach nan Cabar, the lowest point of the long undulating ridge between Stuc a'Chroin and Beinn Each. The ascent of the tortuous and knobbly south-west ridge of Stuc a'Chroin from there needs care in misty weather, for it twists and turns and has many humps and hollows, however the remains of an old fence show the way.

The route from Callander is longer than the ones just described, but the going is easy. From Braeleny farm continue along the private road to Arivurichardich and take the path north across the grassy side of Meall Odhar to the col between it and Stuc a'Chroin. (This is the southern half of the right of way from Callander to Ardvorlich). From the col (603m) climb the long grassy south-east ridge of Stuc a'Chroin.

To reach Ben Vorlich by the same approach, continue north-east from the col slightly downhill across the peaty slopes of Gleann an Dubh Choirein to reach the foot of the south-east ridge at the ruins of the Dubh Choirein shieling. This ridge

Ben Vorlich from Meall na Fearna, with Stuc a'Chroin just showing behind

leads directly to the summit, but a diversion from it across the south face shortly before reaching the summit leads to the foot of the south-facing rocks which give a good scramble; certainly worth the extra effort on a warm sunny day.

The Glen Artney approach leads up the track and path along the Allt an Dubh Choirein to the foot of Ben Vorlich's south-east ridge, and one can go south-west across the corrie to reach the south-east ridge of Stuc a'Chroin. The continuation up the last three kilometres of the Gleann an Dubh Choirein to the bealach at its head is hard going through peat hags.

Beinn Each *(horse hill)* (813m)
This hill is a distant outlier of Stuc a'Chroin, being two kilometres away from it along its tortuous south-west ridge, and separated from it by the Bealach an Cabar. The shortest ascent of Beinn Each is from Ardchullarie More by the right of way from there to Glen Ample. One and a half kilometres from the start leave the track and climb steeply up the north side of a burn which flows down in a series of small waterfalls. Follow the north branch of this stream to its source and above it continue by a line of fence posts to the summit.

Meall na Fearna *(alder hill)* (809m)
This is a flat-topped and very peaty hill to the east of Ben Vorlich, separated from it by the pass at the head of Glen Vorlich through which goes the right of way from

Callander to Ardvorlich. Meall na Fearna may be climbed from Ardvorlich by following the right of way almost to the head of Glen Vorlich, and then bearing south-east across undulating high-level peat bog.

An alternative route is from Glen Artney. Follow the track which starts near Glenartney Lodge and goes up Srath a' Ghlinne for about four kilometres and then strike west up steep ground, following a burn towards Pt.742m. Continue west across a peaty col and up grassy slopes to Meall na Fearna.

Uamh Bheag *(little cave)* (665m)

To the south of a line from Callander to Glen Artney the high moorland drops gradually towards the River Teith and the Allan Water. The highest point of this generally featureless area is Uamh Bheag, a flat-topped hill six kilometres north-east of Callander. The nearest approach by road is at Severie near Loch Mahaick. From there a gradual rise across heather leads to Uamh Mhor where there are some caves on the western shoulder at a prominent scarp of rock. Close by is a tiny rift valley known locally as Rob Roy's Cattle Fank. From there it is only a short climb north-east to Uamh Bheag.

Am Bioran (613m)

Two kilometres south of St Fillans at the east end of Loch Earn is the fine little hill called Am Bioran. Its most impressive feature is the north-east ridge which appears from Strath Earn to be a narrow rocky crest dropping from the summit right down to the valley. The ascent of this ridge is a pleasant short climb with the possibility of some scrambling on the many rock outcrops on the way up. The climb may be started from the old church near Wester Dundurn farm. From Am Bioran a broad undulating ridge of heathery hills extends westwards for about five kilometres and gives a good high-level walk which can be completed by descending to Glen Vorlich.

Ben Halton (621m)

This hill and its slightly higher neighbour Mor Bheinn (640m) lie a few kilometres south-east of St Fillans, between the River Earn and Glen Artney. Their north side overlooking the River Earn is forested and craggy. Ben Halton can best be climbed from Glen Artney, starting at Mailerbeg, crossing the Water of Ruchill and climbing north to reach a road which contours round the south side of the hill at about 300m. Go north along this road to a disused quarry and reach the summit of Ben Halton from there.

PATHS AND WALKS

Ardchullarie More to Edinample. This walk follows a right of way, starting from the A84 road beside Loch Lubnaig. Take a path uphill and through the forest to join a higher forest road. Follow this north to its end and continue over the pass to Glen Ample by a good footpath. In due course another road is reached and followed down to Glenample. There cross the Burn of Ample by a footbridge and go down the west side of the burn by a path to rejoin the road and follow it down to the Falls of Edinample. (10 kilometres).

Callander to Glen Artney. Take the narrow road from the centre of Callander sign-posted to the Bracklinn Falls. Continue past Braeleny farm almost to the end of the road at a bridge across the Keltie Water. Follow a footpath uphill north-east for half a kilometre to join another track which is followed east to Glen Artney. The end of the public road is reached at Glenartney Church (grid reference 711 160). (14 kilometres).

Callander to Ardvorlich. Follow the preceding route to the bridge over the Keltie Water. Keep on north past the cottage of Arivurichardich and along the path up the hillside to the col between Meall Odhar and Stuc a'Chroin. Descend north-east across the peaty slopes of Gleann an Dubh Choirein (the path is not well defined) and reach the site of the Dubh Choirein shieling. Follow the stream up the east side of Ben Vorlich to the pass where the going is boggy and trackless. After crossing the pass descend on the east side of the burn in Glen Vorlich where path eventually reappears and leads down to Ardvorlich. (18 kilometres).

SKI MOUNTAINEERING

Ben Vorlich from Ardvorlich is the tour most likely to give good skiing and the minimum of walking. The upper part of Coire Buidhe holds snow well.

Only in rather exceptional circumstances is the ascent of Stuc a'Chroin likely to be worthwhile on skis as there is a long approach at low level from Braeleny farm to the foot of the hill. However, if there is good snow cover down to 250m and it is possible to reach Braeleny by car, then this tour is worth considering. The terrain of the south-east ridge of the mountain gives good skiing.

CLIMBING

The east face of Stuc a'Chroin attracted the attention of early Scottish climbers, and several winter ascents were made of the gullies on that side of the mountain. By modern standards these climbs are all very easy, and they are seldom climbed nowadays.

The south face of Ben Vorlich gives pleasant easy climbing on rocks that are generally cleaner and drier than those on Stuc a'Chroin.

CHAPTER 11

Ben Chonzie and Glen Almond

Ben Chonzie	931m	773 309
Auchnafree Hill	789m	808 308
Creag Uchdag	879m	708 323
Creagan na Beinne	888m	744 369

ACCESS
The A85 road from Lochearnhead to Crieff and Gilmerton, the A822 and A826 roads from Gilmerton to Aberfeldy, and the minor roads from Amulree to Kenmore and from there along the south-east side of Loch Tay to Killin. The road up Glen Lednock to the Loch Lednock Reservoir is public, and the road from Crieff to the Loch Turret Reservoir is private but at the time of writing cars are allowed to go up it to a car park at the dam.

TRANSPORT
Bus: Perth to Crieff, Comrie and St Fillans; daily. Stirling to Crieff; daily.
Perth to Aberfeldy; Mondays to Saturdays.

ACCOMMODATION
Hotels in Lochearnhead, St Fillans, Comrie, Crieff, Amulree, Aberfeldy, Kenmore and Ardeonaig.
Youth hostel at Killin.
Camp and caravan sites at Killin, Comrie and Crieff.

MAPS
Ordnance Survey 1:50,000, Sheets 51 and 52.
Bartholomew 1:100,000, Sheet 48.

The region described in this chapter lies between Loch Tay and Strath Earn; it is bounded on the east by the road from Crieff to Aberfeldy, and extends as far west as Glen Ogle. It is an area composed almost entirely of rolling heather and grass-clad hills and high moorland with no outstanding features of a mountainous nature.

This expanse of hills and moorland is intersected by several glens, of which Glen Almond is the longest and finest from the scenic point of view. It runs from west to east through the centre of the area, and there are some quite attractive corries in the hills on the south side of the glen. Glen Quaich is in the north-east corner of the region, and a minor road through it goes from Amulree over the moors to Kenmore.

Ben Chonzie and Glen Turret from Knock of Crieff

To the south and south-west of Glen Almond two more glens lead into the hills from Strath Earn: Glen Turret above Crieff and Glen Lednock above Comrie.

There is a public road up Glen Lednock for nine kilometres to the dam on the Loch Lednock Reservoir, and a right of way (which in places is submerged under the raised waters of the loch) continues north-west to Ardeonaig on Loch Tay. In Glen Turret a private road leads for seven kilometres to the dam at the foot of the Loch Turret Reservoir and at present public access by car is permitted to the dam. In Glen Almond the road is private and cars are not permitted along it; a bicycle is a great help in reaching the head of the glen sixteen kilometres from the public road in the Sma' Glen. The continuation of the road and path in Glen Almond leads over a low pass and down Gleann a'Chilleine to Ardtalnaig on Loch Tay. This route is a right of way.

This area is mostly given over to sheep farming and grouse shooting, with a few deer in the higher corries, and it should be avoided in the shooting season. A feature of interest is the very large number of mountain hares of Ben Chonzie; few other mountains in Scotland seem to support such a large population.

These hills and glens are essentially hillwalkers' country; their unspectacular nature, and the fact that only one of them is in the list of the Munros, makes them much less frequented than, for example, Ben Lawers and the Tarmachan hills on the

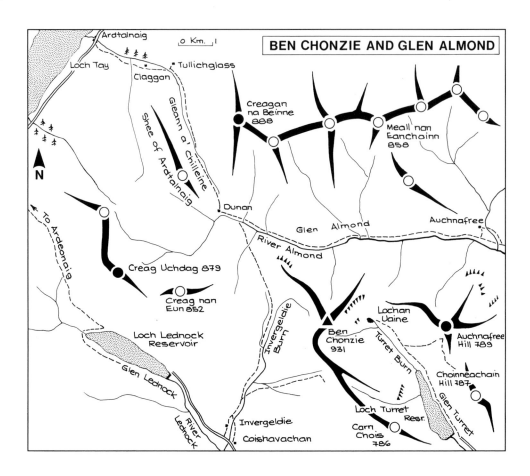

opposite side of Loch Tay. There is a solitude among them that is not found in the more popular hills of the Highlands. In winter there is the possibility of some excellent and easy ski-touring along the smooth broad ridges, but the hills are too low to hold much snow in springtime.

For the rock-climber the main feature of interest is Balnacoul Castle, a small hill on the south-west side of Glen Lednock with a very steep rocky face overlooking the glen opposite Invergeldie.

THE HILLS

The hills in this area can be subdivided into two groups, one to the north of Glen Almond and the other to the south. The former group is a long, broad and undulating ridge which runs from east to west and culminates at its western end in the broad dome of Creagan na Beinne. To the south of Glen Almond, Ben Chonzie is the highest hill and it has just sufficient extra height to enable it to stand out above the surrounding hills and plateaux and make it a recognisable landmark from distant viewpoints, particularly from the south. To its west is Creag Uchdag above the Loch Lednock Reservoir, and to its east Auchnafree Hill is the highest point on an undulating ridge which extends further east towards the Sma' Glen.

Ben Chonzie *(probably mossy hill)* (931m)
Seen from the south, the hills on the north side of Strath Earn form a long gently undulating plateau. At their centre, between the indentations of Glen Lednock and Glen Turret, Ben Chonzie is clearly the highest of the group, its flat summit rising above the surrounding hills.

The best impression of Ben Chonzie is had from Loch Turret. From that viewpoint the summit appears as a rounded dome above the crags on the south-west side of Glen Turret, and the corrie at the head of this glen is the most interesting feature of the hill.

Although the approach from Loch Turret is not the shortest route to the hill, it is scenically the best. From the car park at the dam, walk along the track on the north-east side of the reservoir. This track continues further than is shown on the OS 1:50,000 map past an area of well-preserved moraines and ends at Lochan Uaine. From there one can either climb fairly directly towards the summit of Ben Chonzie, or make a detour to the north to reach the summit up the north-east ridge. The crags above Lochan Uaine are fairly broken and easily avoided.

The summit plateau is rather featureless, but three fences converging near the cairn make it easy to find even in very thick weather. In good weather it would be worthwhile to return to the Loch Turret dam along the spine of the hill, going south-west, then south-east along the fence and continuing south-east along the broad undulating ridge over Carn Chois (786m) and so back to the dam.

The approach from Glen Lednock starts at Coishavachan and follows the right of way up the Invergeldie Burn for one and a half kilometres before taking a track across the burn at a small dam. Follow this track eastwards onto the broad ridge of Ben Chonzie, reach the line of the fence on this ridge near Pt.841m and follow it north-west then north-east to the summit.

Auchnafree Hill *(hill of the field of the deer forest)* (789m)
This is a flat-topped hill midway between the head of Loch Turret and Auchnafree in Glen Almond. The top of the hill is rather featureless, and the tall summit cairn is about a hundred metres south of the fence which crosses the top from north-west to south-east.

The shortest ascent of Auchnafree Hill is from Loch Turret, following the track along the loch and then back onto the southern slopes of the hill. This track reaches a height of 700m less than one kilometre south of the summit. An alternative route is to climb fairly steeply north-east from the dam to reach the south-east ridge of Choinneachain Hill (787m). There is a track up this broad ridge along the top of Creag Chaisean, but it does not go right to the summit of the hill. Leave the track

The Shee of Ardtalnaig with the Lawers range beyond

near a cairn at 776m, go over the top of Choinneachain Hill and then cross a very wide and shallow col northwards to reach Auchnafree Hill.

If one cycles up Glen Almond as far as Auchnafree, the ascent of Auchnafree Hill from there is quite short. Follow the track above Larichfraskhan to the ridge of Crom Chreag one and a half kilometres north-east of the summit.

The continuation of the broad grassy ridge eastwards from Auchnafree Hill leads south-east at first to a peaty col just north of Blue Craigs. At that point the ridge turns slightly north of east and continues, with a faint path for most of the way, over several humps and hollows to Meall Dubh. It is worth keeping to the north edge of this ridge to get some pleasing views downwards into the corries above Glen Almond. In one of these, Coire Chultrain, the Kirk of the Grove was once a meeting place of the Covenanters.

A very good circular traverse starting and finishing at the Loch Turret dam can be made over Choinneachain Hill, Auchnafree Hill, Ben Chonzie and Carn Chois.

Creag Uchdag *(crag of the hollows)* (879m)
Some distance to the west of Ben Chonzie, and separated from it by the headwaters of the Invergeldie Burn, there is a group of three hills of which Creag Uchdag is the central and highest. The hill has rather a craggy south-west side, and it is easily

Loch Freuchie in Glen Quaich

climbed either from Glen Lednock or Ardeonaig on Loch Tay-side by the path between them which is a right of way. This path crosses the south-west shoulder of the hill at about 560m. At its south-east end the path is submerged by the raised waters of the Loch Lednock Reservoir, but there is no difficulty in traversing along the hillside above the loch.

Creagan na Beinne *(hill of the rocks or crags)* (888m)
This is a smooth rounded hill which forms the western end of the long ridge of hills on the north side of Glen Almond. Unless one plans to traverse some of these hills in addition to Creagan na Beinne, the most convenient ascent of this hill is from Ardtalnaig on Loch Tay-side. The track, which is the right of way from Ardtalnaig to Glen Almond, passes along the western side of the hill which can be climbed almost anywhere.

The other hills on the north side of Glen Almond can be easily climbed by their southern ridges above the glen. There are several bulldozed tracks on these slopes which may give easy routes, but they are scars on the landscape. Of these hills Meall nam Fuaran (805m) is the most prominent, with steep crags overlooking Glen Lochan, the narrow pass between Glen Quaich and Glen Almond. This hill is easily reached by taking the track from Glenquaich Lodge towards Glen Lochan for half a kilometre and then climbing the rounded east ridge.

PATHS AND WALKS

Newton Bridge (Sma' Glen) to Ardtalnaig. This right of way leads all the way up Glen Almond by a private road which deteriorates to a path one and a half kilometres before Dunan. From there another track leads north over a low pass to Gleann a'Chilleine to reach Ardtalnaig. (22 kilometres).

Glenquaich Lodge to Auchnafree. This pass linking Glen Quaich to Glen Almond may be used as a shorter start to the previous walk. From Glenquaich Lodge on the south-west side of Loch Freuchie go south-west along a track to Lochan a'Mhuilinn. A path continues through the narrow Glen Lochan enclosed by the crags of Meall nam Fuaran and Beinn na Gainimh, past the tiny Lochan Uaine (which almost disappears in dry weather), through the narrow pass and down to Auchnafree. (6 kilometres).

Coishavachan (Glen Lednock) to Ardtalnaig. Follow the track and path up the Invergel-die Burn and over the pass (633m) to Dunan at the head of Glen Almond. Continue from there to Ardtalnaig by the track through Gleann a'Chilleine. This route is a right of way. (15 kilometres).

Glen Lednock to Ardeonaig. From the end of the public road at the Loch Lednock Reservoir dam go along the north-east side of the reservoir to reach the path near its head. Continue along the path over the lower slopes of Creag Uchdag to descend past old shielings to the Finglen Burn. The path goes down the hillside to the north of the burn to reach Ardeonaig. This route is a right of way. (10 kilometres).

CLIMBING

The main climbing interest is at Balnacoul Castle Crag in Glen Lednock. This crag is about six kilometres up the glen from Comrie, on the south-west side of the glen opposite Invergeldie. A large number of rock climbs have been done on this low-lying crag, most of them being of a high standard of difficulty.

More recently Creag na h-Iolaire on the east side of Glen Lednock opposite Balnacoul Castle has been explored and climbs done on it. A full description of these routes is currently published in the Scottish Mountaineering Club's guide to *Creag Dubh and Craig a' Barns* by D. Cuthbertson and will be updated in the Scottish Mountaineering Club's *Climbers Guide to Highland Outcrops*, edited by K.Howett, to be published in 1992.

In Glen Almond the corrie on the north-east side of Meall Dubh contains a big broken buttress on which a number of climbs were recorded many years ago. More recently, in 1985, a Grade II winter route has been reported in this corrie.

SKI MOUNTAINEERING

The character of the hills surrounding Glen Almond is very suitable for easy ski mountaineering, given an adequate snow cover. Ben Chonzie gives a good short tour, either from Glen Lednock or from Glen Turret; it was in fact one of the earliest Scottish mountains to be skied, in 1904. Auchnafree Hill and Choinneachain Hill can also be easily traversed from Glen Turret.

Possibly the best long expedition in these hills is the ridge on the north side of Glen Almond. The traverse from Glenquaich Lodge to Ardtalnaig is likely to give an excellent day in the right conditions, for the nature of the terrain is ideal for ski touring and the cols between successive hills are quite high.

CHAPTER 12

Glen Dochart to Glen Lyon

Meall Ghaordaidh	1039m	514 397
Beinn nan Oighreag	909m	542 412
Meall nan Subh	806m	461 397
Beinn Heasgarnich	1076m	413 383
Creag Mhor	1048m	391 361
Cam Chreag	885m	375 346
Beinn Chaorach	818m	359 328
Ben Challum	1025m	387 322
Meall Glas	960m	431 322
Sgiath Chuil	935m	463 318
Beinn nan Imirean	849m	419 309

The mountains described in this chapter might very aptly be described as the Glen Lochay mountains, for with only two exceptions they lie round that glen and can be very conveniently climbed from it. The area is bounded on the north by the River Lyon and on the south by the River Fillan, which becomes the River Dochart below Crianlarich. Glen Dochart on the south side of the mountains carries the A85 road from the south to Crianlarich, and is thus an important part of the road system in this part of the Highlands. Between Crianlarich and Killin, Glen Dochart is a wide strath with an attractive variety of scenery: natural woodland and densely planted conifers, the river winding through farms and fields and above them rough moorland rising gradually to the hills which (with the notable exception of Ben More) stand well back from the glen and give it a feeling of spaciousness which is not characteristic of all Highland glens.

Glen Lochay and Glen Lyon are both closed by mountains at their western ends and have no through roads, so they are quiet by comparison. Glen Lochay is rather an attractive and unfrequented glen, and as there is no through road it is usually fairly traffic-free. For the first ten kilometres above Killin, where the River Lochay enters Loch Tay, the glen is pleasantly wooded, there are farms and cottages and the river flows through quiet rocky pools. At Kenknock farm the public road ends and the glen becomes desolate and almost treeless. A private road, not accessible to cars, continues up the glen for a further five kilometres to the cottage at Batavaime, and another private road goes north over the hills by the Learg nan Lunn to Lubreoch

Looking up Glen Lochay to Ben Challum

in Glen Lyon. There are gates on this road, but at present they are not kept locked, and it appears that the public are permitted to drive from one glen to the other.

Glen Lyon is very much finer, but although it is the northern boundary of the area described in this chapter, it provides access to only one or two of the hills and a full description of the glen is reserved for Chapter 14 dealing with the mountains on its north side.

On the whole the Glen Lochay mountains lack any very distinctive features. Certainly none of them can be compared with their near neighbours Ben Lawers, Ben More, Stob Binnein or Ben Lui. They provide the hillwalker with some fine wild country well off the beaten track of the more popular hills, and in winter the ski mountaineer can fine good tours on nearly every one of them.

A good impression of the group may be had from the end of the public road near Kenknock in Glen Lochay. Looking up the glen the steep pointed peak of Ben Challum dominates the view, looking much steeper from this viewpoint than it does from Strath Fillan to its south. Just to its north the twin spurs of Creag Mhor's horseshoe ridge are visible, but the summit of this mountain is hidden. The north side of the glen is filled with the great bulk of Beinn Heasgarnich, and opposite it the crescent-shaped ridge of Meall Glas and its lower Top, Beinn Cheathaich enclose a shallow grassy corrie.

ACCESS
By the A85 road through Glen Dochart, the A82 road from Glasgow up Loch Lomond to Crianlarich and the minor narrow roads up Glen Lochay and Glen Lyon. The private road from Glen Lochay to Glen Lyon is at the time of writing open for public use, but the situation may change. This road may not be kept clear of snow in winter and in snowy conditions is likely to be impassable.

TRANSPORT
Bus: Glasgow to Crianlarich and Tyndrum; daily.
Stirling to Callander and Killin; Mondays to Fridays. Also on Saturdays connecting with postbus.
Postbus: Crianlarich to Killin, with connections to Callander and Stirling; Mondays to Saturdays
Aberfeldy to Lubreoch (Loch Lyon dam); Mondays to Saturdays. Connects with the bus from Perth to Aberfeldy.
Train: Glasgow to Crianlarich and Tyndrum.

ACCOMMODATION
Hotels at Tyndrum, Crianlarich, Luib (Glen Dochart) and Killin.
Youth hostels at Crianlarich and Killin.
Camp and caravan sites at Tyndrum, Luib (Glen Dochart) and Killin.

MAPS
Ordnance Survey 1:50,000, Sheets 50 and 51.
Bartholomew 1:100.000, Sheet 48.

THE HILLS

Meall Ghaordaidh *(possibly from the Gaelic gairdean, meaning a shoulder, arm or hand)* (1039m)
This rather isolated mountain lies between Glen Lochay and Glen Lyon about nine kilometres north-west of Killin. On the Glen Lochay side it rises in uniform and rather featureless slopes in a single sweep from glen to summit, but on the Glen Lyon side the shape of the mountain is more interesting, with two prominent ridges jutting out above the glen, both ending in steep craggy buttresses, Creag Laoghain and Creag an Tulabhain. To the west of Meall Ghaordaidh there is a stretch of lower hills towards the Learg nan Lunn.

The simplest route of ascent of Meall Ghaordaidh is from Glen Lochay. Start just west of the bridge over the Allt Dhuin Croisg near Duncroisk farm and follow a track north-east then north through fields and onto the open hillside. Just beyond a sheepfank bear north-west up the broad south-east shoulder of the hill and high up pass a few small rocky outcrops just before reaching the summit.

The ascent from Glen Lyon is best made from the bridge over the River Lyon near Stronuich. From there follow the Allt Laoghain up into the corrie between the two northern spurs and reach the ridge of Meall Ghaordaidh just over half a kilometre east of the summit.

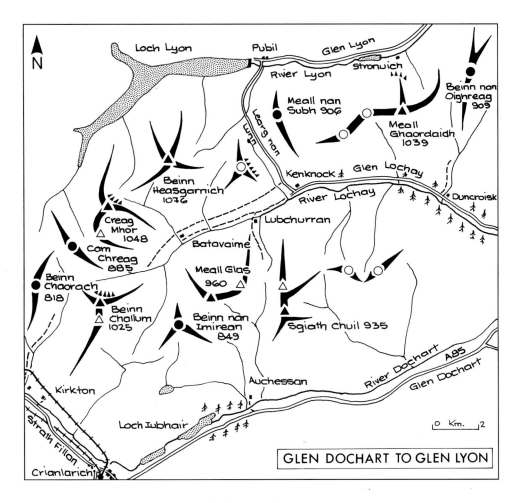

GLEN DOCHART TO GLEN LYON

Beinn nan Oighreag *(cloudberry hill)* (909m)
This hill, which lies about four kilometres north-east of Meall Ghaordaidh, forms a long ridge running from south to north between Glen Lochay and Glen Lyon. On its east side is the Lairig Breisleich, a right of way once used as a route between these two glens; there are the remains of many old shielings near the summit of this pass. The hill itself has no distinctive features, being smooth and grassy. The summit is rather hummocky and has three tops, of which the middle one is the highest. In 1932 it was suggested by J.G.Inglis that Beinn nan Oighreag was just over 3000 feet high and thus a Munro, but measurements by J.A.Parker contradicted this, and the most recent work of the Ordnance Survey places this hill as one of the highest of the Corbetts.

   The ascent may be easily made from Glen Lochay, starting as described opposite for Meall Ghaordaidh. Beyond the sheepfank continue north past the remains of shielings on the west side of the Allt Dhuin Croisg and climb up the long grassy south ridge of the hill over the barely perceptible south top to the summit.

Beinn Heasgarnich (centre) and Creag Mhor (right) from the north across Loch Lyon

Beinn Heasgarnich *(perhaps sheltering or peaceful hill)* (1076m)
This is a large sprawling mountain at the heart of the Forest of Mamlorn between
Glen Lochay and Loch Lyon. It is difficult to get a good impression of Beinn
Heasgarnich from any viewpoint, possibly because its ridges, corries and crags lack
any well-defined shape or character. Nevertheless it is the highest of the Glen Lochay
hills and holds snow well, which makes it popular as a ski-mountaineers' mountain.

The narrow road over the Learg nan Lunn gives close access to Beinn Heasgarnich, but in winter this road may not be passable. In that case the nearest point of
access is at the end of the public road in Glen Lochay near Kenknock. From that point
the route to the hill goes west-north-west up grassy slopes to about 700m. Continue
north, descending slightly across a shallow peaty corrie past Lochan Achlarich and
follow the Allt Tarsuinn up into Coire Ban Mor to reach the summit.

If a start is made from the Learg nan Lunn road, the Allt Tarsuinn can be followed
almost all the way from the highest point of the road to the summit.

Beinn Heasgarnich can readily be climbed along with its western neighbour
Creag Mhor. In this case its south-west ridge is traversed. This ridge rises quite
steeply above the pass between the two mountains and then continues in a more
northerly direction over a few knolls to the summit of Beinn Heasgarnich.

The southern slopes above Glen Lochay are rather featureless. A hydro road traverses across this hillside at a height of about 400m and provides a good cycle route to the head of the glen.

Meall nan Subh *(hill of the soo or raspberry)* (806m)
This hill rises immediately to the east of the Learg nan Lunn road, from which it can be climbed in little more than an hour. The hillside is quite steep and rocky in places, but the only difficulty in thick weather will be finding the true summit. There are three or four knolls on the flat summit area of the hill, and the highest one is on the eastern side. In clear weather there is a good view westwards towards Loch Lyon from the northernmost of these summit knolls.

Creag Mhor *(big rock)* 1048m
Three kilometres to the south-west of Beinn Heasgarnich, and partly hidden by it in the view up Glen Lochay, is Creag Mhor. The summit of this mountain stands at the head of Coire-cheathaich, and the lower Top, Stob nan Clach (958m), is on the southern spur enclosing this corrie. The northern spur, Sron nan Eun (837m), rises above the cottage of Batavaime, the highest habitation in Glen Lochay. On the north side of Creag Mhor a third ridge runs north to Meall Tionail (895m) and beyond that point it drops towards the head of Loch Lyon.

Creag Mhor is one of the remotest mountains in the Southern Highlands judged by its distance from the nearest public road and the fact that it is surrounded by other mountains. From no point on any public road can one get a clear view of it.

The ascent is almost invariably made from Glen Lochay, starting at the gate just west of Kenknock farm. From there walk or cycle up the private road in the glen to Batavaime and climb north-west up a track to the hydro road about 130m above the cottage. This point can be reached equally well along the hydro road itself, which starts from the Learg nan Lunn road not far above Kenknock. Continue the ascent up the steep lower slopes of Sron nan Eun to reach the higher more level ridge where a fair path leads to the summit of Creag Mhor. To complete the circuit of Coire-cheathaich, go west then south-west along the ridge round the head of the corrie to Stob nan Clach. Continue south-east along the knolly ridge to Sail Dhubh and descend its rocky end with care to reach grassy slopes and the hydro road.

If traversing from Creag Mhor to Beinn Heasgarnich, do not descend directly north-east from the summit of Creag Mhor to the col between the two mountains; the hillside is steep and rocky. Instead go north-west then north along the north ridge for three-quarters of a kilometre and then turn east and descend an easy grassy corrie to the col in which is situated the tiny Lochan na Baintighearna.

Cam Chreag *(crooked crag)* (885m)
This unfrequented hill, standing remotely between its two higher neighbours Creag Mhor and Ben Challum, is at the very head of Glen Lochay. However, Cam Chreag is not only Glen Lochay's most remote hill, its western flanks are part of the River Orchy headwaters and southwards from it the streams flow to join the River Fillan. There are thus at least three quite distinct approaches to this hill.

The approach from Glen Lochay is the same as that for Creag Mhor, but one continues along the hydro road to its end at the foot of the east ridge of Cam Chreag. From there climb the easy-angled ridge to a top at 870m which is connected to the summit by a nearly level crest one kilometre long. The north-east face of the hill drops steeply below the summit ridge along its whole length.

From the west the approach starts from the A82 road near Auch. Walk down the private road past Auch and up the Auch Gleann under the great arches of the West Highland railway. Turn right along a track up Glen Coralan and beyond the end of the track continue south-east, climbing to the col between Cam Chreag and Beinn Chaorach. There one finds the remains of a small wind generator, now broken, which at one time provided power for electric fences on Beinn Chaorach and Cam Chreag. Now all that remains is an extensive network of wires on these two hills, liable to trip up the unwary walker. Finally from the col climb north-east then east to the summit of Cam Chreag.

The southern approach from Strath Fillan is best made by traversing Beinn Chaorach as described below.

Beinn Chaorach *(sheep hill)* (818m)
This is another rather modest hill between higher neighbours, and it is one of only two hills described in this chapter which are not within the Glen Lochay catchment area. It is an unremarkable grassy hill which is easily climbed from the south, starting at the bridge which carries the A82 road over the River Fillan. Follow the private road to Auchtertyre farm and a track north to the foot of the south ridge of Beinn Chaorach. The ascent of this ridge gives a perfectly easy ascent. In winter beware of tripping over the several low fences which may be buried under snow. One of these fences goes up the crest of the south ridge.

To continue to Cam Chreag descend north-north-east along the broad ridge to the col with the derelict generator and continue to Cam Chreag as described above.

The return to Auchtertyre from Cam Chreag is best made down Gleann a'Chla-chain on the east side of Beinn Chaorach. Keep above the stream on the west side of the glen to reach the track leading down to the farm.

Ben Challum *(Malcolm's hill)* (1025m)
In the view up Glen Lochay, Ben Challum is the prominent pointed peak at the head of the glen, and it has a striking outline. However, its appearance as seen from the south, from Strath Fillan or Crianlarich, is very different. From that direction the mountain appears as a broad grassy mass rising at a shallow angle from the strath to the rounded South Top (997m), behind which the summit is hidden. The two sides of Ben Challum, north and south, are very different.

The highest part of the mountain is in the shape of the letter **T**, with ridges going south, east and north-west from the summit. Between the east and north-west ridges the north face overlooking the head of Glen Lochay is quite steep and rocky.

The usual route of ascent, but not the best in terms of its mountain character, is from Strath Fillan. The start may be made at Kirkton farm, going uphill past the graveyard of St Fillan's Priory and crossing the West Highland Railway to reach the open hillside. The route up this wide open slope needs no description, for one can climb almost anywhere in a north-easterly direction towards the knolls of Creag Loisgte. The only hazards may be electrified fences, so it is advisable to look for the gates in these fences. Beyond the level part of the ridge at 650m the route continues north-north-east where an old fence is a guide, and above it the broad ridge leads to the South Top. From there careful route-finding is needed in bad visibility as a simple compass bearing to the summit will lead one into difficulty. Descend westwards from the cairn of this top to cross a narrow hollow and reach the ridge on its west side. This ridge leads north across a slight drop to the summit of Ben Challum.

The approach from Glen Lochay is much longer, but scenically finer, and can be shortened in time by cycling to the end of the hydro road at the foot of the Allt Challum. From there climb south to reach the east ridge near Stob a'Bhiora and climb this ridge over a knoll at 864m.

The north-west ridge rising above the Bealach Ghlas Leathaid is less accessible than the other two ridges, but it can be climbed as part of a traverse coming from Cam Chreag. A dry stone dyke crosses the bealach and goes a short way up the ridge towards Ben Challum.

The north face of Ben Challum is not steep nor rocky enough to give serious climbing, but it might give an interesting ascent in winter conditions. It is accessible above the end of the hydro road in Glen Lochay, or alternatively by walking up Gleann a'Chlachain from Auchtertyre and crossing the Bealach Ghlas Leathaid.

Meall Glas (*greenish-grey hill*) 960m
Sgiath Chuil (*back wing*) (935m)
The high ground to the east of Ben Challum between Glen Lochay and Glen Dochart has no distinctive mountainous character, but is more in the nature of high undulating moorland whose highest points are Meall Glas and Sgiath Chuil and their Tops, Beinn Cheathaich and Meall a'Churain. These hills appear from Glen Dochart as rather flat-topped hills; there is a craggy escarpment round the south side of Meall Glas and Sgiath Chuil has a prominent summit on a little crag which from certain viewpoints looks like the prow of a ship. Both hills can be climbed together from Auchessan in Glen Dochart or from Lubchurran in Glen Lochay, and they are described accordingly.

In Glen Dochart there are few convenient parking places on the A85 road near the private road to Auchessan, and cars have to be left some distance to the east or west. There is a good parking place 800 metres east. After passing the house and farm at Auchessan climb north up the open hillside which higher up becomes rough heathery moor. Cross the Allt Glas and follow the Allt Coire nam Moine towards the escarpment of Meall Glas which is easily climbed by a grassy break in the crags, above which the summit of the hill is a short distance to the west.

The ridge eastwards follows a wide crescent past a prominent cairn at 908m to Beinn Cheathaich (937m). Go a short distance north from that Top before descending east, quite steeply at first, to the wide col at the head of the Allt Riobain. On its east side climb a steep grassy slope to Meall a'Churain (918m) and traverse south along the short level ridge to Sgiath Chuil. The return to Auchessan goes fairly directly south-west across moorland to cross the Allt Riobain and rejoin the uphill route near Creag nan Uan.

The approach from Glen Lochay starts from the end of the public road near Kenknock. Continue west along the private road and cross the River Lochay by the bridge at Lubchurran. From there one can either climb the north ridge of Meall a'Churain or the north ridge of Beinn Cheathaich to join the traverse described above. If returning to Lubchurran from Meall Glas it is perfectly simple to take a direct line diagonally across Coire Cheathaich.

Beinn nan Imirean *(hill of the ridge)* (849m)
This hill is in reality the south-west outlier of Meall Glas, although the drop between the two hills is sufficient for Beinn nan Imirean to have Corbett status. In other respects it is an unremarkable hill. The ascent is made from Auchessan in Glen Dochart. From the farm bear north to Creag nan Uan and then north-west past Meall Garbh to the summit. It is perfectly straightforward to descend north-east from the top to the col below Meall Glas and climb this hill from there as a prelude to the traverse described above.

PATHS AND WALKS

Duncroisk (Glen Lochay) to Bridge of Balgie (Glen Lyon) by the Lairig Breisleich. This is an old right of way, but it is now pathless for much of the way. Although the 1:50,000 map indicates that the path in Glen Lochay starts well to the east of Duncroisk, the easier and shorter route starts just west of there on the west side of the Allt Dhuin Croisg and follows a track on that side of the burn for some distance uphill. Continue north past the scattered remains of old shielings through the Lairig Breisleich and descend beside the Allt Breisleich to cross the Allt Bail a'Mhuilinn and reach the road which crosses from Loch Tay to Glen Lyon. Go down this road to Bridge of Balgie. (12 kilometres).

Lubchurran (Glen Lochay) to Auchessan (Glen Dochart). This is the easiest cross-country route between these two glens. A bulldozed track leads south from Lubchurran on the west side of the Lubchurran Burn for some distance. Beyond it continue over the pass between Beinn Cheathaich and Meall a'Churain and descend on the west side of the Allt Riobain to Auchessan. (10 kilometres).

There are other cross-country routes starting in Glen Lochay and going to the head of this glen, from where one can cross either the pass on the east side of Ben Challum to Crianlarich, or the Bealach Ghlas Leathaid between Ben Challum and Cam Chreag to Auchtertyre in Strath Fillan. These routes are not rights of way, nor are there paths for their whole lengths, but they are quite well-defined.

Sgiath Chuil from Auchessan in Glen Dochart

SKI MOUNTAINEERING

Several of the mountains described in this chapter give good and fairly easy ski tours in favourable snow conditions.

Meall Ghaordaidh can be easily climbed on skis by the walking route described from Glen Lochay. Beinn Heasgarnich is a very short ascent if one can drive up the road over the Learg nan Lunn and put one's skis on near Lochan Learg nan Lunn at a height of 500m. There is very pleasant skiing to be had up the Allt Tarsuinn and in Coire Ban Mor, but it should be remembered that the road over the Learg nan Lunn may not be passable in winter. In that case the snow-covered road itself may provide an easy route to the mountain from Glen Lochay.

Ben Challum is a popular skiers' mountain, with easy slopes all the way from Kirkton farm to the South Top which give a good downhill run. The final ridge from the South Top to the summit is a bit more interesting.

Meall Glas and Sgiath Chuil can be climbed from Glen Dochart by the walking routes described earlier in this chapter. The best snow conditions and skiing in this group may well be found in Coire Cheathaich on the north-east side of Meall Glas.

CHAPTER 13

Ben Lawers and the Tarmachans

Ben Lawers	1214m	636 414
Beinn Ghlas	1103m	626 404
Meall Garbh	1118m	644 437
Meall Greigh	1001m	674 438
Meall Corranaich	1069m	616 410
Meall a'Choire Leith	926m	612 439
Meall nan Tarmachan	1043m	585 390
Meall nam Maigheach	779m	586 436

These two groups of mountains lie between Loch Tay and Glen Lyon, and are bounded on the west by the well-defined pass, the Lairig Breisleich, which goes between Glen Lochay and Glen Lyon. Ben Lawers is at the centre of a continuous ridge of seven distinct peaks over 900m; the connecting ridge is about twelve kilometres long and at no point drops below 780m. The whole range is the biggest single mountain massif in the Southern Highlands; the Carn Mairg range on the opposite side of Glen Lyon may rival it in area, but certainly not for height and grandeur.

The Tarmachan hills are separated from Ben Lawers by the road from Loch Tay to Glen Lyon over the Lochan na Lairige pass. There are four distinct peaks in this range and the highest of them, Meall nan Tarmachan, gives its name to the whole group.

The traveller going northwards from Lochearnhead has a grand view of these mountains as he crosses the pass at the head of Glen Ogle and descends towards Glen Dochart. Near at hand, above the town of Killin, the four peaks of the Tarmachans show their distinctive knobbly outline, and beyond them Ben Lawers and its satellites have a very different appearance with long grassy ridges rising from Loch Tay to their high summits.

Ben Lawers and the Tarmachans are among the most popular mountains of the Southern Highlands, and access to both groups is easy from the Lochan na Lairige road which reaches 550m at the lochan. The southern side of Ben Lawers is owned by the National Trust for Scotland, and there is an information centre and car park about one and a half kilometres south of the lochan at grid reference 609 379. The

ACCESS
The A827 road from Killin to Aberfeldy gives access to the south side of these mountains, and the road from Fortingall up Glen Lyon gives access to the north side. The minor road from Loch Tay to Glen Lyon passes between the Lawers and Tarmachan groups, but this road may not be kept open in winter and in conditions of heavy snow it may be impassable.

TRANSPORT
Bus: Stirling to Callander and Killin; Mondays to Fridays. Connects with postbus service to Killin on Saturdays.
Postbus: Callander to Killin; Mondays to Saturdays. Connects with the bus service from Stirling to Callander.
Aberfeldy to Fortingall and Lubreoch (Loch Lyon dam); Mondays to Saturdays. Connects with the bus service from Perth to Aberfeldy.
Aberfeldy to Fearnan and Lawers Hotel; Mondays to Saturdays. Connects with the bus service from Perth to Aberfeldy.

ACCOMMODATION
Hotels at Killin, Lawers, Fearnan, Kenmore and Fortingall.
Youth hostel at Killin.
Camp and caravan sites at Killin, Loch Tay (five kilometres north-east of Killin on the A827 road) and Kenmore.

MAPS
Ordnance Survey 1:50,000, Sheet 51
Bartholomew 1:100,000, Sheet 48

'tourist route' to the mountain and a nature trail start at this point. Both mountain groups are famous for their alpine plants which attract botanists as well as climbers and walkers in early summer. Unfortunately this popularity has brought with it the inevitable erosion of footpaths and damage to flora, and on Ben Lawers the National Trust for Scotland has done much work to repair footpaths.

Some of the Ben Lawers peaks are also very popular for ski mountaineering in winter. At one time Coire Odhar on the south-western slopes of Beinn Ghlas was the centre of skiing in Scotland; the first ski races were held there in the nineteen thirties and the Scottish Ski Club built a small hut in the corrie which survives to this day. In the nineteen fifties Coire Odhar was often crowded with skiers at good winter weekends, and a rudimentary rope-tow operated occasionally. However, the development in the last three or four decades of skiing facilities elsewhere in the Highlands has resulted in skiers going to other mountains and corries, and Ben Lawers is now the preserve of ski-mountaineers rather than downhill skiers.

The Tarmachans are quite different in character from Ben Lawers. Whereas the ridges and summits of the latter are rather smooth and regular in outline, the Tarmachans are knobbly peaks with some craggy faces, and the linking ridges are themselves in places mazes of little knolls and hollows. These hills have a character all of their own.

Looking across Loch Tay to Ben Lawers

THE HILLS

Ben Lawers itself is the central and highest point of the twelve kilometre ridge which connects all the peaks of the range. The traverse of all these peaks in a single day is a very fine and energetic expedition, but most hillwalkers will prefer to take two or three days to climb them separately, and in the following descriptions they are described with that in mind. In this way the whole range can be explored more completely than is possible if one is traversing it in a single day.

Ben Lawers *(from the Gealic labhar, meaning loud and describing the noise of a stream)* (1214m)
Beinn Ghlas *(greenish-grey hill)* (1103m)
Ben Lawers is the highest mountain in the Southern Highlands, and one of the best-known in all the Highlands. It rises in long grassy slopes from the fields and farms along the north side of Loch Tay. The north ridge of the peak drops over the spur of Creag an Fhithich (1047m) down to a col, the Bealach Dubh (942m), and rises to the peak of An Stuc (1118m). Although not a separate Munro, this Top is probably the finest peak of the Ben Lawers massif for it is sharply pointed and steep-sided, particularly on its east face overlooking Lochan nan Cat. The entire east side of the ridge from Ben Lawers to An Stuc is steep and rocky, making the corrie which holds Lochan nan Cat the most impressive corner of the range.

Ben Lawers from Beinn Ghlas

The west side of Ben Lawers drops in uniform grassy slopes towards the head of the Allt a'Chobhair which flows down to Glen Lyon. The south-west ridge leads down to the col from where the north-east ridge of Beinn Ghlas rises to that peak.

The summit of Ben Lawers has a large cairn and an indicator. The cairn is all that remains of an imposing one seven metres high built by thirty men and two masons one summer's day in 1878. Presumably the organiser of this feat, one Malcolm Ferguson of Glasgow, hoped to raise Ben Lawers to the select company of Scotland's 4000ft mountains, but his cairn has failed to survive the ravages of time.

Beinn Ghlas is a much less distinguished peak than its higher neighbour, but it is the one that is seen from the National Trust for Scotland's visitor centre. The south and west slopes drop towards Coire Odhar. The north corrie drops steeply just below the small cairn on the summit, but it is not particularly rocky.

The 'tourist route' to Ben Lawers starts at the visitor centre and goes up a well constructed path which crosses to the east side of the Burn of Edramucky and climbs the grassy slopes to the crest of the south ridge of Beinn Ghlas. Continue up the path along this ridge to the summit of this peak and traverse the connecting ridge to Ben Lawers. In summer the route is obvious as the path along the ridges is very eroded. Return to the visitor centre by the same route.

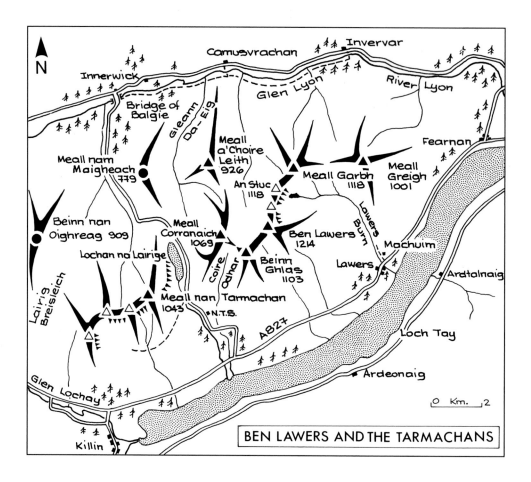

BEN LAWERS AND THE TARMACHANS

A more attractive approach to Ben Lawers, avoiding the crowds which on a good summer's day are likely to be on the 'tourist route', starts at Lawers village and goes up the Lawers Burn. The few farms and cottages at the foot of this stream are all that now remain of the once-thriving village of Lawers, which at one time had a population of about a thousand and was the centre of the flax spinning industry in Scotland. There were once, it is said, about a dozen mills along the lower part of the Lawers Burn, but only three or four remain, none of them working.

One route to Ben Lawers starts just east of the Burn up the private road to Machuim farm and continues along a footpath on the east side of the Burn. In about five kilometres Lochan nan Cat is reached in its fine setting. From the south-west corner of the lochan climb south up a little stream by grassy slopes to reach the east ridge of Ben Lawers about half a kilometre from the summit.

A more direct, but less attractive route goes uphill from the Lawers Hotel, at first through fields and past many old shielings along the line of the old (but now

Ben Lawers from Beinn Ghlas

non-existent) pony track. This route leads to the east ridge of Ben Lawers more than a kilometre from the top, but it is rather featureless and probably better suited for a fast descent.

It should be borne in mind that there is very little space for car parking at the side of the A827 road near Lawers village. Such space as there is may be private land.

Ben Lawers (left) and An Stuc from Meall Greigh

Meall Garbh *(rough hill)* (1118m)
Meall Greigh *(hill of horse studs)* (1001m)
These two hills are at the north-eastern end of the Ben Lawers range, both of them rising above the Lawers Burn. Meall Garbh is joined to An Stuc by a high ridge which drops to 991m at the col between them; its south-east face is fairly steep and craggy above the head of the Lawers Burn, as is the west face above the head of the Fin Glen. North-eastwards from the summit a long ridge drops towards Glen Lyon and a shorter branch of this ridge goes east to the Lairig Innein (834m), the col between Meall Garbh and Meall Greigh.

Meall Greigh is a big grassy hill, well seen from the Lawers Hotel, but it has few distinguishing features. It marks the eastern end of the Ben Lawers massif, and beyond it to the north-east long featureless slopes drop gradually towards Fearnan and the foot of Glen Lyon.

The traverse of these two hills is most conveniently done from Lawers village. Take the private road past Machuim farm and continue up the path on the east side of the Lawers Burn for about a kilometre. It is then very straightforward to climb the broad south ridge of Meall Greigh over the little knoll of Sron Mhor (805m) direct to the top. From the summit go north-west past a lower cairn 200 metres away across the little plateau, and bear west along the very broad ridge to the Lairig Innein.

Careful route-finding is needed in thick weather. From the col climb west up a steeper slope and in less than a kilometre reach the crest of the north-east ridge of Meall Garbh. Follow this ridge to the summit where there is a small cairn on the narrow crest of the hill.

The descent from Meall Garbh can be made by returning towards the Lairig Innein and going down one of the headstreams of the Lawers Burn to the dam. Alternatively, one can descend due south from the summit to Lochan nan Cat. Any descent in a south-easterly direction is inadvisable as the lower slopes above the outflow of Lochan nan Cat are craggy.

It is possible, though longer, to climb these two hills from Glen Lyon. The closest starting point is at the car park at Invervar, though Camusvrachan further up the glen can be used as a starting point for Meall Garbh.

Meall Corranaich *(perhaps notched, prickly, hooked or crooked hill, or possibly hill of lamenting)* (1069m)
Meall a'Choire Leith *(hill of the grey corrie)* (926m)
These are the western hills of the Ben Lawers range; they form a fairly continuous ridge running from south to north, and on their western side Gleann Da-Eig and Lochan na Lairige mark the end of the massif.

Seen from the south, Meall Corranaich appears prominently rising on the west side of Coire Odhar, but Meall a'Choire Leith is hidden behind it. Only from Glen Lyon does one get a view of the latter hill, rising at the end of a long ridge on the east side of Gleann Da-Eig.

The most convenient place from which to traverse these two hills is near the highest point of the Lochan na Lairige road not far from a prominent cairn. There is a rather small parking place nearby. From the cairn cross a low peaty ridge eastwards to reach the head of the Allt Gleann Da-Eig and climb south-east up this stream to reach the south-west ridge of Meall Corranaich not far from the summit. The cairn is close to the edge of the steep north-east face of the hill.

Continue the traverse down the north ridge and after one kilometre keep to the east side of the ridge to avoid going down the spur on the west side of Coire Gorm. In bad visibility it would be quite easy to do this. The route continues down between the shallow depression of Coire Gorm and the steep crags of Coire Liath to the col at 775m. From there climb north up the rounded summit dome of Meall a'Choire Leith.

To return to the road near Lochan na Lairige descend south-west across the lower part of Coire Gorm and continue in the same direction up Gleann Da-Eig to reach the cairn at the starting point.

Meall Corranaich can easily be climbed from the National Trust for Scotland's visitor centre up its south ridge, and an alternative approach to Meall a'Choire Leith is from Glen Lyon, starting at Camusvrachan and climbing the north ridge of the hill.

The complete traverse of the Ben Lawers range is probably the best day's hill-walking in the Southern Highlands, giving a splendid high-level expedition. The highest starting point is at the top of the Lochan na Lairige road, and from there the route starts by doing in reverse the traverse of Meall a'Choire Leith and Meall Corranaich as described above. From Meall Corranaich there is quite a steep descent east-south-east to the col at the head of Coire Odhar and a similar re-ascent of the north-west ridge of Beinn Ghlas. From there traverse the well-worn path along the ridge to Ben Lawers and continue down its north ridge over the knoll of Creag an Fhithich, across the Bealach Dubh and up the south ridge of An Stuc. The descent north-eastwards from this peak to the col linking it to Meall Garbh is very steep and rocky; it is the only part of the traverse that is in any way awkward and in winter the descent or ascent of this slope calls for considerable care. From the col the ascent to Meall Garbh is straightforward and the traverse ends along the route already described to Meall Greigh and down to Lawers village.

In the absence of public transport services, the traverse described above needs two cars or a friendly driver. If one is committed to starting and finishing at the same point, all the Ben Lawers peaks except Meall Greigh can be quite conveniently climbed by starting and finishing at Camusvrachan in Glen Lyon.

Meall nan Tarmachan *(hill of ptarmigan)* (1043m)
To the west of the road from Loch Tay to Glen Lyon over the Lochan na Lairige pass the four peaks of the Tarmachans have a very distinctive outline. Alone among the mountains of Breadalbane they are distinctly steep and rocky. The highest of the four is Meall nan Tarmachan, and low down below its north-east ridge dark crags overlook Lochan na Lairige. Next to it is Meall Garbh (1026m), characterised by its sharply pointed summit and the steep crags of Cam Chreag, its south-east face. Beinn nan Eachan (c.1000m) is the next peak along the ridge and finally at its south-west end Creag na Caillich (916m) has on its east face the highest and most continuous cliff in the Tarmachans; its steep profile is well seen from Killin. The connecting ridge is in places remarkably tortuous, not following a straight line from peak to peak but twisting over little knolls and across rocky hollows. Were it not for the well-defined path along this ridge, route finding might be quite difficult in bad visibility, and this point should be borne in mind in winter when the path is masked by snow.

The best point from which to start the traverse of the Tarmachans is just over half a kilometre north-west of the National Trust for Scotland's visitor centre where a rough track branches off the road to Glen Lyon. It is not possible to drive along this track as there is a locked gate a few hundred metres along it. From the gate climb west up easy grassy slopes to reach the crest of the south ridge of Meall nan Tarmachan and continue up this ridge over a distinct knoll. The height of this knoll is about 920m and the drop beyond it at least 30m, so it might almost qualify to be included in Munro's Tables as a Top. From the col beyond it climb more steeply north-west to a rocky band which can either be climbed direct or outflanked by a rising traverse to the right along an obvious wide grassy rake above which the summit of Meall nan Tarmachan is reached.

Meall nan Tarmachan from Meall Corranaich

Meall Garbh

The traverse continues south-west along a broad ridge which drops to the col before Meall Garbh. Just below this col on its north side is a tiny lochan and the ridge up to Meall Garbh is quite rocky. The summit of this peak is a pointed rock with hardly room for a cairn. The continuation of the traverse is along a narrow level ridge followed by a steep drop to the next col. From there the route is rather tortuous, following a path over and round a few knolls to Beinn nan Eachan.

The last part of the traverse goes down a broad ridge to the col at the head of Coire Fionn Lairige and up to the top of Creag na Caillich which is at the north end of the fairly level summit ridge of this peak. To return to the starting point, retrace the route for a few hundred metres almost to the col and descend south-east into Coire Fionn Lairige. Aim for the disused quarry and from it follow the track for about four kilometres back to the Lochan na Lairige road.

Other routes exist to the summits of the Tarmachans. A pleasant and relatively unfrequented way up Meall nan Tarmachan starts from the prominent cairn near the top of the Lochan na Lairige road and goes up the north ridge of the peak over Creag an Lochain and across knolly ground near Lochan an Tairbh-uisge. There are fine views from this ridge down to Lochan na Lairige.

The quickest ascent of Creag na Caillich is from Bridge of Lochay (at the north end of Killin), climbing north directly towards the peak and finishing up its south ridge above the crags of the east face.

Beinn nan Eachan with Meall Garbh to the right

Probably the best expedition on the Tarmachans is the traverse by the routes described above from the north end of Lochan na Lairige to Bridge of Lochay, but it does require two cars or a friendly driver.

Meall nam Maigheach *(hill of the hare)* (779m)
This rather modest hill lies to the west of Meall a'Choire Leith, midway between Lochan na Lairige and Bridge of Balgie. On earlier maps it was called Meall Luaidhe *(hill of lead)*, a name indicative of the lead mining once, but no longer, carried out on the hill. On the present Ordnance Survey maps this name appears to apply to the north-west shoulder of the hill.

The shortest approach to Meall nam Maigheach is from the south, starting from the Lochan na Lairige road near a hut just west of its summit. Much of this side of the hill is rough peat bog and heather, and the best route goes north from the hut to a wall which leads up onto the summit.

A longer, but much more interesting route can be made from Glen Lyon, starting from Camusvrachan, crossing the river to Roroyere and taking the path up the west side of the Allt Gleann Da-Eig. Once the north-facing crags of Creag nan Eildeag are passed, climb onto the long north-north-east ridge of Meall nam Maigheach and follow it to the summit.

CLIMBING

Nearly all the climbing recorded in this area has been done in winter on the vegetatious crags of Ben Lawers and the Tarmachans. Few of the routes are serious or difficult by modern standards, but they have possibly been unjustifiably neglected over the years.

On the Ben Lawers group in the corrie of Lochan nan Cat the *Cat Gully* on An Stuc is a long easy gully (Grade I) in a fine situation ending close to the summit of that peak. A little further south in the same corrie *Raven's Gully* splits the north-east facing crag of Creag an Fhithich above Lochan nan Cat.

On Meall nan Tarmachan the south-facing crag just north-west of the Lochan na Lairige dam is very accessible, being only a few hundred metres from the dam and not far above it. On its left side a prominent chimney, *Arrow Chimney* (Grade III), was climbed many years ago. More recently the buttress to its right has been climbed (Grade IV), as has the slanting gully at the right-hand side of the crag (Grade III).

Cam Chreag on the south-east side of Meall Garbh (Tarmachans) is a long broken crag which reaches its highest extent below the summit of the peak. There are many gullies and chimneys of Grade I/II standard, most of which have been climbed without detailed records. There is also scope for more difficult routes, avoiding the easy gullies and climbing the broken crags between them. One such route (Grade III) has recently been recorded.

The east face of Creag na Caillich is the most impressive feature of the Tarmachans from the climbers' point of view, and it was the scene of some notable attempts many years ago. At the north end of the cliff there is a wide gully which gives an easy climb. South of this is a broad buttress crossed by discontinuous ledges on which an indeterminate summer climb has been done. To its south is *Great Gully* (130m, Grade III) which required more than one attempt by such great names as H.Raeburn and G.Winthrop Young before it was climbed in 1902.

SKI MOUNTAINEERING

Ben Lawers is the mountain par excellence for ski mountaineers in the Southern Highlands, and one of the best in all the Highlands. In general the nature of the mountain, its smooth slopes, broad ridges and grassy terrain with few crags, give excellent skiing. All the peaks, except possibly An Stuc, give good and undemanding routes, generally following the walking routes described earlier in this chapter.

The car park at the National Trust for Scotland's visitor centre is the most popular starting point for ski tours. The south ridge of Meall Corranaich is an easy ascent with good views of Ben Lawers to the east and the Tarmachans to the west. The traverse of Beinn Ghlas and Ben Lawers is the classic tour. The ascent of Beinn Ghlas may best be made up its shallow south corrie, and if the snow on the north-east ridge of this peak is not in good condition, there may be a better run down the broad shelf

Ben Lawers from the north-west ridge of Beinn Ghlas

just on the south-east side of the ridge with a short re-ascent to the col below Ben Lawers. On the return from Ben Lawers it is not necessary to climb Beinn Ghlas again as a traverse from this col below the north side of Beinn Ghlas leads to the col at the head of Coire Odhar from where a long easy run leads back to the car park.

The ascent of Meall nan Tarmachan on skis is another excellent short tour. The corrie on the west side of the south ridge may well hold better snow than the ridge itself, and as the steep upper crags of the peak are reached a rising traverse rightwards enables one to ski right to the summit. There is good skiing northwards down Coire Riadhailt to the Lochan na Lairige road, but it leads a long way away from the day's starting point.

CHAPTER 14

Glen Lyon to Loch Rannoch

Schiehallion	1083m	714 548
Farragon Hill	783m	841 553
Meall Tairneachan	787m	807 544
Carn Mairg	1041m	635 501
Creag Mhor	981m	695 496
Meall Garbh	968m	646 517
Carn Gorm	1028m	635 501
Beinn Dearg	830m	609 497
Cam Chreag	862m	536 491
Stuchd an Lochain	960m	483 449
Meall Buidhe	932m	498 499
Sron a'Choire Chnapanich	837m	456 453
Meall Buidhe	907m	427 450

The extensive area covered by this chapter forms the north-eastern corner of the Southern Highlands. It is bounded on the south by Glen Lyon and the River Tay, on the east by the River Tummel, on the north by Loch Rannoch and the River Tummel and on the west by the eastern edge of the Moor of Rannoch and the pass leading from there through Gleann Meran to Loch Lyon.

The principal mountains in this area are Schiehallion, the Carn Mairg group a few kilometres to its south-west, and Stuchd an Lochain some eighteen kilometres west-south-west of Carn Mairg. With the exception of Schiehallion, whose conical peak is one of the best-known landmarks of the Highlands, the other mountains just mentioned and many of the lower ones in this area are rather flat-topped and lacking in distinctive features. Only on Stuchd an Lochain is there a corrie of any notable size or steepness. These mountains and their surrounding moors are extensively used for deer stalking and grouse shooting, and this should be borne in mind by hillwalkers during the seasons when these activities are in progress.

The hills at the western end of this area above the head of Loch an Daimh are just about the most remote and least visited of all the hills in the Southern Highlands, and the head of this loch is a very desolate place.

Looking west up Glen Lyon

In general the southern sides of the mountains overlooking Glen Lyon are quite steep; however, on the north the hillsides are more in the nature of heather covered moorland with some extensive areas of forest. If the mountains, Schiehallion excepted, lack outstanding character or features, the same certainly cannot be said of Loch Rannoch and Loch Tummel on their north or Glen Lyon on their south.

Loch Rannoch, Loch Tummel and Strath Tummel form one of the most beautiful straths in the Highlands; wide and spacious, and backed by moorland rising to distant hills. There is a wonderful variety of scenery from the Black Wood of Rannoch, one of the remnants of the Old Caledonian Forest, and birch-fringed Loch Rannoch to the splendid mixed landscape of woodland, farms and fields on the hillsides above Loch Tummel.

Glen Lyon is without question the grandest glen in the Southern Highlands, and deserves exploration for its own sake without any thought of climbing the hills which enclose it. It ranks with Glen Affric, with which it has many features in common, as one of the finest of all Scotland's glens. It is about fifty kilometres long from its headwaters to the confluence of the rivers Lyon and Tay, and in this distance there is almost every type of Highland scenery from the high mountains around Loch Lyon to the woodland and farms of the lower reaches.

ACCESS
The principal route of access is the road up Glen Lyon. The start of this road at Fortingall
is reached from the A827 road along Loch Tay and the River Tay either at Fearnan,
Kenmore or Aberfeldy. Two other roads cross the hills on the south side of Glen Lyon, one
from Glen Lochay by the Learg nan Lunn and the other from Loch Tay to Bridge of Balgie.
Both may be impassable in winter if there is deep snow. Access to the north side of the
area is by the B846 road from Aberfeldy or the B8019 road from Pitlochry to Kinloch
Rannoch, and from there along the south side of Loch Rannoch.

TRANSPORT
Postbus: Aberfeldy to Lubreoch (Loch Lyon dam); Mondays to Saturdays. (Connects with
the bus service from Perth to Aberfeldy).
Pitlochry to Kinloch Rannoch and Rannoch Station; Mondays to Saturdays.
Train: Glasgow to Rannoch. (West Highland Line); daily.

ACCOMMODATION
Hotels at Kinloch Rannoch, Rannoch Station, Coshieville and Fortingall.
Camp and caravan sites at Tummel Bridge and Kinloch Rannoch.

MAPS
Ordnance Survey 1:50,000, Sheets 51 and 52
Bartholomew 1:100,000, Sheet 48

The village of Fortingall near the foot of the glen has many features of interest,
including several thatched houses which give it a rather un-Highland appearance,
and the oldest tree in Europe, a yew tree which is thought to be over 3000 years old
growing in the churchyard. The standing stone called Carn na Marbh on the south
side of the village marks the spot where victims of the Black Plague were buried in
the 14th century. Fortingall is also said to have been the birthplace of Pontius Pilate.

One kilometre west of the village the road enters the narrow Pass of Lyon where
the outlying spurs of Ben Lawers and Carn Mairg close in and the River Lyon rushes
through a narrow twisting defile. The glen is magnificently wooded, the beech trees
being particularly fine, and five great larches stand at the point in the gorge where,
in the 16th century, Gregor Macgregor leapt across the river to escape from pursuing
Campbells and their bloodhounds. The place is still known as Macgregor's Leap,
but the only person who has tried to repeat the feat died in the attempt.

Above the Pass of Lyon the glen opens out and for about fourteen kilometres the
river flows more placidly between farms, fields and woodland. Between Invervar
and Bridge of Balgie there is a minor road on the south side of the river, in places
little more than a farm track. It gives a very pleasant walk, but is not suitable for cars.
At Bridge of Balgie, where the road from Loch Tay crosses the river, the character of
the glen begins to change again. Meggernie Castle, once the stronghold of the
Campbells of Glenlyon and still a splendid building, stands in the middle of the glen
flanked by avenues of lime and beech trees, and the public road climbs high on the
hillside above it at the approach to the wild upper reaches of Glen Lyon. There is a

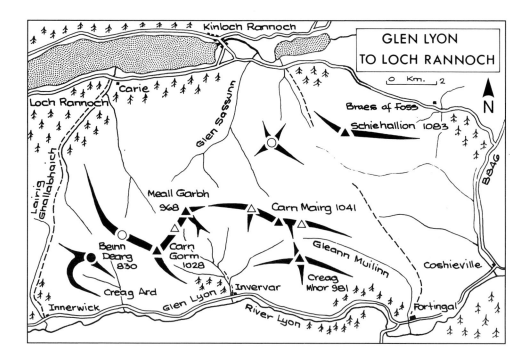

fine pine wood, a remnant of the Old Caledonian Forest, where the Allt Conait tumbles down from Loch an Daimh, and beyond that point the glen becomes more bare , with few trees.

A side road leaves the main Glen Lyon road just east of the Allt Conait and climbs to the dam at the eastern end of Loch an Daimh. This is a hydro-electric reservoir whose waters include the former lochs Giorra and Daimh. The old farm and house at Lochs has been submerged and the new Loch an Daimh is over five kilometres long.

One kilometre below Cashlie there is a hydro-electric power station and reservoir, and just beyond Cashlie are the remains of the ancient forts of Glen Lyon. There were at one time four of these forts, but all that now remain are some not very obvious piles of stones which were once their circular walls. The most obvious remains (on the north side of the road) are of the fort called Caisteal an Duibhe, *the castle of the dark hero*. Tradition associates these forts with Fionn, the legendary Scottish king of the Iron Age, whose stronghold was in Glen Lyon. There is an old Gaelic saying:

> 'Twelve castles had Fionn
> In the crooked glen of the stones.'

The crooked glen of the stones can only be Glen Lyon.

At Pubil the road passes a group of grey cottages, hardly a village, built for hydro-electric workers but long-since deserted. A kilometre further the road ends

Schiehallion from the River Tummel

at Lubreoch below the the huge concrete face of the Loch Lyon dam. The new and greatly enlarged loch is nine kilometres long, with a side arm up Gleann Meran, and it fills the head of Glen Lyon. The old right of way to Auch and the River Orchy, along which the Macgregors carried their dead to the clan's burial ground at Glenorchy Church, is now flooded and the walker heading westwards must find his way along the steep hillside above the loch by sheep-tracks.

The western end of Loch Lyon is a lonely and desolate spot, and far above it, in the corries of Beinn Achaladair, Beinn a'Chreachain and Creag Mhor, the River Lyon has its highest sources on the watershed of the Highlands.

THE HILLS

Schiehallion *(the fairy hill of the Caledonians)* (1083m)
This is the outstanding mountain in the north-east corner of the Southern Highlands, and is one of the best-known of all Scottish peaks. It is quite isolated, with deep glens on all sides, and it has a simplicity of shape which is very striking, consisting as it does of a single hump-backed ridge running from east to west with steeply falling slopes to north and south. The finest view of Schiehallion is from the north side of Loch Rannoch, from where the mountain has a perfect conical appearance, possibly framed by the birch trees along the side of the loch. The Queen's View at the east

Schiehallion from Meall Garbh in the Carn Mairg group

end of Loch Tummel is also a well-known viewpoint for the mountain, although from there its symmetrical appearance is somewhat lost. Another striking view of the mountain is had from the Buachaille Etive Mor over 45 kilometres away to the west. From there the isolated peak of Schiehallion is easily recognised beyond the vast expanse of the Moor of Rannoch.

The evenly weathered quartzite of which Schiehallion is composed has given the mountain its regularity of outline, and it was its isolation and regular shape that led Maskelyne, then the Astronomer-Royal, to carry out his pendulum experiment on the slopes of the mountain to determine the Earth's mass. The upper part of the mountain is largely composed of quartzite boulders and small outcrops. Lower down the slopes are grassy and heathery, and where these two regions meet there are some areas of mixed heather, grass and boulders - a most unpleasant combination.

The most frequented route of ascent starts from the road which passes round the north side of Schiehallion. A short distance east of Braes of Foss farm there is a Forestry Commission car park at the edge of an area of forest. A plaque nearby commemorates the experiment of Maskelyne. From the car park a path goes south-west across the grassy moor, past a prominent cairn and across the track leading onto the hillside from Braes of Foss. Higher up the path climbs more steeply up the

An Stuc and Ben Lawers from Glen Lyon

hillside onto the east ridge of the mountain and there is very unsightly erosion where the path is worn into the soft peaty ground. On the ridge itself the nature of the terrain changes again and the last part of the ascent is along a broad expanse of quartzite stones and boulders whose hard, sharp nature make for rough walking. There are cairns at regular intervals along the upper ridge.

On the north-west side of Schiehallion there is a track up the east side of the Tempar Burn which gives easy access to the stony upper slopes of the mountain where a path leads up the screes to the summit.

Farragon Hill (783m)
Meall Tairneachan (787m)
These two hills are the highest points of an area of high moorland between Loch Tummel and Strath Tay. Near both hills there are recently developed mine workings for barytes, and roads have been driven across the moors to give access to these mines. The hills themselves have no features of particular interest, but their position between Strath Tay to their east and the higher mountains such as Schiehallion and Ben Lawers to their west give some good views from their summits.

Farragon Hill can be approached either from Strath Tay, starting from Edradynate on the road between Aberfeldy and Grandtully, or from the side of Loch Tummel at the foot of the Frenich Burn. The former route leads uphill by a track past the west side of Loch Derculich and over the ridge one kilometre east of Farragon Hill. This track may be developed for the extraction of barytes from the nearby mine down to Strath Tay.

Meall Tairneachan can most easily be climbed from the west, leaving the B846 road at a parking place about three kilometres due west of the summit, or alternatively and less aesthetically by walking up the track which leaves this road two kilometres further north and leads to the barytes mine on the east side of the hill.

Carn Mairg *(perhaps from Gaelic marag, pudding)* (1041m)
Creag Mhor *(big rock)* 981m
Meall Garbh *(rough hill)* 968m
Carn Gorm *(blue hill)* 1028m
This range of mountains forms a continuous ridge, in places almost a plateau, which extends for about nine kilometres from east to west on the north side of Glen Lyon. The ridge is not straight, but forms a big semicircle so that most of the streams which flow southwards converge above Invervar, which is the focal point of the range.

Although they might be likened to the Cairngorms or other hills of the eastern Grampians because of their extensive flat summits, the Carn Mairg group lack the height and grandeur of the Cairngorms and their magnificent corries. Only the southern slopes of Creag Mhor which rise steeply above Chesthill and the Pass of Lyon give any impression of steepness. Elsewhere, and particularly on their northern slopes, these hills appear rather unimposing and the summit ridges are featureless. Nevertheless the complete round of them is a good hillwalking expedition, and

Stuchd an Lochain from Creag an Fheadain

in suitable conditions in winter or spring the traverse on skis is one of the best expeditions of its kind in the Southern Highlands. The owners of the North Chesthill estate, which includes the southern part of these hills, have expressed the wish that hillwalkers should make the traverse from west to east to minimise interference with deer management on the estate.

   The traverse starts at Invervar, where there is a car park just off the Glen Lyon road. A track leads north through forest for a short distance and then up the east side of the Invervar Burn. In just over a kilometre cross the burn by a footbridge and follow a path to the north corner of the forest on the west side of the burn. From there the ascent to Carn Gorm goes west up rising moorland and steeper slopes to the summit cairn. There is an Ordnance Survey trig point about a hundred metres further north-west.

   From there descend quite steeply north to the next col from where the Top of An Sgorr (924m) is only a short climb. Alternatively, it can be avoided by a traverse across its north-west side to the col below Meall Garbh. This is the least interesting of this group of hills, having a flat featureless summit adorned by the rusting remains of a large iron fence. There are two tops, the north-west one (on the fence) being the higher by a metre or so.

Continue east along the line of fence posts past a lochan to another wide col and up a long rise to Meall a'Bharr (1004m) whose summit is a level ridge with the cairn on a rocky outcrop. Beyond the next col and a little knoll the ridge turns south-east and becomes bouldery and quite narrow for a short distance before the summit of Carn Mairg with its large cairn is reached.

To continue the traverse descend east, being careful in bad visibility to avoid a crag just below the summit. Once level ground is reached at the saddle between Carn Mairg and Meall Liath (1012m) turn south down grassy slopes, across a wide col and up to the broad summit ridge of Creag Mhor. There are two tops, the summit being the north-east one which is recognisable as a little rocky tor. Finally, go due west from this summit to reach the grassy ridge on the south side of the Allt Coire Chearcaill and descend this ridge to its foot at the track beside the Invervar Burn a few hundred metres above the forest.

There are other possible routes to the various summits of the Carn Mairg group. For example, from Fortingall it is possible to reach Carn Mairg and Creag Mhor up the path in Gleann Muilinn, and from Kinloch Rannoch there is a track for a long way up Glen Sassunn ending not far from Meall Garbh. However, these routes are less interesting than the Invervar approach, which is the one almost invariably used for the traverse of these hills.

Beinn Dearg *(red hill)* (830m)
Three kilometres west of Carn Gorm is the lower rounded mass of Beinn Dearg. The most prominent feature of this hill is its southern spur Creag Ard which rises steeply above Glen Lyon and is prominent in views up the glen between Invervar and Camusvrachan. The south-western slopes of Beinn Dearg rise at a uniform angle above Innerwick and provide an easy route of ascent which can be extended by going out along the level ridge to Creag Ard.

Cam Chreag *(crooked crag)* (862m)
The hillside to the north of Meggernie Castle rises very steeply in forested slopes to Ben Meggernie which is the end of the long south-east ridge of Cam Chreag. The ascent of this hill can be made from Innerwick, taking the track which goes up the Allt a'Choire Uidhre. In about four kilometres, at the foot of Coire Odhar, leave the track and climb south-west to reach the broad south-east ridge of Cam Chreag, which is climbed to the summit.

The hill can also be climbed by its south-western slopes, possibly starting at the Loch an Daimh dam, but this route is rather featureless and uninteresting.

Stuchd an Lochain *(peak of the little loch)* (960m)
This mountain occupies a commanding position between Loch an Daimh and Glen Lyon, and its bulk fills the view as one looks up the glen from Bridge of Balgie. The summit is at the west end of a broad, crescent-shaped ridge which encloses the north-facing Coire nan Cat. This corrie is the finest feature of the mountain, with the little circular Lochan nan Cat nestling 250m below the summit. The headwall of the

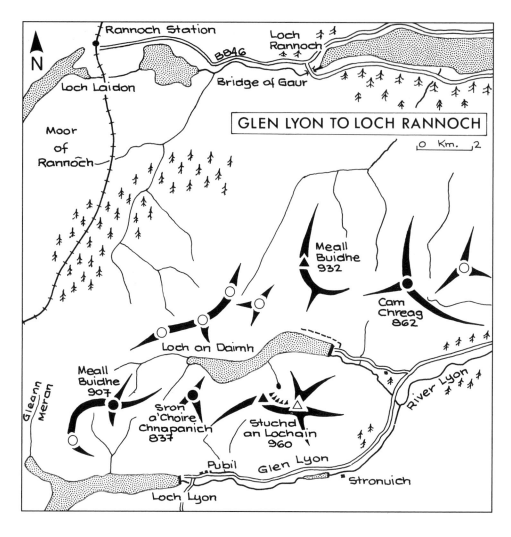

GLEN LYON TO LOCH RANNOCH

corrie is quite steep, but the crags are grassy and there does not seem to be any possibility of good climbing on them.

The first recorded ascent of Stuchd an Lochain appears to have been made about 1590 by Colin Campbell, he who built the original tower of Meggernie Castle. It is recorded that 'On the brow of the hill, Stuic-an-Lochain - a huge rock beetling over a deep circular mountain tarn - they encountered a flock of goats'. It is one of the first accounts of the ascent of any Scottish mountain.

The ascent of Stuchd an Lochain from the Loch an Daimh dam is quite easy as the road end at the dam is at an altitude of about 400m. From the car parking place walk along the road to the south end of the dam and continue west for a short distance. Then climb due south up steep grassy slopes (where there is a faint path) to reach the east ridge of Creag an Fheadain at a line of fence posts. Go west up the ridge over this top, then south-south-west across a dip in the broad ridge to Sron Chona Choirein (c.920m) and finally west to Stuchd an Lochain. By keeping to the north side of the ridge there are some fine glimpses down to the little circular Lochan nan Cat far below. The summit is a few metres beyond the highest point of the fence at the very edge of the cliffs above the lochan.

Another route can be made from Pubil just below the Loch Lyon dam up the south-west slopes of Stuchd an Lochain. Follow sheep paths beside the Allt Camaslaidh to the rather boggy ground near its source from where the summit is easily reached. This way is rather featureless, but it does enable the ascent to be combined with Sron a'Choire Chnapanich, the Corbett which lies three kilometres west of Stuchd an Lochain.

Meall Buidhe *(yellow hill)* (932m)
This hill lies to the north of the Loch an Daimh dam, and like Stuchd an Lochain it is an easy short climb from there. Meall Buidhe is the highest point of a broad ridge running north from Loch an Daimh towards the west end of Loch Rannoch, but the approach from that side is much longer. The east side of this ridge drops quite steeply into the Glas Choire.

The ascent from Loch an Daimh goes north from the dam up the featureless hillside; for part of the way there is a discernible path and some low-relief rocky ribs give firm dry going. Aim for the grassy col just west of Meall a'Phuill (878m) on the southern rim of the Glas Choire. From there go west then north along the fairly level ridge round this corrie, past several small cairns to reach the large cairn on the summit of Meall Buidhe.

The ascent from the north involves a much longer approach from Camghouran or Bridge of Gaur on the south side of Loch Rannoch. There is a track for about seven kilometres up the Allt Camghouran and another track south from Bridge of Gaur for about five kilometres. A bicycle would be useful along these tracks, both of which end not far from Garbh Mheall, the northern outlying spur of Meall Buidhe.

Sron a'Choire Chnapanich *(nose of the lumpy corrie)* (837m)
This hill which overlooks the west end of Loch an Daimh is not named on the 1:50,000 Ordnance Survey map, and its existence as a Corbett was not recognised by earlier maps which showed its height very inaccurately. However, the present Landranger Series map shows the height of the hill and its separation from Stuchd an Lochain correctly, thus confirming its Corbett status, even though the name Creag Doire nan Nathrach on the map is rather misleading.

The ascent can be made very easily from Pubil in Glen Lyon. There is a track above this group of cottages which goes up to about 500m, and beyond it one climbs due north up the grassy corrie of the Allt Phubuill to Sron a'Choire Chnapanich. The north side of the hill drops very steeply down to the head of Loch an Daimh. Returning to the col at the foot of the south-south-east ridge at a height of 640m, it

The northern spurs of Meall Ghaordaidh above the Stronuich Reservoir

is easy to continue to Stuchd an Lochain up the Meall an Odhar ridge over Pt.815m one kilometre west of its summit.

Meall Buidhe *(yellow hill)* (907m)
The range of mountains along the north side of Glen Lyon ends at Meall Buidhe (not to be confused with its higher namesake north of Loch an Daimh). To its west is Gleann Meran which is the boundary between the Glen Lyon and the Orchy hills.

Meall Buidhe is rather hidden behind its lower outlier Meall Phubuill, and its neighbour Meall Daill, which rises steeply above Loch Lyon, is a more prominent hill in views up the glen.

The ascent starts from the Loch Lyon dam with a rising traverse across the south side of Meall Phubuill to reach the 700m col between that hill and Meall Buidhe. From there climb north to reach the fairly level summit ridge of Meall Buidhe at two small lochans and traverse this ridge west for one kilometre to the summit.

PATHS AND WALKS

Fortingall to Kinloch Rannoch. Follow the hill track from Fortingall north then north-west over a col at about 700m and down to Glenmore Bothy. Continue downhill to reach the stream in Gleann Mor at some old shielings. The cave called Uamh Tom a'Mhor-fhir near that point is rather difficult to find as its entrance is an inconspicuous hole in the ground about a hundred and fifty metres north-west of the stream junction at the shielings. Continue north-west, leaving the stream after about one kilometre to reach a little bothy at the end of the track on the west side of Schiehallion. Finally go down this track on the east side of the Tempar Burn to reach the road three kilometres east of Kinloch Rannoch. (15 kilometres).

Innerwick (Glen Lyon) to Carie (Loch Rannoch). This is a right of way over the Lairig Ghallabhaich. There is a track all the way which goes through Rannoch Forest for five kilomteres at its northern end. (11 kilometres).

Glen Lyon to Bridge of Orchy. Except where it is forced uphill by the raising of the level of Loch Lyon, this route follows an old right of way used by the Macgregors on their way from Glen Lyon to the clan's burial ground at the foot of Glen Orchy. The first part from the Loch Lyon dam is along the north shore of the loch, following a path for the first four kilometres. There is a diversion round the arm of the loch which extends into Gleann Meran and a pathless section below the steep slopes of Beinn Mhanach leads to Srath Tarabhan near the head of the loch. Go up this glen to reach the pass at its head. There a track is reached which leads down the Auch Gleann for several kilometres to the great viaduct of the West Highland Railway. To reach Bridge of Orchy without any road walking, go along the Old Military Road, now the West Highland Way, which goes parallel to the railway for the last five kilometres to Bridge of Orchy. (23 kilometres).

SKI MOUNTAINEERING

The best ski tour in this area is the traverse of the four hills of the Carn Mairg group, following the same route as that described for the walking traverse of these hills. This is a long, but easy tour, possibly best suited for Nordic skis.

Schiehallion can give a good day on skis provided the rough bouldery summit ridge is well covered. On the lower slopes the shallow corrie just north of the path may well give good skiing from the ridge down to the moor above Braes of Foss.

CHAPTER 15

The Bridge of Orchy Hills

Beinn Dorain	1076m	326 378
Beinn an Dothaidh	1002m	332 408
Beinn Achaladair	1039m	346 433
Beinn a'Chreachain	1081m	373 441
Beinn Mhanach	954m	373 412
Beinn a'Chaisteal	886m	348 364
Beinn nam Fuaran	806m	361 381
Beinn Odhar	901m	338 339
Beinn Udlaidh	840m	280 333
Beinn Bhreac-liath	802m	303 339

The mountains described in this chapter can be described briefly as those which overlook the headwaters of the River Orchy and two of its principal tributaries, the Water of Tulla and the Allt Kinglass. All these mountains are easily accessible from Bridge of Orchy or from the A82 road a few kilometres to the north or south of there. The western slopes of most of them are a familiar sight to travellers on the road or the West Highland Railway between Tyndrum and the southern edge of the Moor of Rannoch, but one or two of the hills are partly hidden behind their higher western neighbours. The eastern boundary of the area described extends round the head of Loch Lyon, a remote and lonely corner of the Southern Highlands.

The finest mountains of this group are the four highest ones which form a more or less continuous twisting ridge from Beinn Dorain to Beinn a'Chreachain. The western and north-western sides of these peaks drop steeply and without interruption to Loch Tulla and the headwaters of the River Orchy, and this continuous and impressive rampart forms the north-western perimeter of the mountains of Breadalbane and the Southern Highlands. From their summits the climber looks out across the vast expanse of the Moor of Rannoch to the Black Mount and the mountains of Lochaber.

These peaks are themselves well seen by the traveller between Tyndrum and the Moor of Rannoch. In particular the view of the great cone of Beinn Dorain from the summit of the A82 road just north of Tyndrum is one of the grandest sights in the

ACCESS
The main route of access to these hills is by the A82 road from Tyndrum to Bridge of Orchy and points further north. The A85 road from Tyndrum to Dalmally and the B8074 road through Glen Orchy give access to Beinn Udlaidh.

TRANSPORT
Bus: Glasgow to Tyndrum and Bridge of Orchy; daily.
Glasgow to Tyndrum and Dalmally; daily.
Postbus: Aberfeldy to Lubreoch (Loch Lyon), Mondays to Saturdays. (Connects with bus service between Perth and Aberfeldy).
Train: Glasgow to Tyndrum and Bridge of Orchy; daily.
Glasgow to Tyndrum and Dalmally; daily.

ACCOMMODATION
Hotels at Tyndrum, Bridge of Orchy and Inveroran.
Bunk house at Bridge of Orchy hotel.
Camp and caravan site at Tyndrum.

MAPS
Ordnance Survey 1:50,000, Sheet 50
Bartholomew 1:100,000, Sheet 48

Southern Highlands, and the upsweep of the mountainside completely dwarfs the railway line which contours round its base. Further north, the three other mountains are well seen from the road where it climbs above the north end of Loch Tulla.

The Bridge of Orchy mountains are in general steeper and rockier than the smooth grassy hills further south-east. There are some impressive corries on Beinn an Dothaidh, Beinn Achaladair and Beinn Udlaidh with steep but not very high cliffs. Most of these crags are very vegetatious and consequently the climbing on them is more suited to winter than summer conditions. Although these corries and the routes in them were slow to be discovered, the last twenty years has seen considerable exploration, and the Bridge of Orchy hills have now become a popular winter climbing area.

THE HILLS

Beinn Dorain *(from the Gaelic dobhran, hill of the streamlet)* (1076m)
Although not quite the highest mountain of the group, Beinn Dorain is certainly the best known landmark among them by virtue of the impressive upsweep of its flanks above the West Highland Railway and its sharp conical summit. The shape of the mountain is starkly simple; from the summit it drops steeply for almost 900m to the west, south and east, while to the north a broad grassy hillside drops gradually towards Coire a'Ghabhalach. The western flanks in particular are seamed by many shallow gullies down which streams cascade in wet weather, probably explaining the mountain's name.

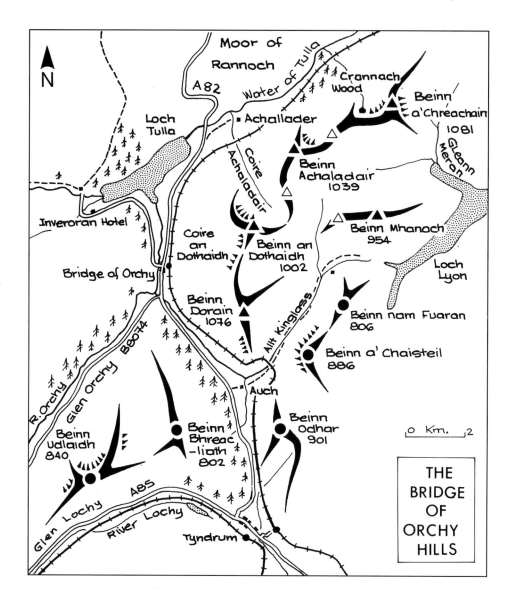

The usual approach to the summit is from Bridge of Orchy, starting at the station. After going under the railway line bear left for a short distance to follow the path up the south side of the Allt Coire an Dothaidh. This path has become very eroded and leads up into Coire an Dothaidh between the crags of Beinn Dorain and Beinn an Dothaidh. Near the head of the corrie follow the path left towards the prominent Y-shaped gully on the flank of Beinn an Dothaidh and reach some old fence posts. Climb uphill and make a rising traverse rightwards (south-east) below the crags of Beinn an Dothaidh to reach the col between it and Beinn Dorain, marked by a cairn.

Beinn an Dothaidh and Beinn Dorain from the north-west across Loch Tulla

From the col climb south along the rocky crest of a little crag for a few hundred metres and continue up the broad grassy north ridge of Beinn Dorain which leads to a large well-built cairn. This is not, as might be thought in misty conditions, the summit, which is about 300 metres further beyond a short drop and re-ascent. In clear weather it is worth descending a short distance south from the summit to get the very impressive view downwards to the West Highland Railway curving round the foot of Beinn Odhar and over the viaduct across the Auch Gleann. It is a view which puts the work of man into its true perspective.

Other ascent routes of Beinn Dorain are a good deal more strenuous than the one described above. The south ridge rising above Auch is a long relentless grind; there are some crags on the west side of this ridge low down which must be avoided if descending this route. Further round to the east above the Auch Gleann the flanks of Beinn Dorain are steep, wild and rocky high up near the summit and any ascent route on that side of the mountain is likely to give rough climbing.

Beinn an Dothaidh *(hill of the scorching or singeing)* (1002m)

This peak is the continuation northwards from Beinn Dorain of the high mountain rampart overlooking Loch Tulla. Like Beinn Dorain it has steep gully-scarred western flanks, but it lacks its neighbour's pointed summit, having a rather flat plateau with three bumps on it. The best view of Beinn an Dothaidh is from the north,

Beinn Dorain from the south

looking into Coire Achaladair, at whose head the north face of the mountain has a long line of cliffs - impressive to look at, but rather too grassy to give good climbing except in winter. One of the most prominent features of the cliffs is the West Gully which forms a small subsidiary corrie below the West Top (1000m).

The ascent of Beinn an Dothaidh from Bridge of Orchy follows the same route as for Beinn Dorain to the col between the two mountains. From there climb north-east up the grassy slopes on the south side of Beinn an Dothaidh. The summit is the middle one of the three bumps on the edge of the north face. It is worth going half a kilometre west to the West Top as it commands a better view to the west and north-west. From there the return to the col is due south.

From Achallader farm (where cars can be parked) there are two or three possible routes to Beinn an Dothaidh, all starting up Coire Achaladair which is easily reached by a path behind the farm which leads to a footbridge over the West Highland Railway. The path continues up the rising moorland on the west side of the Allt Coire Achaladair. The most direct route leaves the path about a kilometre beyond the railway and goes due south up steepening slopes to the ridge which forms the west edge of the north face and leads to the West Top.

Going further up Coire Achaladair one reaches the foot of a fairly well-defined ridge which drops steeply north-north-east from the summit. This ridge gives a

The north-east face of Beinn Achaladair above Crannach Wood

pleasant climb with some very easy scrambling. Beyond it the Beinn an Dothaidh face of Coire Daingean (as the upper part of Coire Achaladair is called) falls back and is mostly steep grass. The col at the head of the corrie is easily reached and bearing west from there the south-east ridge of Beinn an Dothaidh leads to the summit over the lower South-east Top.

Beinn Achaladair (1039m)

This fine mountain rises directly above Achallader farm and is probably named after the settlement which existed there. The ruined Achallader Tower was once a hunting lodge of the Stuart kings. The north-west face of the mountain rises above the farm and the West Highland Railway in long steep slopes, boulder-strewn and scarred by many little gullies. This side of the mountain has been the scene of at least two serious accidents and is best avoided. It would in any case be a tedious route of ascent. The crest of the mountain is a long fairly level ridge connecting the summit to the South Top (1002m) and dropping from there to the col at the head of Coire Daingean. The south-east side of this ridge forms the open and rather featureless Coire nan Clach. The finest feature of the mountain is its north-east corrie which drops steeply between the north and east ridges at the head of the Allt na Crannaich.

The mountain is almost invariably climbed from Achallader farm, either by Coire Achaladair or by its northern slopes reached by walking up the Water of Tulla to

Beinn Achaladair from Meall Buidhe

Crannach Wood. For the Coire Achaladair approach it is probably better from the railway above the farm to go up the east side of the Allt Coire Achaladair. One kilometre up the corrie one can bear south-east up steep but quite easy slopes to reach the ridge of Beinn Achaladair at the col between the summit and the South Top. Continue north-east up the gradually rising ridge to the level crest where the summit is at the end overlooking the north-east corrie.

An easier but longer alternative to the route described above is to walk all the way up Coire Achaladair and Coire Daingean to the col at its head and there turn north up the easy-angled ridge to the South Top. This is the best route, probably the only reasonable route, for skiing up Beinn Achaladair.

The ascent of Beinn Achaladair from the north is a little longer, but more interesting than the routes described above. Start along the track from the farm up the Water of Tulla to reach Crannach Wood, a fine remnant of the Old Caledonian Forest. Go uphill beside the Allt na Crannaich to the upper edge of the trees and then climb the north ridge which leads directly to the summit of the mountain.

The east ridge of Beinn Achaladair drops steeply with some rocky steps round the southern edge of the north-east corrie to reach the Bealach an Aoghlain (813m). From there it is possible to descend steep grassy slopes to the head of the Allt na Crannaich.

Looking south from Beinn a'Chreachain to the Tyndrum hills

Beinn a'Chreachain *(hill of the rock or hill of the clamshell)* (1081m)
The continuation north-eastwards from the Bealach an Aoghlain along the high ridge of the Bridge of Orchy peaks leads over the level crest of Meall Buidhe (977m) to the rounded dome of Beinn a'Chreachain, the highest mountain in this group.

The finest features of Beinn a'Chreachain are its northern and eastern corries. Coire an Lochain, lying to the north-west of the summit below Meall Buidhe is particularly fine with Lochan a'Chreachain backed by dark cliffs.

The eastern corries are the remotest and least accessible part of the mountain, seldom visited by climbers. North-eastwards from the summit a long ridge stretches far out towards the Moor of Rannoch.

Beinn a'Chreachain can readily be traversed from Beinn Achaladair across the Bealach an Aoghlain and along the level ridge of Meall Buidhe, finishing up a long bouldery slope from the 924m col at the foot of its west face.

If climbing Beinn a'Chreachain direct from Achallader farm, take the track along the Water of Tulla to reach Crannach Wood, and climb east through the pine trees and their upper fringe of scattered birches to reach the Allt Coire an Lochain. Continue south-east up grassy slopes to a little col on the north-east ridge which is followed to the summit.

Looking up the Auch Gleann to Beinn Mhanach

Although these four mountains have been described separately, the complete traverse of all of them is one of the best hillwalking expeditions in the Southern Highlands , and is recommended.

Beinn Mhanach *(monk hill)* (954m)
This retiring mountain and its slightly lower Top, Beinn a'Chuirn (924m) lie between the main mountain chain just described and the head of Loch Lyon. They are among the more remote mountains of the Southern Highlands, hidden by their higher western neighbours. The best impression of them is gained from a point on the A82 road about five kilometres north of Tyndrum. From there they are seen at the head of the Auch Gleann framed between the steep sides of Beinn Dorain and Beinn a'Chaisteal; the left-hand summit is Beinn a'Chuirn and the right-hand one is Beinn Mhanach. The latter hill is also prominently seen from the Loch Lyon dam as one looks up the loch.

The two mountains are connected by a broad mossy ridge which drops at its lowest point to 849m. On their north-west side a col at 638m separates them from Beinn Achaladair. On all their other sides they are quite steep, and the west end of Beinn a'Chuirn and the north face of Beinn Mhanach are also quite rocky. Elsewhere the flanks are grassy, and lacking in distinctive features.

One possible approach to Beinn Mhanach is up the Auch Gleann, starting from the A82 road five kilometres north of Tyndrum. It should be noted that the road from the A82 down to Auch is private and cars should not be driven down it. There are few suitable parking places on the main road. From Auch walk along the track under the arches of the West Highland Railway viaduct and up the Auch Gleann beside the Allt Kinglass to the ruined cottage of Ais-an t-Sidhean. The celebrated Gaelic poet Duncan Ban MacIntyre lived in this cottage for several years while he was shepherd and keeper on the slopes of Beinn Dorain, and his love of the mountain inspired him to write his great poem *Moladh Beinn Dobhran - In Praise of Beinn Dorain*. Continue along the track beyond the cottage for a further kilometre and then climb steeply north up grassy slopes towards Beinn a'Chuirn, whose flat summit is marked by a very small cairn. An easy walk of one and a half kilometres leads north-east to the col and then east to Beinn Mhanach with its rather larger cairn.

An alternative route to these two hills may be made from Achallader farm. It is no longer and has no car parking problems at the start. Go up Coire Achaladair and Coire Daingean to the col at its head as described for Beinn Achaladair. From the col traverse north-east along an indistinct path across the grassy flank of Beinn Achaladair, descending slightly to reach the broad peaty col at 638m below Beinn a'Chuirn. From there follow a fence south-east to the col between Beinn Mhanach and Beinn a'Chuirn. If this route is used, it is a simple matter to combine the ascent of these two hills with Beinn Achaladair.

Beinn a'Chaisteal *(hill of the castle)* (886m)
Beinn nam Fuaran *(hill of the well)* (806m)
These two hills are on the east side of the Auch Gleann, from which they rise very steeply in a discontinuous line of crags four kilometres long. Beinn a'Chaisteal in particular looks impressive when seen from the A82 road above Auch, its western prow rising abruptly above the viaduct of the West Highland Railway. Beyond it, further up the Auch Gleann, Beinn nam Fuaran is rather hidden from view. The east side of these hills drop almost as steeply, but less rockily to the Abhainn Ghlas which flows into the head of Loch Lyon.

These two hills can very conveniently be traversed together and the best starting point is at the private road from the the A82 down to Auch, although as noted above this is not a particularly good place for car parking. Go up the Auch Gleann as for Beinn Mhanach (with which these hills could be combined in a fairly long day) to within one kilometre of Ais-an t-Sidhean and climb steeply south-east to the Mam Lorn, the flat peaty col between Beinn nam Fuaran and Beinn a'Chaisteal. From the col Beinn nam Fuaran is quickly reached up a short bouldery slope.

Return south-west following a fence along the broad grassy ridge to Beinn a'Chaisteal. The very steep slopes to the west of the summit and the crags of Creagan Liatha to the south prevent a direct descent to Glen Coralan, so go south-east down an easier ridge following a fence for a kilometre and then descend south to this glen. There is a track down it to return to Auch.

The direct ascent of Beinn a'Chaisteal from the foot of the Auch Gleann is a very steep climb, mostly grass but with a few little crags high up that can be avoided. In dry conditions there is no undue difficulty although the terrain is in places not particularly pleasant, but if wet the grassy slope is steep enough to be potentially dangerous.

Beinn Odhar *(dun-coloured hill)* (901m)

The steep conical shape of Beinn Odhar makes it a prominent hill, looking in some views like a smaller version of Beinn Dorain. Rising as it does immediately above the A82 road at its highest point between Tyndrum and Bridge of Orchy, it is very accessible and gives a short and pleasant climb with a fine view which on a clear day is an excellent reward for the modest effort required to reach the summit.

Start from the A82 road near a bridge over the West Highland Railway one and a half kilometres north of Tyndrum. Follow a grassy track up the broad ridge on the west side of the Crom Allt to the remains of a disused mine and continue north up stony slopes past a tiny lochan to the summit. There was at one time lead mining on the slopes of the hill as the disused mine and the corrie on the north side of the hill, Coire Luaidh *(corrie of lead)*, indicate.

Beinn Udlaidh *(dark or gloomy hill)* 840m
Beinn Bhreac-liath *(speckled grey hill)* 802m

These two hills are on the south side of Glen Orchy about six kilometres south of Bridge of Orchy. The north side of Beinn Udlaidh is deeply scalloped by corries, and one of these, Coire Daimh, has a continuous line of cliffs round its head. The ice-climbing on these crags in winter is of a very high quality, and the corrie has become very popular at that time of year when hard frosty conditions prevail.

The south side of these two hills overlooking Glen Lochy is forested along much of its length, and there is only limited access through the trees onto the higher slopes.

Probably the most pleasant traverse of these two hills is from Glen Orchy. Start near Invergaunan and climb open grassy slopes southwards up the broad north ridge of Beinn Udlaidh. At about 650m a very prominent quartzite dyke, which is clearly seen from a distance crossing the north side of the hill, is reached. Above it the climb continues at an easier angle to the flat summit of Beinn Udlaidh which is about 200 metres from the rim of Coire Daimh.

Continue south then east down steepening slopes to a wide flat col (587m) with some knolls and tiny lochans on it. From there climb north-east up a stony slope to Beinn Bhreac-liath. The descent from there to Glen Orchy goes down the long north ridge to Invergaunan.

It is possible to reach the col between the two hills through the forest from Arinabea in Glen Lochy, and a short ascent of Beinn Bhreac-liath can be made from the A82 road three kilometres north of Tyndrum. However, although these two routes are shorter than the Glen Orchy approach, they are no more attractive.

The ice-fall in Salamander Gully, Beinn an Dothaidh

PATHS AND WALKS

Glen Lyon to Bridge of Orchy. This route has been described in the preceding chapter.

Tyndrum to Bridge of Orchy. This walk follows the West Highland Way along the old military road round the base of Beinn Odhar and Beinn Dorain. (10 kilometres).

CLIMBING

There are good crags and corries on most of the mountains described in this chapter, but they all tend to be very vegetatious and consequently the climbing on them is much better suited for winter than summer. A few of the early climbs were done in summer, but they are seldom if ever climbed nowadays. However, in good winter conditions there is a fine selection of ice climbs of all grades, some of them very accessible and suitable for short days. All these climbs are described in the Scottish Mountaineering Club's *Climbers Guide to Arran, Arrochar and the Southern Highlands* by K.V.Crocket and A.Walker, published in 1989. The following notes summarise the climbing.

The path up the Allt Coire an Dothaidh from Bridge of Orchy station gives access to two crags near the col between Beinn Dorain and Beinn an Dothaidh. Creag an Socach is the steep crag forming the south side of Coire an Dothaidh on the Beinn

Dorain side of the col. Near the left side of the crag is a narrow gully, usually wet in summer, which gives a steep ice climb, *False Rumour Gully* (60m, Grade IV).

D.Stewart's original summer route (Very Difficult) starts about 25 metres right of this gully and there are two more recent winter routes on the same section of the crag. Further right the crag is more impressive with steep waterworn slabs separated by grass ledges. The highest appears from below as a very steep wall of clean grey rock. The summer climb *Scorpion* (105m, Very Severe) is on this part of the crag and further right there are five hard winter routes, one of which, *Messiah* (90m, Grade VI) is reputed to be one of the finest lines in the Southern Highlands.

On the Beinn an Dothaidh side of the col, Creag Coire an Dothaidh is in summer a rather damp crag, being below some springs further up the hillside. These springs provide a source of water which in hard winter conditions freezes to give several good ice climbs. On the left side of the crag *Salamander Gully* (150m, Grade III/IV) is an obvious gully with an icefall high up, and on the right side of the crag several days of hard frosty weather leads to the build-up of a series of icefalls which give very enjoyable ice climbing up to Grade IV standard.

The earliest climbs on Beinn an Dothaidh, four long Grade I snow gullies, are on the north face of the mountain above Coire Achaladair. The most prominent of these is *West Gully*, a well-defined snow corridor below the West Peak. Its left wall is North Buttress, and to its right are North-West, West and Far West buttresses. The ascent of *Taxus* (240m, Grade III) on North Buttress in 1969 was the start of extensive winter exploration in the corrie, particularly on West Buttress where there are now several routes of Grade III to Grade V standard. *Haar* (135m, Grade III) is a prominent open gully on the left side of West Buttress, and *Cirrus* (135m, Grade III/IV), the steep narrow gully between West Buttress and Far West Buttress, gives one of the best climbs in the corrie. This is an excellent area for winter climbing within easy reach of Achallader farm.

The north-east corrie of Beinn Achaladair has two or three easy gullies in the western half of the corrie, the best of which leads directly to the summit (Grade I). The eastern half of the corrie has a very steep headwall on which four routes, Grade II to IV, have been done. Further to the north-east, beyond the Bealach an Aoghlain, there is a long broken crag on the flank of Meall Buidhe to the west of its summit. The most prominent feature is *Forked Gully* (105m, Grade II) near the left side of the crag, and to its right there are several routes of Grade II to Grade IV standard of a not too serious character.

In Coire an Lochain on Beinn a'Chreachain the lochan is backed by three buttresses, separated by easy gullies. Three winter routes have been done, one on the central and two on the right-hand buttress, all Grade III.

On Beinn a'Chaisteal four routes have been done on the steep craggy hillside opposite the small plantation in the Auch Gleann on the lower slopes of Beinn Dorain. The routes are in the gullies and icefalls high up on the hillside. (Grade III and IV).

Beinn Udlaidh offers the best selection of winter climbs in the Bridge of Orchy area on the north-facing crags of Coire Daimh. Water draining across the upper slopes of the hill and down the cliffs make it possible in freezing conditions to get excellent ice climbing on spectacular columns of water-ice without the need for a fall of snow. When snow does fall, there are several more conventional climbs in the many gullies of the corrie. There are about 30 routes of Grade II to Grade V, some of them of excellent quality which in the right conditions make modest Beinn Udlaidh an ice-climber's playground.

Prominent landmarks in the corrie are the left- and right-slanting Central and West gullies, both Grade II. Between them is Central Buttress, with *Doctor's Dilemma* (180m, Grade IV) a fine route up the icefalls in the middle of the buttress. The section of cliff to the right of West Gully is West Wall, marked high up by the prominent wide icefall of *Organ Pipe Wall* (75m, Grade IV/V). Further right, near the right-hand side of West Wall, is the steep and obvious gully of *The Smirk* (90m, Grade IV/V), another fine winter route.

To the left of Central Gully are *Sunshine Gully* and *Ramshead Gully*, both Grade III. Further left, beyond a square-cut buttress, is *South Gully of the Black Wall* (120m, Grade IV) and to its left is the Black Wall which when ice-draped after a spell of hard frosty weather displays an impressive array of icefalls and huge icicles. There are several very hard routes on the wall. To the left of the Black Wall is *Quartzvein Scoop* (90m, Grade III/IV), and to its left the cliffs diminish.

Below the main line of cliffs and just left of the foot of Central Gully there is a smaller line of quartzite crags on which there are two chimneys, the left-hand one giving a good climb (30m, Very Difficult). This climb, with Ramshead Gully, Quartzvein Scoop and South Gully of the Black Wall, were first climbed in summer conditions by J.B.Nimlin and his companions in the nineteen thirties, but Coire Daimh was neglected from then until the nineteen seventies when the exploration of winter routes began in earnest.

SKI MOUNTAINEERING

The four high Bridge of Orchy mountains all give good ski mountaineering. The best access route to Beinn Dorain and Beinn an Dothaidh is up the Allt Coire an Dothaidh to the col between them. The north side of Beinn Dorain in particular has very good snow-holding slopes at the head of Coire a'Ghabhalach, and this corrie may well give an excellent run towards the Auch Gleann, but one should resist the temptation to ski right down to the glen. It is easier to return to Bridge of Orchy back over the col.

The only feasible ski-route to Beinn Achaladair is from Achallader farm right up to the col at the head of Coire Daingean and along the ridge over the South Top. The continuation to Beinn a'Chreachain over Meall Buidhe is a fine traverse, and there is an excellent, if steep, run from the north-east end of the level Meall Buidhe ridge down to Crannach Wood.

INDEX OF PLACE NAMES

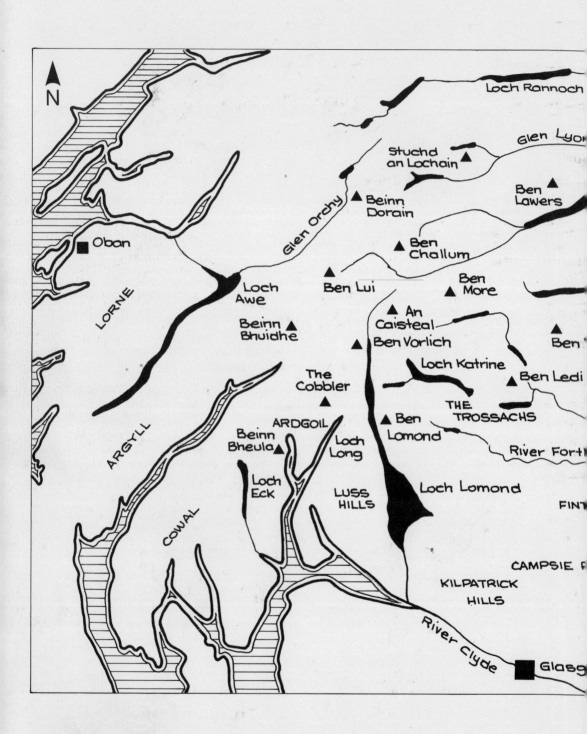